P9-DFT-811

Includes
365 OF THE BEST PILSNERS, STOUTS, TRIPELS, AND MORE!

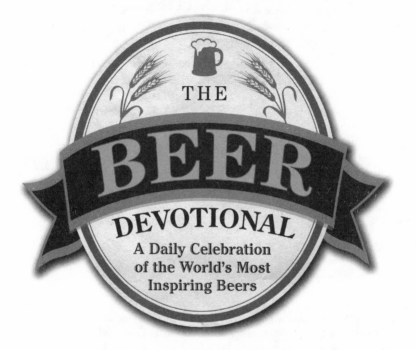

THE BEER DEVOTIONAL

A Daily Celebration of the World's Most Inspiring Beers

JESS LEBOW

adamsmedia
Avon, Massachusetts

Copyright © 2010 by F+W Media, Inc.
All rights reserved.
This book, or parts thereof, may not be reproduced in any
form without permission from the publisher; exceptions are
made for brief excerpts used in published reviews.

Published by
Adams Media, a division of F+W Media, Inc.
57 Littlefield Street, Avon, MA 02322. U.S.A.
www.adamsmedia.com

ISBN 10: 1-4405-0357-5
ISBN 13: 978-1-4405-0357-3
eISBN 10: 1-4405-0702-3
eISBN13: 978-1-4405-0702-1

Printed in the United States of America.

10 9 8 7 6 5 4 3 2 1

Library of Congress Cataloging-in-Publication Data
is available from the publisher.

This publication is designed to provide accurate and authoritative information with regard to the subject matter covered. It is sold with the understand-
ing that the publisher is not engaged in rendering legal, accounting, or other
professional advice. If legal advice or other expert assistance is required, the
services of a competent professional person should be sought.

—From a *Declaration of Principles* jointly adopted by a Committee of the
American Bar Association and a Committee of Publishers and Associations

Many of the designations used by manufacturers and sellers to distinguish
their product are claimed as trademarks. Where those designations appear in
this book and Adams Media was aware of a trademark claim, the designations
have been printed with initial capital letters.

This book is available at quantity discounts for bulk purchases.
For information, please call 1-800-289-0963.

Special Thanks

Thanks first must go to my editor, Peter Archer, for his help and guidance. This book truly would not have been possible without you. Cheers.

Next to Sybil Grieb, who put up with me storing all our food in a camping cooler, so there would be more space in our refrigerator for the beer. Psst . . .

Thanks also to the tireless support of my "research" assistants: Dean Orion, Alex Arko, Sylvia Grieb, Greg Hughes, Linda Matsumi, Troy Hewitt, Joe Mullenix, Jessica Moore, Cassie Bannister, Cory Herndon, S.P. Miskowski, Anna Murchison, Gavin Irby, Sara Kang, Will Kielar, Robert Land, Marc Hernandez, Steve Bannister, Phil and Deanne Athans, Dave and Connie Beetlestone, Nate and Erica Levin, John Zipperer, Andrew Beegle, Mat Staltman, Nancy Shelton, Chris Pramas, Nicole Lindroos, Bobby Stein, Clay Holly, Kinsley Earl, Cole Downing, Matt Smith, and Robin Thyssen.

And to our bottle cap girl: Kasey Arko.

And finally to Steve Whitman and Phil Tasca, because, well, you know why.

BEER PRAYER

Our lager, which art in barrels, hallowed be thy drink.

Thy will be drunk, at home as in the tavern.

Give us this day our foamy head, and forgive us our spillages,

as we forgive those who spill against us.

And lead us not into incarceration, but deliver us from hangovers.

For thine is the beer, the bitter, and the lager, for ever and ever,

Barmen.

Contents

Introduction

Brothers and sisters, now is a good time to be a beer devotee.

Over the centuries, beer has meant many things to many people. In times of cheer, it has provided happiness to celebrants, added joy to the mundane, and served as sustenance to the devout. In darker times, beer has provided solace to the suffering, given comfort when there was none, and delivered hope of a future when all was thought lost. By more than one account, beer has saved human civilization, from threats as large as monsters of legend and as small as microbes in the water.

Beer is delicious, nutritious, refreshing, intoxicating, dependable, commendable, undying, and even portable. It can be as simple as four ingredients or as complicated as a 2,700-year-old recipe found in King Midas's tomb.

Beer has suffered through drought, plague, depression, holocaust, politics, wars, intolerance, temperance, and even prohibition. Beer has been worshiped, had temples erected to its glory, and priests and priestesses appointed in its name. It has been legislated, criminalized, demonized, and even banned. Yet, through all that, it has persevered, even prospered.

Perhaps it is even safe to say that there has been, in the breadth of human history, no better time to be a connoisseur, lover, or disciple of beer than right now. Thousands of years of experience, recipes and accounts from generations of master brewers, handbooks on the science of fermentation and the technology to employ them, even college diplomas in the brewing arts—these are the tools that make this such an exciting time to enjoy beer. But it is not the tools themselves that make today's world and our time here such a delightful place in the history of all things. No, rather, it is the creativity and spirit of the craft brewer—the men and women who use these tools, both those steeped in tradition and those who are charting new ground—that promises to deliver to the pious believers the hope of new brews to come.

It is indeed a good time to be devoted to beer.

Cheers.

Jess Lebow

🍺 Total Domination IPA

"For we could not now take time for further search [to land our ship], our victuals being much spent, especially our beer."
—LOG OF *THE MAYFLOWER*

TYPE: India pale ale
COLOR: Amber
SMELL: Citrus hops and pine
TASTE: Bright, hoppy, light- to medium-bodied beer with flavors of grapefruit, mandarin, cumin, fennel, and honey followed by a long piney finish.
FOOD PAIRING: Swordfish with corn chutney
AVAILABILITY: Year round

JAN

1

*Beer***fact**

When the pilgrims arrived in Plymouth they had plenty of fresh water, but they had completely depleted their supply of beer, which they believed would cure them of the sickness running rampant through the colony. When several of the *Mayflower's* crew began to come down with the same sickness, the ship's captain, Captain Jones, allowed the governor of the colony to requisition some ale for the ill.

Ninkasi Brewing Company
272 Van Buren Street
Eugene, OR 97402
www.ninkasibrewing.com

 Believer Double Red

"One can drink too much, but one never drinks enough."
    —GOTTHOLD EPHRAIM LESSING

TYPE: Double red ale
COLOR: Deep red
SMELL: Sweet malt and citrus hops
TASTE: A medium-bodied beer with lots of rich caramel, a touch of nuttiness, and a hint of cocoa. Nicely balanced by citrus and grassy hops with a soft bitter finish.
FOOD PAIRING: Applewood-smoked bacon BLT
AVAILABILITY: Year round

JAN

2

Beerfact

On the label of Believer Double Red appear these words: "The Ancient Sumerians Worshipped the beer they made, and praised the Goddess Ninkasi for the miracle of fermentation. Beer is a staple of civilization. Worship the Goddess."

I'll drink to that.

Ninkasi Brewing Company
272 Van Buren Street
Eugene, OR 97402
www.ninkasibrewing.com

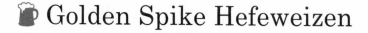 Golden Spike Hefeweizen

"Good beer needs no passport."
—ANONYMOUS

TYPE: Hefeweizen
COLOR: Cloudy orange amber
SMELL: Fresh baked bread and lemon
TASTE: A creamy, light-bodied beer with flavors of wheat, yeast, and citrus. Finishes crisp and refreshing.
FOOD PAIRING: Beer-battered true cod with thick-cut fries served with tartar sauce and a lemon wedge
AVAILABILITY: Year round

JAN
3

Beerfest

2009 Great American Beer Festival Winners by Category:
German-Style Wheat Ale: Hefeweizen, Triumph Brewing Co. of New Hope, New Hope, PA
Belgian-Style Witbier: ZON, Boulevard Brewing Co, Kansas City, MO
French- and Belgian-Style Saison: Saison Vautour, McKenzie Brew House, Glen Mills, PA
Belgian- and French-Style Ale: Carnevale, The Lost Abbey, San Marcos, CA

Uinta Brewing Company
1722 South Fremont Drive (2375 West)
Salt Lake City, UT 84104
www.uintabrewing.com

🍺 Live Oak Big Bark Amber Lager

"When the water of a place is bad, it is safest to drink none that has not been filtered through either the berry of a grape or else a tub of malt."
—SAMUEL BUTLER

JAN

4

TYPE: Vienna-style lager

COLOR: Reddish amber

SMELL: Yeast and sweet malt with citrus and pine

TASTE: Flavors of soft, freshly baked bread with more than a suggestion of malty sweetness followed by a bitter hop finish.

FOOD PAIRING: Steamed asparagus drizzled with sesame oil and lemon juice

AVAILABILITY: Year round

Beer*words*

Microbrewery: A brewery that produces less than 15,000 barrels (17,600 hectoliters) of beer per year with 75 percent or more of its beer sold off site. Microbreweries sell to the public by one or more of the following methods: the traditional three-tier system (brewer to wholesaler to retailer to consumer); the two-tier system (brewer acting as wholesaler to retailer to consumer); and, directly to the consumer through carryouts and/or on-site tap-room or restaurant sales.

—Beertown.org (The Brewers Association website)

Live Oak Brewing Company
3301 E. 5th Street #B
Austin, TX 78702
www.liveoakbrewing.com

 Smoked Porter

"Sometimes too much drink is barely enough."
—MARK TWAIN

TYPE: Porter
COLOR: Oily brown
SMELL: Like the smoke from an open campfire
TASTE: Seductive, smooth, and oily, there are layers of coffee and roasted meat under the delicious tutelage of alder smoke.
FOOD PAIRING: Cold-smoked sockeye salmon, sliced thinly and served with crème fraise and a sprinkle of black caviar
AVAILABILITY: Vintage batches released at the end of each year

**JAN
5**

Brewtip

Alaskan brewers Geoff and Marcy Larson worked with their local Juneau neighbor, Sandro Lane, who owns Taku Smokeries, to get just the right smoke on their malt.

Special stainless steel racks hold the malt but still allow the smoke to circulate among the grains. The moistened malt is smoked at a relatively cool temperature over alder wood. It takes about seventy-two hours to create enough of the smoked malt to make a small batch of porter. After it comes out of the smoker, the grain rests and cools for another twelve hours.

Several months later, the vintage smoked porter is released. Ah.

Alaskan Brewing Company
5429 Shaune Drive
Juneau, AK 99801-9540
www.alaskanbeer.com

🍺 Hairy Eyeball

"I pray thee let me and my fellow have, A hair of the dog that bit us last night, And bitten were we both to the brain aright. We saw each other drunk in the good ale glass."
—JOHN HEYWOOD, AUTHOR

TYPE: American strong ale

COLOR: Like dark brown sugar in liquid form

SMELL: Malt and hops but each distinct from the other

TASTE: Thick on the tongue, it has a sweet, malty, molasses flavor with hints of licorice that are cut by a solid amount of hops. A balancing act between the heavy sweetness, the 8.7% alcohol by volume, and the refreshing hops.

FOOD PAIRING: Crumbly, crystalline five-year cave-aged Gouda and some almonds.

AVAILABILITY: Winter seasonal

JAN
6

Beerthought

Imagine yourself in a cabin, high up in the mountains. It's winter. The sun is just peeking its head over the horizon. You rock gently in your chair and tuck your toes under the warm fur of your trusty pooch, lying at your feet. You take a sip from your bottle of Lagunitas Hairy Eyeball. It tastes just as good going down this morning as it did last night. Thank goodness for dogs.

Lagunitas Brewing Company
1280 North McDowell Blvd.
Petaluma, CA 94954
www.lagunitas.com

🍺 Brown Ale

"Then to the spicy nut-brown ale."
—JOHN MILTON

TYPE: English dark ale
COLOR: Very dark brown
SMELL: Roasted malt, chocolate, and dried fruit
TASTE: Flavors of toasted malt, chocolate, caramel, and deeply roasted coffee along with a little nuttiness. A medium-bodied beer that goes down easy and feels lighter than you might expect.
FOOD PAIRING: Shredded pork in a mild mole sauce over white rice
AVAILABILITY: Year round

JAN
7

Beerfood
BEER BREAD

1 can or bottle of beer
3 cups self-rising flour
3 tablespoons honey

Grease a 9" × 5" bread loaf pan. Mix the flour and sugar together first, then add the beer. Stir until you have a nice ball of dough, then knead 10 to 15 minutes. Bake in the loaf pan at 350 degrees for about 50 minutes.

New Orleans Lager and Ale Brewing Company
3001 Tchoupitoulas Street
New Orleans, LA 70130
www.nolabrewing.com

🍺 Celebration Ale

Sam: *"Whaddya say, Norm?"* Norm: *"Well, I never met a beer I didn't drink."*
—CHEERS

TYPE: India pale ale
COLOR: Deep orange
SMELL: Caramel and pine
TASTE: A medium- to full-bodied beer with flavors of sweet malt and spice paired nicely with grapefruit and pine hops. A well-balanced beer with a solid heft to it.
FOOD PAIRING: Beef and Italian sausage meatloaf
AVAILABILITY: Winter seasonal

**JAN
8**

Beerfun
Six-Cup Beer Pong

Required supplies: Ping-pong table, twelve keg cups, two ping-pong balls, beer

Place six keg cups in a pyramid at each end of a ping-pong table. Fill each cup one-third to one-half full of beer. Teams of two take turns throwing or bouncing their ping-pong balls at the other team's cups. If a ball lands in a cup, the team that owns the cup drinks the beer. The team that eliminates all the cups from their opponent's side of the table wins.

Sierra Nevada Brewing Company
1075 East 20th Street
Chico, CA 95928
www.sierranevada.com

🍺 Krystal

"The problem with the world is everyone is a few drinks behind."
—HUMPHREY BOGART

TYPE: American style
COLOR: Almost clear, slightly golden
SMELL: Very light, just a whiff of hops and roasted wheat
TASTE: One of those thirst quenchers that goes down fast to keep you cool. A light buttery flavor gives way to tangy malt as it goes down by the great mouthful.
FOOD PAIRING: Ice-cold lettuce wrapped around ground beef and rice with corn salsa and plenty of hot sauce
AVAILABILITY: On tap at Morgan Street

JAN

9

Beerfact

The craft brewing industry produced nearly 8.6 million barrels of craft beer in the United States in 2008. Total U.S. craft brewing industry annual dollar volume is $6.3 billion. The U.S. brewery count of 1,525 on July 31, 2009, is the highest total in 100 years. (The 2008 total includes breweries that closed during the year, and the July 2009 count is higher than at any time in 2008.)

Morgan Street Brewery
721 North Second Street
Saint Louis, MO 63102
www.morganstreetbrewery.com

🍺 Pearl Street Porter

"Beersteaks and porter are good belly mortar."
—SCOTTISH PROVERB

TYPE: Porter
COLOR: Dark brown
SMELL: Roasted malt and earthy hops
TASTE: A creamy, medium-bodied beer with flavors of toffee, chocolate, and dark-roasted coffee that are accentuated by a hoppy, bitter finish and a burnt toast aftertaste.
FOOD PAIRING: BBQ chicken drumsticks
AVAILABILITY: Made to celebrate Boulder's 150th anniversary (limited release)

JAN

10

Beerfact

Sir John Lubbock, a noted nineteenth-century biologist who studied, among other things, ants, bees, and wasps, did an experiment during which he got a large number of ants drunk. He discovered that those ants that remained sober would carry their drunken friends back to the nest— but only if they were from the same colony.

Twisted Pine Brewing Company
3201 Walnut Street, Suite A
Boulder, CO 80301
www.twistedpinebrewing.com

🍺 Longboard Island Lager

"Oh, lager beer! It makes good cheer, and proves the poor man's worth; it cools the body through and through, and regulates the health."
—ANONYMOUS

TYPE: Pale lager
COLOR: Golden
SMELL: Baked wheat and citrus hops
TASTE: Smooth and easy to drink, with flavors of pine and warm biscuit. Light enough to go down quick after a long morning of surfing.
FOOD PAIRING: Shrimp and jalapeño ceviche on garlic-rubbed toast
AVAILABILITY: Year round

JAN
11

Beer*fact*

In the United States, a barrel holds 31 gallons of beer. A standard keg, like the ones popular at college parties, holds 15.5 gallons of beer. An "import" keg weighs in at 13.2 gallons. Pony kegs hold 7.75 gallons. The little-known "sixth barrel" keg holds only 5 gallons. The average American consumes 23.1 gallons of beer annually.

Kona Brewing Company
7192 Kalaniana'ole Highway
Inside Hawaii Kai, waterside
Honolulu, HI 96825
www.konabrewingco.com

 Shiva

"(Hops), when put in beer, stops putrification and lends longer durability."
—HILDEGARD OF BINGEN

TYPE: India pale ale
COLOR: Golden honey
SMELL: Floral and citrus hops
TASTE: A medium-bodied beer that leads with citrus and pine hops, but catches its balance nicely with a sweet malty backbone.
FOOD PAIRING: Beer-battered grouper with thin-cut French fries and garlic tartar sauce
AVAILABILITY: Year round

JAN
12

Beersaints
Hildegard of Bingen (born 1098 c.e., died September 17, 1179 c.e.)
Also known as Saint Hildegard and Sybil of the Rhine, Hildegard of Bingen was an author, a scientist, a naturalist, an herbalist, a poet, a composer, and a German Benedictine abbess. She is credited with having founded the monasteries of Rupertsberg in 1150 and Eibingen in 1165. A multitalented woman, her writings include the earliest known reference to adding hops to beer.

Asheville Brewing Company
675 Merrimon Avenue
Asheville, NC 28804
www.ashevillebrewing.com

🍺 Imperial Stout

"Mother's in the kitchen washing out the jugs, Sister's in the pantry bottling the suds, Father's in the cellar mixin' up the hops, Johnny's on the front porch watchin' for the cops."

—ANONYMOUS

TYPE: Imperial stout

COLOR: Dark brown to black

SMELL: Dried fruit, chocolate, and heavily roasted malt

TASTE: Nice medium-bodied beer with strong flavors of chocolate and burnt sugar. In the mouth, this beer is smooth, silky, and creamy, just the way a good stout should be. Though it's 10% ABV, it goes down surprisingly easily, so watch out. This one can sneak up on you.

FOOD PAIRING: Smoked duck with caramelized onions and dried cherry relish

AVAILABILITY: Year round

JAN

13

Beerfest

2010 marked the tenth anniversary of the Big Beers, Belgians, and Barleywines Festival, which takes place in January in Vail, Colorado (*www .bigbeersfestival.com*). This event features both a commercial beer tasting and a homebrew competition. Festival directors define "big" as a minimum of 7.0%. No beer under this ABV qualifies for inclusion.

Left Hand Brewing Company
1265 Boston Avenue
Longmont, CO 80025
www.lefthandbrewing.com

🍺 8 Ball Stout

"A quench of bartenders."
—KAREN HEBERMAN'S WINNING ENTRY IN A COMPETITION
TO FIND A COLLECTIVE NOUN FOR BARTENDERS

TYPE: Stout
COLOR: Dark brown with a tinge of red
SMELL: Roasted malt, chocolate, nuts, coffee
TASTE: A smooth, rich brew that starts off with mocha bean and sweet
   espresso. Then it moves on to roasted malt and a touch of bitterness
   followed by a chocolate and coffee aftertaste.
FOOD PAIRING: Dark chocolate cake with sweet whipped cream
AVAILABILITY: Year round

JAN
14

Beerwords

Irish drinking toasts:

May the saddest day of your future be no worse than the happiest day of your past.

May misfortune follow you the rest of your life, and never catch up.

May you always have a clean shirt, a clear conscience, and enough coins in your pocket to buy a pint!

Lost Coast Brewery
123 West Third Street
Eureka, CA 95501
www.lostcoast.com

🍺 Amber Ale

"And malt does more than Milton can
To justify God's ways to man."
—A. E. HOUSMAN

TYPE: Alt
COLOR: Deep orange or reddish copper
SMELL: Very mild nose with just a touch of banana
TASTE: Light-bodied smooth drinking beer that could easily lull you into drinking one too many. There are flavors of lightly toasted bread surrounded by slices of bitter melon.
FOOD PAIRING: Smoked sausage and mushroom pizza
AVAILABILITY: Year round

JAN
15

Beerfact

Altbier, also called Alt, is a top-fermenting beer that originated in Westphalia and eventually spread to the Rhineland. Alt, which means "old," refers to the older method of using warm top-fermenting yeast to facilitate the production of alcohol and carbonation, as opposed to the colder, bottom-fermenting done with lagers.

Alaskan Brewing Company
5429 Shaune Drive
Juneau, AK 99801-9540
www.alaskanbeer.com

🍺 Riverwest Stein Beer

"Men are nicotine-soaked, beer-besmirched, whiskey-greased, red-eyed devils."
—CARRIE NATION

TYPE: American amber lager
COLOR: Cloudy dark amber with an off-white head
SMELL: Malt and caramel with pine cone and lemon zest
TASTE: Medium-bodied beer with a smooth, silky mouthfeel and a delicious caramel malt flavor. There are hints of grapefruit and orange peel. Smooth all the way to the last drop.
FOOD PAIRING: Authentic German cabbage rolls filled with ground beef and spicy pork sausage
AVAILABILITY: Year round

JAN

16

Beerfact

Fueled by the temperance movement, the United States Senate proposed the 18th Amendment to the Constitution on December 18, 1917. It was approved by thirty-six states and then ratified on January 16, 1919 and put into effect January 16, 1920. As a result, the illegal smuggling and distribution of alcohol—known as bootlegging—became rampant, sparking the creation of tens of thousands of speakeasy clubs across the nation.

Lakefront Brewery
1872 N. Commerce Street
Milwaukee, WI 53212
www.lakefrontbrewery.com

🍺 Shark Attack Double Red Ale

"Beer brewers shall sell no beer to the citizens unless it be three weeks old; to the foreigner they may knowingly sell younger beer."
—GERMAN BEER LAW, 1466

TYPE: Red ale
COLOR: Deep mahogany
SMELL: Caramel malts, pine, and a touch of alcohol
TASTE: A creamy, medium-bodied beer with flavors of caramel, toffee, and roasted malt followed by dried dark fruit and a pine finish.
FOOD PAIRING: Filet mignon with five-pepper sauce
AVAILABILITY: Year round

**JAN
17**

Beerfest

2009 Great American Beer Festival Winners by Category

American Style Amber/Red Ale: Organic Rise Up Red, Hopworks Urban Brewery, Portland, OR

Imperial Red Ale: Shark Attack, Pizza Port Solana Beach, Solana Beach, CA

English Style Mild Ale: Sara's Ruby Mild, Magnolia Gastropub & Brewery, San Francisco, CA

Ordinary or Special Bitter: Big Rapid Red, Beaver St. Brewery, Flagstaff, AZ

Port Brewing Company
155 Mata Way, Suite 104
San Marcos, CA 92069
www.portbrewing.com

🍺 Green Lakes Organic Ale

"No animal ever invented anything as bad as drunkenness—or as good as drink."
—G. K. CHESTERTON

TYPE: Amber ale
COLOR: Amber
SMELL: Sweet roasted malt and citrus
TASTE: A subtly complex beer with hints of molasses and caramel underneath a predominate flavor of roasted malt and a good blending of hops.
FOOD PAIRING: Black bean chili
AVAILABILITY: Year round

JAN
18

Brew*tip*

Did you know that both clear and green glass do not protect your beer from harmful ultraviolet rays? Both sunlight and florescent light can damage the taste of your beer. To avoid this, use only brown glass or ceramic bottles. Kegging your beer will also protect it, though it will be much harder to bring your homebrew with you to parties.

Deschutes Brewery
901 SW Simpson Avenue
Bend, OR 97702
www.deschutesbrewery.com

🍺 Old Bawdy Barley Wine

"You're not drunk if you can lie on the floor without holding on."
—DEAN MARTIN

TYPE: Barley wine

COLOR: Orange amber

SMELL: Aromatic nose of wild herbs against a backdrop of sweet, succulent malted caramel.

TASTE: Rich and spicy, with big hops, malt, and yeast in every gulp. Thick and powerful, it slides over your tongue and assaults your senses with its 10% alcohol by volume.

FOOD PAIRING: Pair with a big, pungent blue cheese like Roquefort or Gogonzola. Then laugh at it while your beer goes toe to toe with the creamy goodness and overpowering flavor.

AVAILABILITY: Year round

JAN

19

Brewtip

Though the name may conjure images of monks stomping on vats of roasted barley, the truth is barley wines are beers, ales in fact, and are made in the same fashion as any other top-fermented brew. Originally brewed in England at the turn of the twentieth century, barley wines are typically very high in alcohol content. On average they range between 7.0% and 12.0% ABV.

The Pike Brewing Company
1415 First Avenue
Seattle, WA 98122
www.pikebrewing.com

🍺 Domaine Du Page

"Yes, sir. I'm a real southern boy. I got a red neck, white socks, and Blue Ribbon beer."
—BILLY CARTER

TYPE: Bière de garde
COLOR: Amber
SMELL: Malt, alcohol, honey, and molasses
TASTE: Flavors of caramel, bittersweet chocolate malt, and toasted honey blend into crisp hops that come through in the finish.
FOOD PAIRING: Persian beef kebabs served with lentil and tomato stew over basmati rice
AVAILABILITY: Year round

**JAN
20**

Beerfact

This story begins with two brothers, good friends, both with a healthy hankering for hefeweisen they picked up in Europe. They open a home-brewing supply shop called The Brewer's Coop in Naperville, Illinois. One night over Sunday dinner, their mother tells them, "You guys either need to open a brewery or shut up about it 'cause you're driving me crazy." In 1996 Two Brothers Brewing Company is born—to this day, a 100 percent family-owned operation.

Two Brothers Brewing Company
30W315 Calumet Avenue
Warrenville, IL 60555
www.twobrosbrew.com

🍺 Red Tail Ale

"Yes, my soul sentimentally craves British beer."
—THOMAS CAMPBELL, AUTHOR

TYPE: Amber ale
COLOR: Dark amber
SMELL: Toasted malt and honey
TASTE: A crisp, easy, medium-bodied beer with flavors of caramel, fresh bread, and sweet honey, followed by a touch of earthy hops.
FOOD PAIRING: Salmon cakes served with fresh tartar sauce
AVAILABILITY: Year round

JAN
21

Beerfact

In 1840, Americans drank 2.5 gallons of spirits per capita, but only about a gallon of beer. But in 1896, they downed 15 gallons of beer. Pre-Prohibition beer consumption reached its high point in 1914 at 21 gallons. When the ban of drinking ended, it took the brewing industry a long time to recover, and it wasn't until 1975 that Americans would drink as much beer as they did in 1914.

Medocino Brewing Company
13351 So. Highway 101
Hopland, CA 95449
www.mendobrew.com

🍺 Krank Shaft

"I drink with impunity . . . or anyone else who invites me."
—W. C. FIELDS

TYPE: Kölsch

COLOR: Light straw

SMELL: Grain, floral hops, and a touch of tree fruit

TASTE: A lighter-bodied beer with flavors of biscuit, pear, white grape, and green apple followed by a touch of grassy hops. It finishes with notes of tree fruit and ends with just a touch of bitter aftertaste.

FOOD PAIRING: Garlic and roasted red pepper hummus served with toasted pita triangles

AVAILABILITY: Year round

**JAN
22**

Publore

They take their beer very seriously at the Map Room. Offering over 300 beers, representing 36 different styles, each is served in its proper glass and rinsed before the pour to ensure proper head retention. Each month they invite a local brewer in to teach about the different styles and how the brewing process works for each.

Visit the Map Room at 1949 N. Hoyne, Chicago, IL 60647.

Metropolitan Brewing Company
5121 N. Ravenswood Avenue
Chicago, IL 60640
www.metrobrewing.com

🍺 Phin & Matt's

"Mean spirits under disappointment, like small beer in a thunderstorm, always turn sour."
—JOHN RANDOLPH (1773–1833)

TYPE: Pale ale
COLOR: Pale golden
SMELL: Grain and citrus
TASTE: A light- to medium-bodied beer that is nicely balanced between sweet, roasted malt flavors and bitter citrus notes. Ends with a touch of caramel and a spicy hop aftertaste.
FOOD PAIRING: Lemon salmon planked on cherry wood
AVAILABILITY: Year round

**JAN
23**

Publore

The Biercafé at Belmont Station keeps seventeen beers on tap (including one cask conditioned), over 1,000 beers in bottles, kegs to go, wine, sake, cider, and mead, and they are a bottle shop on top of it all. Sign up for their Twitter feed (belmontstation).

Visit the Biercafé at Belmont Station at 4500 SE Stark Street, Portland, OR 97215, *www.belmont-station.com*.

Southern Tier Brewing Company
2051A Stoneman Circle
Lakewood, NY 14750
www.southerntierbrewing.com

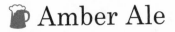 Amber Ale

"Where village statesmen talked with looks profound, And news much older than their ale went round."
—OLIVER GOLDSMITH

TYPE: Amber ale
COLOR: Dark amber
SMELL: Caramel with nice floral hops
TASTE: Flavors of malt and dried stone fruit and nice yeasty bread dominate while citrus hops and notes of chocolate fill out a fairly complex taste profile.
FOOD PAIRING: Charred corn guacamole with blue corn chips
AVAILABILITY: Year round

JAN
24

Beerfact

Just a stone's throw from the Hood River, Full Sail set up shop in 1987 inside what they affectionately call the "haunted Technicolor pigeon cannery," the former Diamond Fruit Cannery. One year later, they bought an Italian bottling line and used the manual still-wine bottling machinery to put Full Sail Amber into the corner grocery store, making it the first craft brew in bottles.

Full Sail Brewery
506 Columbia Street
Hood River, OR 97031
www.fullsailbrewing.com

 I.P.A.

"Here's to a long life and a merry one, A quick death and an easy one, A pretty girl and an honest one, A cold beer and another one!"
—ANONYMOUS

TYPE: India pale ale
COLOR: Deep copper
SMELL: Floral hops
TASTE: A light- to medium-bodied beer with a toasty, malty backbone and waves of floral hops. Crisp and dry, it finishes with a nice hop resin aftertaste.
FOOD PAIRING: Roasted bass with fennel and chives
AVAILABILITY: Year round

**JAN
25**

Publore

Father's Office is a dark hipster hangout with taps all over the back wall and a list of good 750ml bottles to share (served in champagne buckets). The kitchen earns its solid reputation with perfectly cooked burgers, baskets of sweet potato and regular French fries, grilled figs with blue cheese, oatmeal stout ribs . . . even smoked eel. Here are their locations:

Santa Monica:
1018 Montana Ave
Santa Monica, CA 90403

Los Angeles:
3229 Helms Avenue
Los Angeles, CA 90034
www.fathersoffice.com

Harpoon Brewery
306 Northern Avenue
Boston, MA 02210
www.harpoonbrewery.com

🍺 Smokestack Series Double-Wide India Pale Ale

"The problem with some people is that when they aren't drunk, they're sober."
—WILLIAM BUTLER YEATS

JAN 26

TYPE: Double India pale ale
COLOR: Rusty amber
SMELL: Piney and floral hops with a touch of sweetness and a hint of yeast
TASTE: A very smooth, almost oily, medium-bodied beer with warm caramel malt and liquid toffee flavors followed by a huge rush of citrus and pine hops.
FOOD PAIRING: Crumbled sausage and mushroom pizza on a thick bready crust
AVAILABILITY: Year round

Beer*fact*

Other things to do with beer:

- **Fire extinguisher:** Place your thumb over the open mouth of a mostly full beer bottle and shake vigorously. Then point the end at the fire and release your thumb just enough to allow a narrow stream to squirt out and quench the flames.
- **Meat tenderizer:** Poke holes in a steak, place it inside a sealable plastic baggie, fill it with a pale ale, and let it marinate overnight.

Boulevard Brewing Company
2501 Southwest Blvd.
Kansas City, MO 64108
www.boulevard.com

🍺 Old Ruffian

"Flow, Welsted, flow! Like thine inspirer, beer!"
—ALEXANDER POPE

TYPE: Barley wine
COLOR: Caramel copper
SMELL: Sweet malt, citrus, and earthy hops
TASTE: Full bodied and full of life, starting out with sweet flavors of malt, molasses, and caramel that linger as they develop into citrus and pepper. It finishes with a touch of alcohol and leaves with a bitter aftertaste.
FOOD PAIRING: Saint Agur blue cheese with fig spread
AVAILABILITY: January to March

JAN
27

Beerfact

Things you probably didn't know about Great Divide Brewing Company:

Opened in 1994 by homebrewer Brian Dunn, the initial facility was set up inside an abandoned dairy processing plant. In 2008 they were ranked 14th on Ratebeer.com's "The Best Brewers in the World." Beer Advocate ranked them 7th in the 2008 "All-Time Top Breweries on Planet Earth." Whoa.

Great Divide Brewing Company
2201 Arapahoe Street
Denver, CO 80205
www.greatdivide.com

🍺 Mad Hatter

"When I was in that city, I asked a policeman where I could get a glass of beer. 'You see that second street on your right?' the officer said. 'Well, go down there, and the fourth door on your right is a movie theater. That's the only place in town you can buy it.'"
—AMERICAN PROHIBITION JOKE

TYPE: India pale ale
COLOR: Light copper
SMELL: Pine and a touch of yeast
TASTE: Pine first, then grass, then grapefruit, dandelion to finish, and a sharp lemon aftertaste. A very smooth beer with just a touch of sweet malt to hold it all together.
FOOD PAIRING: Poached sole with lemon and thyme
AVAILABILITY: Year round

*Beer**words***
Beer toasts of the world:

Armenian: *Genatz*
Bosnian: *Zivjeli*
Cornish: *Yeghes da*
Greenlandic: *Kasugta*
Latvian: *Prieka*

Mexican: *Slaud*
Occitan: *A la vòstra*
Pakistani: *Sanda bashi*
Russian: *Vashe zdorovie*
Serbian: *Zivjeli*

New Holland Brewing Company
66 E. 8th Street
Holland, MI 49423
www.newhollandbrew.com

🍺 90 Shilling Ale

Sam: "What'll you have, Norm?" Norm: "Well, I'm in a gambling mood, Sammy. I'll take a glass of whatever comes out of that tap." Sam: "Looks like beer, Norm." Norm: "Call me Mister Lucky."
  —*CHEERS*

TYPE: Scottish ale

COLOR: Dark amber

SMELL: Caramel, cinnamon, and floral hops

TASTE: Smooth and balanced, with notes of sweet caramel and roasted malt that balance with citrus and floral hops. A very drinkable, medium-bodied brew that finishes with bitter hops and has a clean finish.

FOOD PAIRING: Sweet sesame chicken wings

AVAILABILITY: Year round

JAN
29

Beerfact

Most Scottish pubs will offer beers that sound like prices: 60 shilling, 70 shilling . . . 90 shilling. This is in fact exactly what they are, or were. The names are based on prices charged per barrel for beer during the nineteenth century. The stronger or better quality the beer, the more it cost.

Odell Brewing Company
800 East Lincoln Avenue
Fort Collins, CO 80524
www.odellbrewing.com

1554

"Merry met, and merry part, I drink to thee with all my heart."

—ANONYMOUS

TYPE: Belgian dark ale

COLOR: Dark brown

SMELL: Roasted malt and ground coffee

TASTE: A medium- to full-bodied beer with a smooth, creamy mouthfeel. Flavors of dark, bittersweet chocolate and roasted coffee blend with sweet, almost tangy malt and a touch of bitter on the finish.

FOOD PAIRING: Masa-harina-and-buttermilk-coated onion rings

AVAILABILITY: Year round

JAN

30

Beerword

Contract Brewing Company: A business that hires another brewery to produce its beer. It can also be a brewery that hires another brewery to produce additional beer. The contract brewing company handles marketing, sales, and distribution of its beer, while generally leaving the brewing and packaging to its producer-brewery.

—Beertown.org (The Brewers Association website)

New Belgium Brewing Company
500 Linden Street
Fort Collins, CO 80524
www.newbelgium.com

🍺 Black Bavarian

"A drink a day keeps the shrink away."
—EDWARD ABBEY, AUTHOR

TYPE: Schwarzbier
COLOR: Black
SMELL: Toffee, sweet malt, coffee, and dried dark fruit
TASTE: Flavors of caramel and roasted malt intermingle with fresh brown bread and brown sugar simple syrup. It finishes smooth with notes of chocolate and coffee, ending with just a touch of smoke.
FOOD PAIRING: Potato gnocchi tossed with oil and covered with shredded aged Gouda and Parmesan cheeses
AVAILABILITY: Year round

JAN 31

Beer*fact*

In the nineteenth century it was a widely held belief that in order for nursing mothers to be able to breast-feed their children they must consume seven pints of beer a day. This myth was debunked by the Munich Health Department in 1876, which decreed that seven pints was excessive and that only two pints were needed.

Sprecher Brewing Company
701 W. Glendale Avenue
Glendale, WI 53209
www.sprecherbrewery.com

🍺 Yellowtail Pale

"Wait it out with a six-pack of beer and a football game."
—FORMER BUFFALO, NY, MAYOR JAMES GRIFFIN'S ADVICE
DURING A 1977 BLIZZARD

TYPE: Kölsch
COLOR: Clear yellow
SMELL: Yeasty with mild citrus
TASTE: A light, easy-to-drink beer with mild yeast flavors and a touch of spicy hops. Great for an easy day in the sun.
FOOD PAIRING: Wild mushrooms baked with Parmesan cheese
AVAILABILITY: Year round

FEB

1

Beerfact
In addition to being a world-class brewery, Ballast Point also happens to distill spirits as well. Starting out in 1992 as Home Brew Mart, their original desire was to help others brew good beer. But by 1996, they had constructed a working brewery behind the retail store. Things went so well that by 2005 they had to open a second brewery.

Ballast Point Brewing Company
10051 Old Grove Road, Suite B
San Diego, CA 92131
www.ballastpoint.com

🍺 Honey Amber Ale

*Sam: "What'd you like, Normie?" Norm: "A reason to live.
Give me another beer."*
  —CHEERS

TYPE: Amber ale
COLOR: Light coppery brown
SMELL: Honey, sweet malt, and floral hops
TASTE: A smooth, medium-bodied beer that starts with flavors of sweet
  malt, caramel, and honey, then balances nicely with mandarin orange
  and citrus hops.
FOOD PAIRING: Curried lamb burgers with sweet potato fries
AVAILABILITY: Year round

FEB

2

Beer*fest*

2009 Great American Beer Festival Winners by Category
German-Style Kölsch: Kolsch, Sierra Nevada Brewing Co., Chico, CA
English-Style Summer Ale: Light Rock Ale, RJ Rockers Brewing Co.,
  Spartanburg, SC
Classic English-Style Pale Ale: Mactarnahan's Amber, Pyramid Brewer-
  ies, Seattle, WA
English-Style India Pale Ale: Beech Street Bitter, Pizza Port Carlsbad,
  Carlsbad, CA

RJ Rockers Brewing Company
226-A West Main Street
Spartanburg, SC 29306
www.rjrockers.com

🍺 Double Crooked Tree

"God made yeast, as well as dough, and he loves fermentation just as dearly as he loves vegetation."
—RALPH WALDO EMERSON

TYPE: India pale ale

COLOR: Beautiful slightly cloudy amber

SMELL: Honey, mandarin orange, and floral hops

TASTE: A thick, luscious, medium- to full-bodied behemoth with a blast of citrus hops that balance nicely with flavors of delicious toffee and spun sugar, continuing on with notes of buttered caramel corn and coffee and ending with a butterscotch and hops finish.

FOOD PAIRING: Spicy lamb burger with roasted red pepper mayonaise

AVAILABILITY: February

FEB

3

Brewtip

International Bittering Units (IBU) is the unit of measure by which brewers describe how much bitterness has been imparted on a beer due to the amount of hops used during the brewing process. Though a beer with a high IBU does in fact have a lot of bitterness in it, the actual flavor of the beer will also be influenced by how much sweet malt it contains. Dark Horse Brewery's Double Crooked Tree IPA boasts an IBU of 98. Pucker up.

Dark Horse Brewing Company
511 S. Kalamazoo Avenue
Marshall, MI 49068
www.darkhorsebrewery.com

🍺 S1NIST0R

"Work is the curse of the drinking classes."
—OSCAR WILDE

TYPE: Black ale
COLOR: Black
SMELL: Chocolate, smoke, and roasted malt
TASTE: A surprisingly light-bodied beer with a smooth mouthfeel, flavors of rich chocolate, dark-roasted malt, and notes of nuttiness.
FOOD PAIRING: Corn hushpuppies dipped in honey
AVAILABILITY: Year round

FEB

4

Beer*words*

How to say you're drunk (in English):

Hammered

Keyed

Legless

Gassed

Fried

Bent

Pissed

Shit-faced

Potted

Trashed

Floored

10 Barrel Brewing Company
20750 High Desert Lane #107
Bend, OR 97701
www.10barrel.com

🍺 Cobblestone Steam Lager

"A bar is better than a newspaper for public discussion."
—JIM PARKER, BREWPUB OWNER

> **TYPE:** Steam beer
> **COLOR:** Dark amber to ruby red
> **SMELL:** Malt and caramel up front with a slightly fainter scent of hops
> **TASTE:** Nice hoppy flavor with very little bitter aftertaste. The sweet malt washes over your taste buds before being cleansed by a subtle taste of pine and the balance of the hops.
> **FOOD PAIRING:** Room-temperature jack cheese on top of toasted French bread and smothered in a jalapeño pepper jelly
> **AVAILABILITY:** On tap at Morgan Street only

FEB

5

Beerwords

Brewpub: A restaurant-brewery that sells 25 percent or more of its beer on site. The beer is brewed primarily for sale in the restaurant and bar. The beer is often dispensed directly from the brewery's storage tanks. Where allowed by law, brewpubs often sell beer "to go" and/or distribute to off-site accounts. Note: BA recategorizes a company as a microbrewery if its off-site (distributed) beer sales exceed 75 percent.

—Official Brewers Association

Morgan Street Brewery
721 North Second Street
Saint Louis, MO 63102
www.morganstreetbrewery.com

🍺 New Grist

"If God had intended us to drink beer, he would have given us stomachs."
   —DAVID DAYE

TYPE: Gluten-free beer
COLOR: Light golden
SMELL: Cooked rice and apple
TASTE: A surprising wheat and malt flavor for a beer with no wheat or barley, blended with a substantial amount of bitter Granny Smith apple.
FOOD PAIRING: Lemon-marinated halibut with grilled zucchini and flourless chocolate cake for dessert
AVAILABILITY: Year round

FEB

6

Beerfact

Gluten intolerance, also known as celiac disease, is a sensitivity to the protein gluten in wheat, barley, and rye—three of the most commonly used ingredients in beer. Being unable to ingest gluten means "no beer for you." That is, unless you can lay your hands on a few bottles of New Grist. Certified gluten free by the United States government, this first-of-its-kind brew is made with sorghum, rice, hops, water, and gluten-free yeast.

Lakefront Brewery
1872 N. Commerce Street
Milwaukee, WI 53212
www.lakefrontbrewery.com

🍺 Woodenhead Ale

"I should like a great lake of ale for the King of Kings."
—ST. BRIGID

TYPE: Amber ale

COLOR: Amber

SMELL: Plum, toasted oak, and grassy hops

TASTE: A complex beer that starts out with flavors of sweet malt, rich toffee, and warm caramel complemented by earthy, herbal hops. Flavors of oak and bourbon emerge, giving you a whole new set of tastes to ponder.

FOOD PAIRING: Lamb burger with garlic aioli and caramelized Brussels sprouts

AVAILABILITY: Year round on draft

FEB
7

Beersaints

Saint Brigid (born 451 C.E., died February 1, 525 C.E.)

Perhaps the second most famous saint in Ireland (behind Saint Patrick), Saint Brigid is said to have taken the beer from one barrel and made it stretch to quench the thirst of the parishioners and clergy from eighteen different churches. There is another legend in which she turned her dirty bath water into beer so that clerics visiting the monastery would have something to drink.

River City Brewing Company
545 Downtown Plaza, Suite 1115
Sacramento, CA 95814
www.rivercitybrewing.net

🍺 Harpoon Munich Dark

"You don't have to be a beer drinker to play darts, but it helps."
—ANONYMOUS

TYPE: Munich dunkel
COLOR: Rich brown
SMELL: Roasted malt, chocolate, dried fruit, and hops
TASTE: A drier, medium-bodied beer that leads with sweet malt and toasted bread followed by the distinct flavor of chocolate. It finishes crisp with a hoppy aftertaste.
FOOD PAIRING: Saurbraten
AVAILABILITY: Year round

FEB

8

Beerfest

2009 Great American Beer Festival Winners by Category
Bock: Troegenator, Tröegs Brewing Co., Harrisburg, PA
German-Style Doppelbock or Eisbock: The Kaiser, Avery Brewing Co., Boulder, CO
Baltic-Style Porter: Duck-Rabbit Baltic Porter, The Duck-Rabbit Craft Brewery, Inc., Farmville, NC
Golden or Blonde Ale: Golden Spike, Tustin Brewing Co., Tustin, CA

Harpoon Brewery
306 Northern Avenue
Boston, MA 02210
www.harpoonbrewery.com

🍺 Dark Night Oatmeal Stout

"Back and side go bare, go bare. Both foot and hand go cold. But, belly, God send thee good ale enough, whether it be new or old."
—BISHOP JOHN STILL (C. 1543–1608)

FEB
9

TYPE: Oatmeal stout
COLOR: Black
SMELL: Coffee, chocolate, and sweet malt
TASTE: A smooth, creamy, full-bodied beer with flavors of chocolate, roasted barely, malted milk, and dried fruit. A very comforting beer with a velvety finish.
FOOD PAIRING: Barron Point oysters
AVAILABILITY: Year round

Beer*fest*

2009 Great American Beer Festival Winners by Category
Extra Special Bitter or Strong Bitter: ESB, Redhook Ales, Woodinville, Woodinville, WA
Scottish-Style Ale: Railbender Ale, Erie Brewing Co, Erie, PA
Irish-Style Red Ale: Ridgetop Red, Silver City Brewery, Silverdale, WA
English-Style Brown Ale: Longboard Brown, Rock Bottom Brewery, La Jolla, CA

Santa Cruz Ale Works
150 Dubois Street
Santa Cruz, CA 95060
www.santacruzaleworks.com

 Witte

"What two ideas are more inseparable than beer and Britannia?"
—SYDNEY SMITH, ENGLISH CLERGYMAN

TYPE: Witbier
COLOR: Cloudy golden yellow
SMELL: Citrus and cloves
TASTE: Opens with flavors of grapefruit, lemon zest, and Valencia oranges that intermingle with fresh wheat, coriander, nutmeg, and clove. It finishes with grain and a citrusy bitter aftertaste.
FOOD PAIRING: Sockeye salmon stuffed with crab and shrimp and drizzled with a beurre blanc sauce
AVAILABILITY: Year round

FEB
10

Beersaints
Saint Columbanus (born 540 C.E., died November 615 C.E.)
Columbanus is credited with having powerful breath. As the story goes, a group of pagans was preparing a huge vat of beer as a sacrifice for a ritual for Wodan. Columbanus asked what the beer was to be used for. When he heard, he took in a deep breath and blew so hard that he destroyed the vat. When asked why he would do such a thing, Columbanus replied that the pagans were wasting good ale.

Brewery Ommegang
656 County Highway 33
Cooperstown, NY 13326
www.ommegang.com

IPA

"Beer is living proof that God loves us and wants us to be happy."
—BENJAMIN FRANKLIN

TYPE: India pale ale
COLOR: A warm golden brown
SMELL: All hops, bitter but not overpowering
TASTE: A light, hoppy India pale ale. Under the bitterness is a warm caramel coupled with a nice grapefruit flavor. There is of course a hop-filled aftertaste.
FOOD PAIRING: A bucket of grilled chicken, mopped liberally with spicy barbeque sauce.
AVAILABILITY: Year round

FEB
11

Beer*thought*

The bitterness resulting from hops is not a punishment. It is instead proof that both god and the brewers at Stone love you. That their devotion to good beer is real, tangible, and here for you through good times and bad. It is a reminder that the hard days and long hours will be rewarded and that happiness can be found at the bottom of your tankard.

Stone Brewing Company
1999 Citracado Blvd.
Escondido, CA 92029
www.stonebrew.com

🍺 The "Censored" Rich Copper Ale

"An oppressive government is more to be feared than a tiger, or a beer."
—CONFUCIUS

TYPE: American amber ale
COLOR: Coppery red
SMELL: Fresh wheat, like bread right out of the oven, only in liquid form and with more kick
TASTE: A little sweet, with a distinct caramel flavor. Not candy, more like melted sugar just as it starts to turn golden brown, a more adult style of sweet.
FOOD PAIRING: Hanger steak just off the grill, served over mashed potatoes.
AVAILABILITY: Year round

FEB

12

Beerthought

Some children grow up never learning good taste. They mature into seemingly functional, fun-loving adults, but underneath it, something is missing. Next thing you know, they've grown up and joined the censorship board. Well we're not going to sit on our hands while good taste is rubber stamped out of our lives. We're going to use those hands to drink our beers.

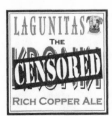

Lagunitas Brewing Company
1280 North McDowell Blvd.
Petaluma, CA 94954
www.lagunitas.com

🍺 Autumn Maple

"Under a bad cloak, there is often a good drinker."
—MIGUEL DE CERVANTES

TYPE: Belgian strong dark ale
COLOR: Light brown
SMELL: Maple, spice, molasses, and yams
TASTE: Brewed with yams, Autumn Maple is a variation on the "pumpkin" beer theme of autumn seasonals. A nice thick, almost sticky, medium- to full-bodied beer with flavors of tart fruit, maple, and spice. Toasted malts, burnt sugar, and dark fruit appear as accent flavors, giving way to a distinctly sweet yam aftertaste.
FOOD PAIRING: Sweet potato (yam) fries with ginger aioli
AVAILABILITY: Fall

FEB

13

Beer*words*

There is some argument about the origins of the phrase "Wet your whistle." One school of thought claims that many years ago, in English pubs, the mugs or cups had a whistle attached to them, so that patrons could simply alert the barkeep of their thirst with a blow. Others point out that during the Middle Ages the word "whistle" was a slang term for "throat." They argue that wetting your whistle simply meant to quench your thirst or dampen your dry throat.

The Bruery
715 Dunn Way
Placentia, CA 92870
www.thebruery.com

🍺 Old Foghorn

"Fermentation and civilization are inseparable."
—JOHN CIARDI, WRITER

TYPE: Barley wine
COLOR: Amber brown
SMELL: Burnt marshmallow and brown sugar syrup
TASTE: Medium-bodied beer with a thick and creamy mouthfeel. Sweet, spicy, slightly fruity flavors that lean toward plum or dried grape. Very light hoppiness at the very beginning with a dry finish.
FOOD PAIRING: Roasted chicken breast with a raspberry demi-glace and a drizzle of sour cream
AVAILABILITY: Year round

FEB
14

Brew*tip*

If you are thinking about taking up homebrewing, remember that getting to the finished product requires patience. As a rule of thumb, ales require a minimum of five weeks before they are ready to drink: one week to ferment, one week to condition, and three weeks to mature. Lagers require double that: two weeks of primary fermentation, two weeks of secondary fermentation, two weeks to condition, and four weeks to mature.

Anchor Brewing Company
1705 Mariposa Street
San Francisco, CA 94107
www.anchorbrewing.com

🍺 Walter's Premium Pilsner

"We're wanted men, we'll strike again, but first let's have a beer."

—JIMMY BUFFETT

TYPE: Pilsner

COLOR: Clear yellow

SMELL: Malt, yeast, and cream

TASTE: One to kick back on the couch with, Walter's is light and easy to drink with flavors of yeast, light malt, and just a hint of citrus.

FOOD PAIRING: Tuna melt

AVAILABILITY: Year round

FEB
15

Beer*fact*

Initially produced by Walter's Brewery in 1874, Walter's Premium Pilsner managed to survive prohibition by being sold as packaged, unfermented wort. The brewery claimed that customers would want it for its "nutritional value," but homebrewers were able to finish the process in their own basements. Sadly, Walter's Brewery shut its doors in 1990. That is, until the spring of 2009, when Northwoods Brewpub relaunched the brand, to the delight of beer drinkers everywhere.

Northwoods Brewpub
3560 Oakwood Mall Drive
Eau Claire, WI 54701
www.northwoodsbrewpub.com

🍺 Ale Diablo

"Milk is for babies. When you grow up, you have to drink beer."
    —ARNOLD SCHWARZENEGGER

TYPE: Blonde ale
COLOR: Hazy pale golden
SMELL: Honey, toasted grain, and citrus
TASTE: A medium-bodied beer with flavors of honey and sweet malt followed by pear, tart green apple, yeast, and spicy hops. Finishes sweet with a slightly spicy aftertaste.
FOOD PAIRING: Grilled eggplant with roasted tomatoes and yogurt
AVAILABILITY: Year round

**FEB
16**

Beerfact
The first American tax on beer was levied in 1862 by the Union Congress. By the early 1900s, taxes on beer and alcohol brought in 40 percent of the nation's revenue. That all stopped, of course, during Prohibition. However, in 1933 when the Twenty-first Amendment ended Dry America, it took only forty-eight hours for American brewers to deliver $10 million in tax revenue, roughly the equivalent of $145 million today.

Steamworks Brewing Company
442 Wolverine Drive
Bayfield, CO 81122
www.steamworksbrewing.com

🍺 Chimay Triple, Cinq Cents

"No soldier can fight unless he is properly fed on beef and beer."

—JOHN CHURCHILL, FIRST DUKE OF MARLBOROUGH

FEB

17

TYPE: Tripel

COLOR: Bronze

SMELL: Yeast, spices, and dried fruit

TASTE: Creamy and smooth, this one starts out with a wave of sweet malt and those familiar Chimay Belgian spices. There are notes of banana, yeast, pear, apple, and dried fig along with a nice citrusy hoppiness.

FOOD PAIRING: Creamy chicken and egg noodles with asparagus and wild rice

AVAILABILITY: Year round

Beer*fest*

2009 Great American Beer Festival Winners by Category

Out of Category – Traditionally Brewed Beer: W '10, Widmer Brothers Brewing, Portland, OR

Gluten-Free Beer: Celia Framboise, The Alchemist, Waterbury, VT

American-Belgo-Style Ale: Exit 4, Flying Fish Brewing Co., Cherry Hill, NJ

American-Style Sour Ale: Rosso e Marrone, Captain Lawrence Brewing Co., Pleasantville, NY

Bieres De Chimay S.A.
Route Charlemagne, 8
6464 Baileux (Chimay)
Belgium
www.chimay.com

🍺 Westmalle Trappist Tripel

"What can the Brits tell us Czechs about the quality of beer? It's as if we Czechs went to France and told them how to make champagne."
—JAN VESLEY, CHAIRMAN OF THE CZECH BREWING AND MALTHOUSE ASSOCIATION

TYPE: Tripel
COLOR: Cloudy amber
SMELL: Citrus, earthy hops, and alcohol
TASTE: A creamy, medium-bodied beer with flavors of sweet malt, freshly baked bread, dark fruit, and bitter hops. Finishes crisp, clean, and dry with slightly bitter aftertaste.
FOOD PAIRING: Smoked whitefish with thin-sliced red onion, lemon, and capers
AVAILABILITY: Year round

FEB

18

Beerfact

The largest producer of trappist beer, Westmalle started its operation in 1836. It was the monks at this abbey that invented the Dubbel and Tripel designations that are now commonplace among breweries worldwide. Westmalle makes two beers, the Dubbel, that makes up 40 percent of their production, and the Tripel, which accounts for most of the other 60 percent.

Brouwerij Westmalle
Malle, 2390
Belgium
www.trappistwestmalle.be

🍺 HopBack Amber

"Drunkards are doomed to hell, so men declare. Believe it not, 'tis but a foolish scare."
—OMAR KHAYYAM, POET

TYPE: Amber ale
COLOR: Dark copper amber
SMELL: Pine and citrus hops over the top of sweet malt
TASTE: A medium-bodied beer with flavors of sweet caramel, roasted malt, and a hint of honey that share space with big pine and a complement of citrus hops. It finishes with the taste of grapefruit and leaves with a slightly spicy aftertaste.
FOOD PAIRING: Beef goulash with egg noodles
AVAILABILITY: Year round

FEB

19

Beer*words*

Beer toasts of the world:

Portuguese: *Saúde*
Slovak: *Na zdravie*
Spanish: *Salud*
Swahili *Afya*
Swedish: *Skal*

Tagalog: *Mabuhay*
Thai: *Sawasdi*
Welsh: *Lechyd da*
Yugoslavian: *Ziveli*
Zulu: *Oogy wawa*

Tröegs Brewing Company
800 Paxton Street
Harrisburg, PA 17104
www.troegs.com

🍺 Smokestack Series Long Strange Tripel

"I went on a diet, swore off drinking and heavy eating, and in fourteen days I lost two weeks."
—JOE E. LEWIS, COMEDIAN

TYPE: Tripel
COLOR: Light cloudy golden orange
SMELL: Sweet, with notes of lemon and orange and just a whiff of alcohol
TASTE: A medium- to full-bodied beer with rich caramel candy malt flavors and earthy hops. A delight to pour into your mouth.
FOOD PAIRING: Duck breast with a molasses glaze
AVAILABILITY: Year round

FEB
20

Brew*tip*

After you've finished boiling your wort, it's time to add your yeast. But if you do it too soon after you remove it from the stove, the liquid will be too hot and the yeast will die. Refrigerate two or three gallons of spring water and pour it cold into your carboy before you add the hot wort. Or, fill your bathtub with ice water, and place your hot brew kettle into it for twenty minutes or a half hour. While you do this, periodically stir the wort to make sure the edges don't freeze.

Boulevard Brewing Company
2501 Southwest Boulevard
Kansas City, MO 64108
www.boulevard.com

🍺 LTD 01

"Give a man a beer, waste an hour. Teach a man to brew, and waste a lifetime!"
—BILL OWENS, PHOTOGRAPHER

FEB

21

TYPE: Bock

COLOR: Dark orange

SMELL: Bread, malt, and caramel

TASTE: Rich malty sweetness with a nice balance of pine sap and citrus zest. This medium-bodied beer rolls smoothly over the tongue and finishes very clean.

FOOD PAIRING: Warm Camembert and pine nuts smeared on a chunk of a giant soft salted pretzel

AVAILABILITY: January and February

Brew*tip*

Brewing Additives

- **Lactic acid:** Lowers the pH of hard water.
- **Lactose:** Also known as milk sugar, lactose is actually not fermentable. It's most commonly added to stouts and porters, where it adds body and sweetness.
- **Licorice sticks:** Used as a flavoring, it goes well in stouts and porters and holiday brews.
- **Maltodextrin:** A nonfermentable carbohydrate that adds a silky mouthfeel to your beer. Using it in lighter beers can lead to an unwanted haze.

Full Sail Brewery
506 Columbia Street
Hood River, OR 97031
www.fullsailbrewing.com

 Wheat

"Drinking wine before beer is a no-no, dear. Topping beer off with wine, that's fine!"
—ANONYMOUS

TYPE: Witbier
COLOR: Cloudy pale straw
SMELL: Fresh baked wheat bread, yeast, and banana
TASTE: Starts out with a touch of sweet malt, yeast, and banana, then delivers subtle spicy notes of coriander and chamomile then finishes clean with a touch of orange zest.
FOOD PAIRING: Skewers of grilled cherry tomatoes sprinkled lightly with fleur de sel
AVAILABILITY: Year round

FEB

22

Publore

If you are looking for an upscale venue in Washington, D.C., to enjoy your handcrafted beers, Brasserie Beck, boasting the largest selection of Belgian beers outside of Belgium, would be a good choice. Catering to the movers and shakers of our nation's capital, the menu lists a bounty of fresh seafood, charcuterie, and impeccably presented European and nuevo-American fare.

Visit Brasserie Beck at 1101 K Street, NW, Washington, DC 20005, *www.beckdc.com.*

Upland Brewing Company
350 W. 11th Street
Bloomington, IN 47404
www.uplandbeer.com

🍺 Dry Irish Stout

"The heart which grief hath cankered hath one unfailing remedy—the tankard."
—C. S. CALVERLEY, POET

TYPE: Stout
COLOR: Black
SMELL: Roasted malt and coffee
TASTE: A smooth, creamy, full-bodied beer with flavors of deep-roasted malt, coffee, and mocha bean. It finishes dry with just a touch of roasted aftertaste.
FOOD PAIRING: Smoked tofu over brown rice
AVAILABILITY: Year round

FEB
23

Beerwords
Irish drinking toast:
> My friends are the best friends, Loyal, willing and able. Now let's get to drinking! All glasses off the table!

Boundary Bay Brewery
1107 Railroad Avenue
Bellingham, WA 9225
www.bbaybrewery.com

🍺 Baltic Porter

"Son, a woman is like a beer. They smell good, they look good, and you'd step over your own mother just to get one."
—HOMER SIMPSON

TYPE: Porter
COLOR: Black
SMELL: Dark chocolate and espresso
TASTE: A smooth, rich, medium-bodied beer with flavors of chocolate, burnt sugar, molasses, rum, and dark-roasted coffee beans. It ends with a strong chocolate flavor and leaves with a slightly burnt aftertaste.
FOOD PAIRING: Wild-rice-and-maple-stuffed pork chops
AVAILABILITY: Year round

FEB
24

Beerfact
The average price of a beer served in a pub in America costs $3.87 a pint. If all the beer consumed in the United States in one year were sold at that price, it would amount to $196 billion, which happens to also be the same amount as the Gross Domestic Product of the county of Columbia.

Uncommon Brewers
303 Potrero Street, Suite 40-H
Santa Cruz, CA 95060
www.uncommonbrewers.com

🍺 Big Swell IPA

"The stronger and staler the beer is, the better the ketchup will be."

— HANNA GLASSE, EIGHTEENTH-CENTURY COOKBOOK
AUTHOR, ON PRESERVING KETCHUP ON LONG SEA VOYAGES

FEB
25

TYPE: India pale ale

COLOR: Light hazy amber

SMELL: Grapefruit, pineapple, and pine

TASTE: A light- to medium-bodied beer with flavors of citrus hops fastened tightly to a core of sweet malt. There are notes of tropical fruit, finishing with a bitter aftertaste.

FOOD PAIRING: Spicy pineapple salsa with blue corn chips

AVAILABILITY: Year round

Beerwords

Polish drinking toasts:

Every shot I take is one more nail in my coffin . . . That's going to be one well-built coffin.

Man's no cactus, drink he must.

Don't drink when driving. You'll spill too much.

Maui Brewing Company
Lahainatown
910 Honoapiilani Highway #55
Lahaina, Maui, HI 96761
www.mauibrewingco.com

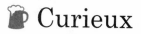 Curieux

"Give me a woman who loves beer, and I will conquer the world."
— KAISER WILHELM II

TYPE: Tripel
COLOR: Cloudy dark gold
SMELL: Bourbon and caramel with a slight floral hop aroma
TASTE: Cellar aged for eight weeks in Jim Beam barrels. Layering of coconut, vanilla, and of course rich bourbon. Undertones of grassy, floral hops complement the sweet, aged barrel flavors.
FOOD PAIRING: Vanilla crème brûlée
AVAILABILITY: Year round

FEB
26

Beer*words*

Here are some basic terms homebrewers use:

- **Adjunct:** Unmalted grain used as a source of sugar.
- **Alpha acid:** A sticky, bitter resin found in hops, which imparts bitterness to the finished beer.
- **Aroma:** The smell produced by the raw ingredients, not the bittering compounds, in beer.
- **Aromatic hops:** Hops used primarily to create aroma and less often for their flavoring properties. Also known as noble hops.
- **Attenuation:** The drop in specific gravity that takes place as the wort ferments.

Allagash Brewing Company
50 Industrial Way
Portland, ME 04103
www.allagash.com

🍺 Derail Ale

"Here sleep in peace a Hampshire grenadier, Who caught his death by drinking cold small beer."
—EPITAPH ON A SOLDIER'S GRAVE

FEB
27

TYPE: India pale ale
COLOR: Golden
SMELL: Caramel, citrus, and floral hops
TASTE: A clean, crisp, bitter beer that hangs pine, citrus, and floral hops on an anchor of roasted, slightly sweet malt and yeast. Ends with flavors of fresh bread and sweet fruit and leaves with a slightly bitter aftertaste.
FOOD PAIRING: Popcorn shrimp served with a lemon aioli
AVAILABILITY: Year round

Beer*fact*

In 1809, President James Madison made a serious attempt to establish a National Brewery. He went so far as to enlist former President Thomas Jefferson's help. Included would have been the creation of a new cabinet-level position for the president's administration—Secretary of Beer. Sadly, Congress did not agree with him, and the effort failed.

Durango Brewing Company
3000 Main Avenue
Durango, CO 813017
www.durangobrewing.com

🍺 Prima Pils

"Men are simple things. They can survive a whole week-end with only three things: beer, boxer shorts, and batteries for the remote control."
—DIANA JORDAN, COMEDIENNE

TYPE: Pilsner
COLOR: Clear yellow
SMELL: Sticky hop resins
TASTE: A nice light-bodied beer with a lot of hoppy heft. Flavors of lemon and grass mix well with Valencia oranges, fresh cut pine, and horseradish.
FOOD PAIRING: Shrimp spring rolls with sweet chili dipping sauce
AVAILABILITY: Year round

**FEB
28**

Beer*fun*

Mary was asleep in bed when her husband, Patrick, crashed through the front door at 3 A.M. and tried to get up the stairs.

"What are you doing?" Mary shouted.

Patrick replied, "I'm trying to get this gallon of beer up the stairs."

"Leave it down there, Patrick," Mary bellowed.

"I can't," Patrick replied. "I've drunk it."

Victory Brewing Company
420 Acorn Lane
Downingtown, PA 19335
www.victorybeer.com

🍺 American Pale Ale

"The letters in 'Brace Beemer' can be arranged to spell 'Embrace Beer.'"
—DAVE BARRY, REFERRING TO THE ACTOR WHO PLAYED THE LONE RANGER ON RADIO

MAR

1

TYPE: Pale ale
COLOR: Light amber
SMELL: Subtle nose of toasted bread crumbs and hop resin
TASTE: A nice combination of bitter pine and smooth butter followed by just a touch of fresh baked bread and finished with tropical floral flavors.
FOOD PAIRING: Spinach salad with almonds, apples, and bacon dressing
AVAILABILITY: Year round

Brewtip

Initially brewed in England, pale ales get their name from the color of the malt they are brewed with—pale malt. The beers themselves are generally amber or copper in color and tend to be of a light to medium body. A good pale ale is well balanced between malt and hops flavors, and at times can be quite pleasantly hoppy.

Stoudt's Brewing Company
Route 272
2800 North Reading Road
Adamstown, PA 19501
www.stoudtsbeer.com

🍺 Deep Water Dopplebock

Sam: "Whaddya know there, Norm?" Norm: "How to sit. How to drink. Want to quiz me?"
—*CHEERS*

TYPE: German-style strong bock
COLOR: Very dark brown with a slight tinge of worn copper
SMELL: Faint citrus—grapefruit
TASTE: Deep chocolate malt flavors with a touch of ash that give way when it warms to flavors of strong, fudgy coffee and roasted toffee.
FOOD PAIRING: Braised chicken with mole negro sauce
AVAILABILITY: Year round

MAR

2

Beerfact

The first commercial release of Deep Water was in 1999, but until the summer of 2007, Deep Water wasn't a true dopplebock because of South Carolina's alcohol limit laws, which didn't allow the brewing or sale of beer over 5% ABV. After the laws were changed, Tom tweaked the recipe again to raise the alcohol and bring the beer back in line with the acceptable standards for a brew of its ilk.

Thomas Creek Brewery
2054 Piedmont Highway
Greenville, SC 29605
www.thomascreekbeer.com

🍺 Supergoose IPA

"Alcohol is my way of life, and I intend to keep it!"
—HOMER SIMPSON

TYPE: India pale ale
COLOR: Dark amber
SMELL: Caramel, pine, and citrus
TASTE: A medium-bodied beer with flavors of grapefruit and bitter hops held together by a caramel malt backbone. Finishes with a touch of sugar and a pine aftertaste.
FOOD PAIRING: Sweet potato fries with miso and wasabi aioli
AVAILABILITY: Limited release

**MAR
3**

Beersaints
King Gambrinus
There is a debate in the beer world about who in fact first invented hopped, malt beer. Some believe this honor goes to King Gambrinus. Often depicted as a round, opulent man with an upraised goblet in one hand and a foot on top of a beer keg, Gambrinus is a symbol of the heritage of beer and beer brewing.

Hale's Ales
4301 Leary Way NW
Seattle, WA 98107
www.halesbrewery.com

🍺 LTD 02

*"But if at church they give some ale, And a pleasant fire
for our souls to regale, We'd sing and we'd pray all the live
long day, Nor ever once from the church to stray."*
—ANONYMOUS

TYPE: American amber lager
COLOR: Golden amber
SMELL: Fresh baked brown bread
TASTE: This light- to medium-bodied beer exhibits flavors of caramel
and honey followed by hoppy bitterness and a touch of dried fruit. The
underlying notes of heady alcohol pair nicely with the rich sweetness
and clean finish.
FOOD PAIRING: Lobster tacos
AVAILABILITY: March through June

MAR

4

Beerfact

It wasn't until about the year 1000 C.E. that beers began to be brewed
with hops. Before that time, brewers used a number of different herbs
and natural additives to spice or balance their brew. In Greece, they added
grapes covered in natural brewer's yeast. The Celts added heather to their
ale. The Scythians used hemp. In northern Europe, they added juniper.

Full Sail Brewery
506 Columbia Street
Hood River, OR 97031
www.fullsailbrewing.com

🍺 Hoppus Maximus

"I was at a bar, nursing a beer. My nipple was getting quite soggy."
  —EMO PHILLIPS

TYPE: Amber ale
COLOR: Hazy golden orange
SMELL: Citrus and mild sweet malt
TASTE: A smooth, light- to medium-bodied beer with flavors of citrus, tropical fruit, sweet malt, and fresh baked cracker.
FOOD PAIRING: Turkey melt with jack cheese and pepper jelly
AVAILABILITY: Year round

MAR

5

Brew*tip*

An easy way to calculate the alcohol in a batch of homebrew is by using the specific gravity scale. Using a hydrometer, a brewer measures how many dissolved solids there are in his unfermented beer. This reading is known as original gravity. To find alcohol content, the brewer takes another hydrometer reading after fermentation has occurred. Since the yeast turns sugar into alcohol, and alcohol is lighter than water, the difference in the readings is the amount of alcohol created during fermentation.

Thirsty Dog Brewing Company
529 Grant Street, Suite B
Akron, Ohio 44311
www.thirstydog.com

🍺 Iowa Pale Ale

"When I heated my home with oil, I used an average of 800 gallons a year. I have found that I can keep comfortably warm for an entire winter with slightly over half that quantity of beer."
—DAVE BARRY

TYPE: Pale ale
COLOR: Amber
SMELL: Sweet malt, toasted grain, and citrus hops
TASTE: A clean, easy-to-drink beer with flavors of toasted malt and caramel infused with grapefruit and lemon. Finishes dry and leaves with a citrus aftertaste.
FOOD PAIRING: Grilled mahi mahi with roasted corn salsa
AVAILABILITY: Year round

MAR
6

Beerfact

In the 1600s and 1700s, midwives in Europe and Colonial America gave delivering mothers "Groaning Ale," which was fermented for seven or eight months and tapped when contractions began. After the birth it wasn't uncommon for the child to be bathed in the remaining ale, since it was often more sanitary that readily available water.

Millstream Brewing Company
835 48th Avenue
Amana, IA 52203
www.millstreambrewing.com

🍺 Easy Street Wheat

"You go out for a night of drinking, and you don't know where you'll wake up the next day. It's like the throw of the dice."
—JIM MORRISON

TYPE: Pale wheat ale
COLOR: Hazy golden
SMELL: Bread, citrus, and spice
TASTE: Smooth, easy-drinking, light-bodied beer that starts with fresh-cut wheat and grass followed by a touch of honey and citrus, ending with a bitter bite and finishing clean.
FOOD PAIRING: Cobb salad with honey-baked ham, hard-boiled eggs, and goat cheese
AVAILABILITY: Year round

MAR

7

Beerfact

Do you collect beer coasters? If so, then you are what is known as a tegestologist. How about old beer bottles and cans? If that's your hobby, then you're a labeorphilist. The largest collection of beer bottles ever recorded belongs to Ron Werner of the USA. At the time the record was set, in 2002, he had 11,644 different beer bottles (representing 1,704 brands), including 7,128 that had not been opened.

Odell Brewing Company
800 East Lincoln Avenue
Fort Collins, CO 80524
www.odellbrewing.com

🍺 Cap City Pale

Woody: "What's going on, Mr. Peterson?" Norm: "A flashing sign in my gut that says, 'Insert beer here.'"
—CHEERS

TYPE: Pale ale
COLOR: Golden
SMELL: Grain and a touch of herbal hops
TASTE: A crisp, light- to medium-bodied beer with complex malt flavors that are balanced nicely as they fade into peppery, herbal hops. You can pick out layers of grape nuts and sweet honey as it finishes, ending with a touch of bitterness.
FOOD PAIRING: Tuscan polenta with fried sourdough croutons
AVAILABILITY: Year round on draft

MAR

8

Beer*words*
Beer toasts of the world:

Asturian: *Gayola*
Breton: *Yec'hed mat*
Creole: *Salud*
Moroccan: *Saha wa'afiab*
Philippine: *Mabuhay*

Rumanian: *Noroc*
Sesotho: *Nqa*
Turkish: *Serefe*
Ukrainian: *Budmo*
Vietnamese: *Chia*

River City Brewing Company
545 Downtown Plaza, Suite 1115
Sacramento, CA 95814
www.rivercitybrewing.net

🍺 Kentucky Breakfast Stout

"Beer. It's not just for breakfast anymore."
—ANONYMOUS

TYPE: Stout
COLOR: Black
SMELL: Chocolate, smoky wood, and roasted malt
TASTE: Brewed with coffee and chocolates then cave aged in oak bourbon barrels for an entire year. Flavors of dark chocolate truffle and mocha bean are a great pair with the thick, smooth mouthfeel. Finishes with notes of burnt sugar and more coffee.
FOOD PAIRING: Chocolate truffle pancakes
AVAILABILITY: Special release

MAR

9

Beer*thought*

Sure the martini gets the dubious distinction of being the breakfast of champions, but beer works at any meal. Throw on some khakis and a polo shirt, and beer is right at home on the golf course or ready for lunch with the in-laws. Pour a barrel-aged ale into a fluted glass, and beer pairs up nicely at even the finest of restaurants.

Founders Brewing Company
235 Grandville Avenue SW
Grand Rapids, MI 49503
www.foundersbrewing.com

🍺 Golden Monkey

"Pretty women make us buy beer. Ugly women make us drink beer."
—AL BUNDY, *MARRIED WITH CHILDREN*

TYPE: Tripel
COLOR: Golden
SMELL: Yeast, floral hops, and alcohol
TASTE: A smooth, medium- to full-bodied brew with flavors of malt, yeast, and alcohol intermingled with spicy hops and a touch of sour apple. It finishes bitter with a sour aftertaste.
FOOD PAIRING: Slow-cooked black pepper beef stew
AVAILABILITY: Year round

MAR

10

Beer*fun*

A clown walks into a bar where there's a guy sitting, just looking at his beer. After watching this man for some time, the clown decides to cheer him up. Going over, the clown takes the beer, holds it up in front of the guy, then drinks it down. The poor man starts crying and says, "This day is the worst of my life. First, I'm late to work and get fired. Then my car gets stolen. I get a cab home and leave my wallet and credit cards in it. When I get home, I find my wife in bed with the gardener. So I come down here, and when I was thinking about ending my life, some clown shows up and drinks my poison . . ."

Victory Brewing Company
420 Acorn Lane
Downingtown, PA 19335
www.victorybeer.com

🍺 Inferno

"Up to age forty, eating is beneficial; after forty, drinking."
—GERMAN PROVERB

TYPE: Belgian strong pale ale
COLOR: Cloudy gold
SMELL: Yeasty with a touch of spicy hops and fruit
TASTE: Lots of fruitiness with flavors of banana, plantain, and pear. Notes of cream of wheat and vanilla in addition to dandelion and peppery hops giving way to an aftertaste of strawberry and alcohol.
FOOD PAIRING: Belgian waffles topped with fried bananas and vanilla whipping cream
AVAILABILITY: Year round

MAR
11

Pub*lore*
A quality beer drinker's kind of place, Downtown Johnny Brown's features seventeen rotating beers on tap, a small but ever-expanding list of beers in bottles, and good cheap bar food. Everything in house will satisfy a seasoned beer connoisseur. Just a few blocks from the harbor, this is a good spot to wind down after a day in the sun.

Visit Downtown Johnny Brown's at 1220 3rd Avenue, San Diego, CA 92101, *www.downtownjohnnybrowns.com.*

The Lost Abbey
155 Mata Way
San Marcos, CA 92069
www.thelostabbey.com

 Burning Bird

"They told me this story while we were waiting for a train. I supplied the beer. The tale was cheap at a gallon and a half."
—RUDYARD KIPLING

TYPE: Pale ale
COLOR: Clear golden
SMELL: Citrus and pine with just a hint of malt
TASTE: Flavors of citrus and pine right up front that fade into more floral notes, followed by a sweet, light malt. Very drinkable and good for those hot days where just one beer won't do you.
FOOD PAIRING: Sweet potato fries with garlic aioli
AVAILABILITY: Year round

MAR
12

Brew*tip*

Hops are rated based on how much alpha and beta acids they contain (alpha acids being used for bittering and beta acids being used for aroma). This number can vary from strain to strain. To figure out how many IBUs their beers contain, brewers use a complex formula that takes into account the amount of hops they use, the amount of alpha acids in the type of hops they have chosen (both the bittering and the finishing hops), and the amount of time the hops are in the wort.

Sonoran Brewing Company
10426 East Jomax Road
Scottsdale, AZ 85255
www.sonoranbrewing.com

🍺 Pipeline Porter

"You know, nobody eats in England. Three or four pints of English beer nigh fills you."
—ANNE DUDLEY, MUSICIAN

MAR
13

> **TYPE:** Porter
> **COLOR:** Dark brown
> **SMELL:** Coffee and dark chocolate
> **TASTE:** Coffee is the other famous brew from Kona, and Pipeline Porter is brewed with it. The sweet malts and chocolate undertones enhance the coffee flavor, balanced out nicely by just a subtle hint of bitter hops.
> **FOOD PAIRING:** Chocolate cream pie with bittersweet chocolate, almonds, and cinnamon
> **AVAILABILITY:** September to March

Beerfest

2010 marks the fifteenth year for the Kona Brewers Festival, held on the big island in March. The festival features more than thirty breweries from both Hawaii and the mainland United States, each of which presents two of their signature brews for tasting. Chefs from twenty-five different restaurants around the islands prepare local foods to enjoy with the fermented beverages, and there is even a beer and food pairing dinner. See *www.konaBrewersFestival.com* for details.

Kona Brewing Company
7192 Kalaniana'ole Highway
Inside Hawaii Kai, waterside
Honolulu, HI 96825
www.konabrewingco.com

🍺 Beatification

"Man, being reasonable, must get drunk; the best of life is but intoxication."
—GEORGE GORDON, LORD BYRON

TYPE: American wild ale
COLOR: Cloudy golden
SMELL: Sour buttermilk
TASTE: Almost like drinking a lime or a grapefruit. It's quite sour with flavors of cider vinegar and yogurt. It's a very enjoyable taste, geared for the more sophisticated beer drinker.
FOOD PAIRING: Tandoori chicken and garlic naan
AVAILABILITY: Year round

MAR
14

Brew*tip*

Before the Middle Ages, vats of cooled wort were exposed to the open air, allowing in wild, uncultivated yeasts to start fermentation. That technique, known as spontaneous fermentation, is used today only by a handful of very skilled brewers. Russian River's Beatification is an excellent example of a modern spontaneously fermented beer. The wild yeasts come not only from the open air but also from the old oak barrels the ale is aged in.

Russian River Brewing Company
725 4th Street
Santa Rosa, CA 95404
www.russianriverbrewing.com

 White

"And I will make it felony to drink small beer."
—WILLIAM SHAKESPEARE

TYPE: Belgian-style witbier
COLOR: Cloudy golden brown, like fermented cider
SMELL: Mild aroma with a soft touch of coriander
TASTE: Light and refreshing. Alaskan White is a suave lady's man, if you will—impressing those who catch his eye with understated charming flavors of sweet pear, white grape, and just a dab of the spice on the neck.
FOOD PAIRING: Spicy shrimp spring rolls with peanut sauce
AVAILABILITY: Year round

**MAR
15**

Beerfact
In 1892 William Painter invented what is known as the "Crown Cap" or "Crown Cork Bottle Cap" for carbonated beverages. The secret to Painter's invention was the thin disc of cork and special paper backing inside the top of the cap. When crimped on top of a bottle, the cork created a seal and held the beverage away from the metal cap, thus preventing it from corroding and keeping both the liquid and the carbonation inside where they belonged.

Alaskan Brewing Company
5429 Shaune Drive
Juneau, AK 99801-9540
www.alaskanbeer.com

🍺 Mothership Wit

"The Puritanical nonsense of excluding children and therefore to some extent women from pubs has turned these places into mere boozing shops instead of the family gathering places that they ought to be."
—GEORGE ORWELL

TYPE: Witbier
COLOR: Pale straw
SMELL: Lemongrass and banana mixed with citrus and a touch of malt
TASTE: Classic wheat flavors of banana, clove, and lemon and orange zest with a fair amount of sweetness and a nice bitter finish.
FOOD PAIRING: Thai fried bananas topped with coconut ice cream and drizzled with honey
AVAILABILITY: Year round

MAR
16

Beerfact

Things you probably didn't know about New Belgium Brewing Company:

Their flagship beer, Fat Tire, was named by founder and brewer Jeff Lebesch for the "fat tires" on the bicycle he rode while on a tour through Belgium. On their one-year anniversary, employees at the brewery become employee owners, garnering a share—and a vote—in the company along with a brand new cruiser bike to commemorate the occasion.

New Belgium Brewing Company
500 Linden Street
Fort Collins, CO 80524
www.newbelgium.com

🍺 Extra Stout

"In a study, scientists report that drinking beer can be good for the liver. I'm sorry, did I say 'scientists'? I meant 'Irish people.'"

—TINA FEY, ACTOR

TYPE: Irish dry stout

COLOR: Black with a tan head

SMELL: Roasted malt, cocoa bean, and smoked peat

TASTE: A silky, medium-bodied beer with a smoky malt taste that blends into dark coffee and a sour dairy undertone. There are notes of toffee and cocoa bean. It finishes mostly dry with just a bit of dark-roasted malt.

FOOD PAIRING: Blue Point oysters on the half shell

AVAILABILITY: Year round

MAR 17

Beerfact

In 2007 a man drove into the Guinness brewery in Dublin just before rush hour. He hitched his truck to a trailer filled with kegs of beer and drove off. How much beer did he get? Three hundred and sixty barrels of Guinness and Budweiser (about half and half), and ninety kegs of Carlsberg. Total value: $235,000. The police caught one man and charged him with possession of one of the stolen kegs. The rest of the heist was never recovered.

Guinness Storehouse
St. James's Gate
Dublin 8
www.guinness.com

🍺 Moose Drool

"Not everyone who drinks is a poet. Some of us drink because we are not poets."
—DUDLEY MOORE, ACTOR

TYPE: Brown ale
COLOR: Cola brown
SMELL: Milk chocolate and roasted malt
TASTE: Leads with dark-roasted malt followed by black coffee and bright lemon. Finishes with mocha bean and leaves with a bitter aftertaste that doesn't linger very long at all.
FOOD PAIRING: Beer-battered onion rings with curry ketchup
AVAILABILITY: Year round

MAR
18

Brewtip

If you've ever done any homebrewing then you know there is always a chance of getting some undesirable flavors or aromas from your brew. Here's a list of those "undesirables" and how they are caused:

- Cabbage, cooked vegetable (from yeast)
- Rubber (from yeast)
- Sour milk (by-product of bacterial action—sometimes this sour flavor is produced on purpose for aged or sour beers)
- Skunk (result of light reacting with the hop resins)

Big Sky Brewing Company
5417 Trumpeter Way
P.O. Box 17170
Missoula, MT 59808
www.bigskybrew.com

🍺 Austin Amber Beer

"Oh no! What have I done? I smashed open my little boy's piggy bank, and for what? A few measly cents, not even enough to buy one beer. Wait a minute, lemme count and make sure . . . not even close."
—HOMER SIMPSON

MAR
19

TYPE: Amber ale
COLOR: Amber
SMELL: Fresh baked bread and sweet malt
TASTE: A light- to medium-bodied beer with flavors of toasted malt and fresh baked bread followed by earthy hops and a touch of lemon. The finish is crisp and dry with an herbal hoppy aftertaste.
FOOD PAIRING: Venison sausage
AVAILABILITY: Year round

Beer*fun*
Beer Bomb
Required supplies: Two card tables, plastic keg cups, ping-pong balls, beer
Place card tables several paces apart. Place a keg cup half full of beer on each table. Players take turns bouncing a ping-pong ball off the near table and trying to land it in the keg cup on the other table. Landing a ball in the cup allows a player to make any other player drink the beer in the cup. Missing the opposite table altogether forces the shooting player to take a drink.

Independence Brewing Company
3913 Todd Lane #607
Austin, TX 78744
www.independencebrewing.com

🍺 Up The Creek Extreme IPA

"Reality is an illusion that occurs due to the lack of alcohol."

—ANONYMOUS

TYPE: India pale ale

COLOR: Golden cola brown

SMELL: Initially big malt with a whispy hint of hops that fades after a few minutes

TASTE: Roasted coffee and leather with bitter orange peel, pear, and dandelion. The hops and malt really come forward as the beer grows closer to room temperature.

FOOD PAIRING: BBQ pork ribs rubbed with brown sugar, smoked paprika, and garlic powder and pecan pie for dessert

AVAILABILITY: Year round

MAR 20

Brewtip

Thomas Creek heats the mash for Up The Creek at a lower temperature to increase the amount of fermentable sugars and reduce the sweetness of the beer. Then the brewers finish the batch with a triple dry hopping. Be warned, this beer does not fool around. The alcohol is well hidden, and before you know it, you've downed quite a bit of the stuff. At 12.5% ABV, this beer packs the same punch as a typical Bordeaux.

Thomas Creek Brewery
2054 Piedmont Highway
Greenville, SC 29605
www.thomascreekbeer.com

🍺 Tower 10 IPA

"Ah, beer. The cause of and the solution to all of life's problems."
—HOMER SIMPSON

TYPE: India pale ale

COLOR: Translucent pumpkin

SMELL: Surprisingly malty for an IPA with a touch of mandarin orange

TASTE: A fair amount of caramel and toffee bordering on burnt molasses that transitions into chocolate and finishes with flavors of citrus and pine.

FOOD PAIRING: Oak-roasted chicken breast (with the skin and ribs still attached) and truffled potato wedges

AVAILABILITY: Year round

MAR
21

Beerfact

Named for the lifeguard tower on the beach in Southern California, Tower 10 IPA marks the beginning of a long venture. The brewery was founded in the mid 1980s and named for master brewer, Karl M. Strauss, who is the cousin of one of the company's co-founders, Chris Cramer. Initially opened as a simple brewpub, the brewery now produces over thirty beers a year and distributes its wares to over 2,500 bars and package stores.

Karl Strauss Brewing Company
5985 Santa Fe Street
San Diego, CA 92109
www.karlstrauss.com

Oatmeal Coffee Stout

"Nothing ever tasted better than a cold beer on a beautiful afternoon with nothing to look forward to than more of the same."
—HUGH HOOD, AUTHOR

TYPE: Stout
COLOR: Dark brown
SMELL: Sweet malt and coffee
TASTE: A smooth, slippery, light- to medium-bodied beer with flavors of dark coffee and sweet malt that finishes with piney hops and a slightly bitter aftertaste.
FOOD PAIRING: Profiteroles filled with fresh whipped cream and sprinkled with cocoa
AVAILABILITY: Limited release

MAR
22

Beer*words*

Irish Saint Patrick's Day toast:

Saint Patrick was a gentleman, Who through strategy and stealth, Drove all the snakes from Ireland, Here's a toasting to his health. But not too many toastings, Lest you lose yourself and then, Forget the good Saint Patrick, And see all those snakes again.

Good People Brewing Company
1035-B 20th Street South
Birmingham, AL 35205
www.goodpeoplebrewing.com

🍺 Chouffe Houblon

"There cannot be good living where there is not good drinking."
—BENJAMIN FRANKLIN

TYPE: Belgian strong pale ale

COLOR: Cloudy golden

SMELL: Yeast and floral hops

TASTE: A light- to medium-bodied beer with flavors of soft bread, ripe fruit, sugar crystals, and grassy hops. There are notes of spice and a touch of spicy bitterness.

FOOD PAIRING: Tuna nicoise salad with Parmesan crackers

AVAILABILITY: Year round

MAR
23

Beerfact

Belgium ranks fourth among European nations, behind Germany, France, and the United Kingdom, for total number of breweries, at 125. They produce about 800 year-round brews, but nearly 9,000 seasonals and special releases. The average Belgian drinks about 93 liters of beer a year. That's approximately 24.57 gallons, slightly higher than the 23.1 gallons the average American drinks.

Brasserie d'Achouffe
Rue du Village 32
Achoufee, 6666
Belgium
www.achouffe.be

🍺 Bikini Blonde

"I don't have a drinking problem except when I can't find a drink."
—TOM WAITS, MUSICIAN

TYPE: Munich Helles lager
COLOR: Light golden
SMELL: Floral hops, spices, and fresh bread dough
TASTE: A nice, crisp, clean beer with flavors of yeast, honey, biscuit, and lemon zest. An easy-to-drink beer that will pair well with delicate foods.
FOOD PAIRING: Miso-glazed black cod
AVAILABILITY: Year round

MAR
24

Publore

Upstairs in The Kitchen you will find a beer and wine lounge with high-end "rustic" bar food. Downstairs is more formal dining. But no matter where you choose to sit or eat, you will find a fine selection of beers from all over the U.S. and even a few from exotic locals, such as Denmark, Belgium, and Canada.

Visit The Kitchen at 1039 Pearl Street, Boulder, CO 80302, *www.thekitchencafe.com.*

Maui Brewing Company
Lahainatown
910 Honoapiilani Highway #55
Lahaina, Maui, HI 96761
www.mauibrewingco.com

🍺 Hop Karma Brown IPA

"There are only two times when I drink beer: when I'm alone and when I'm with someone else."
—ANONYMOUS

MAR
25

TYPE: India brown ale
COLOR: Root beer brown with a nice tan head
SMELL: Crisp, grassy hops
TASTE: A cross between an IPA and an English brown ale. Flavors of mocha bean, cola, and a touch of licorice are followed by the crisp bitterness of grapefruit zest.
FOOD PAIRING: Lime-marinated rock shrimp quesadillas with plenty of cilantro and hot Serrano chilies.
AVAILABILITY: Year round

Brewtip
Brewing Additives
- **Papain:** Often sold as a meat tenderizer, papain is an extract of the papaya. When added to beer it helps prevent chill-haze.
- **Polyclar:** Stabilizing additive that helps prevent oxidization and removes haze.
- **Wood chips:** Used to add a spicy twang. Before adding to your brew, make sure to sanitize the wood by boiling or baking.

Terrapin Beer Company
265 Newton Bridge Road
Athens, GA 30607
www.terrapibeer.com

🍺 Venom Pale Ale

"I drink no more than a sponge."
—FRANÇOIS RABELAIS

TYPE: Pale ale
COLOR: Copper
SMELL: Citrus and caramel malt under a fair amount of hop resin
TASTE: Lots of rich malt flavors, warm burnt sugar, and fresh biscuits.
Smooth, creamy, and delicious, balanced out nicely by tart citrus notes
and bitter piney hops.
FOOD PAIRING: Spiced lamb stew served over fresh spaetzle
AVAILABILITY: Year round

MAR
26

Beerfact
Hangover Helper

Take a high-potency B-complex supplement before you go to bed. The
B vitamins aid your body in metabolizing carbohydrates (alcohol being
a carbohydrate) and dilate your blood vessels, compensating for dehydra-
tion. Additionally, they grant you an energy boost, combating that tired,
sluggish feeling the next morning. If you forget to take them before you
go to bed, pop them first thing when you get up. Not as good, but every
little bit helps.

DuClaw Brewing Company
901 S. Bond Street
Baltimore, MD 21231
www.duclaw.com

🍺 Raison D'Être

*"We are here to drink beer . . . and live our lives so well
that Death will tremble to take us."*
—CHARLES BUKOWSKI, POET

TYPE: Belgian strong dark ale

COLOR: Molasses

SMELL: Chocolate and burnt sugar

TASTE: A medium-bodied beer that means business (8% ABV), Raison
D'être starts out with flavors of caramel, malt, honey, and brown sugar,
and finishes with the taste of sweet sugar crystals.

FOOD PAIRING: Hangar steak with shallots caramelized in Raison
D'être

AVAILABILITY: Year round

MAR
27

Publore

In 1995 when Dog Fish Head Brewings & Eats opened, it was the smallest commercial brewery in America, brewing beers on a system that produced just twelve gallons at a time. To keep up with demand in the restaurant, they had to brew three times a day, five days a week. Though this was exhausting, it gave the brewers the ability to try multiple different recipes. Within a year the reputation of their beer had grown and they began bottling. By 2002 they had to move their facilities into a 100,000-square-foot converted cannery.

Dogfish Head Craft Brewery
6 Cannery Village Center
Milton, DE 19968
www.dogfish.com

🍺 Patriot Pale Ale

"My companion at the press drank every day a pint before breakfast, a pint at breakfast with his bread and cheese, a pint in the afternoon about six o'clock, and another when he'd done his day's work."
—BENJAMIN FRANKLIN

TYPE: Pale ale
COLOR: Hazy copper
SMELL: Sweet malt and earthy hops
TASTE: A medium-bodied beer with light caramel malt and biscuit flavors up front followed by citrus hops and a distinctly lemon finish.
FOOD PAIRING: Roast beef and Yorkshire pudding
AVAILABILITY: Year round

**MAR
28**

Publore

Delux Burger, a trendy little burger joint/beer bar, cuts right to the punch, giving its patrons exactly what they want. The food menu is short and sweet, with burgers, sandwiches, soups, salads, and desserts. They offer flights of three beers for those who want to try more than a few of their impressive beer selection.

Visit Delux Burger at 3146 E. Camelback, Phoenix, AZ 85016, *www.deluxburger.com.*

RJ Rockers Brewing Company
226-A West Main Street
Spartanburg, SC 29306
www.rjrockers.com

🍺 Great Northern Porter

"Stick with the beer. Let's go and beat this guy up and come back and drink some more beer."
—ERNEST HEMINGWAY, *TO HAVE AND HAVE NOT*

TYPE: Porter
COLOR: Dark brown with a reddish tinge
SMELL: Coffee, burnt malt, sweet toffee, and roasted peanuts
TASTE: A light- to medium-bodied beer. Coffee, cola, burnt malt, bitter baking chocolate, and brown sugar, followed by a slightly sweet finish and a subtle burnt aftertaste.
FOOD PAIRING: Grilled New York Steak and eggs
AVAILABILITY: Year round

MAR
29

Beerfact

Things that happened in 1986:
- The space shuttle challenger exploded.
- The Soviet nuclear reactor at Chernobyl melted down.
- Mad cow disease was identified.
- Summit Brewing Company was formed.

One out of four isn't bad.

Summit Brewing Company
910 Montreal Circle
St. Paul, MN 55102
www.summitbrewing.com

🍺 Thomas Jefferson's Tavern Ale

"I am lately become a brewer for family use, having had the benefit of instruction to one of my people by an English brewer of the first order."

—THOMAS JEFFERSON TO JOSEPH COPPINGER, APRIL 25, 1815

TYPE: American strong ale
COLOR: Golden amber
SMELL: Sweet malt and dried fruit
TASTE: A medium-bodied beer with flavors of caramel, sweet malt, and toffee blended with grapefruit and citrus hops. It finishes with a touch of alcohol and leaves with bitter lemon.
FOOD PAIRING: Grilled steak salad with blue cheese crumbles
AVAILABILITY: Year round, part of the Ales of Revolution series

**MAR
30**

Beerfact

There is a lot of documentation showing that Thomas Jefferson was a complete beer hound. Not only did he brew his own beer, but by 1814, the fully functional brew house at his Monticello plantation included a sixty-gallon cask and a malting room where he sprouted his own grain. He was known to have liked his beer stronger than many of the public houses served, which led him to use more malt in his recipes (upping it by a third in some cases) to create brews more to his liking.

Yards Brewing Company
901 N. Delaware Avenue
Philadelphia, PA 19123
www.yardsbrewing.com

🍺 Downtown Brown

"I never trust a man that doesn't drink."
—JOHN WAYNE, ACTOR

TYPE: Nut brown ale
COLOR: Deep amber brown
SMELL: Roasted coffee
TASTE: A light-bodied beer with flavors of cola and mocha that provide a counterpoint to substantial notes of grapefruit and bitter orange. Finishes with a quick flash of chocolate then leaves with a lemon aftertaste.
FOOD PAIRING: Smoked trout
AVAILABILITY: Year round

MAR
31

Beersaint

Saint Amand (born 584 C.E., died 675 C.E.)

The patron saint of brewers, inn keepers, bartenders, and hop growers, Saint Amand was one of the Christian apostles of Flanders (a region that exists in what today are parts of France, the Netherlands, and Belgium, and is, thanks to Amand, known for its ale). He founded many monasteries within Belgium, many of which brewed beer.

Lost Coast Brewery
123 West Third Street
Eureka, CA 95501
www.lostcoast.com

🍺 Brooklyner-Schneider Hopfen-Weisse

"In my opinion, most of the great men of the past were only there for the beer."

—A.J.P. TAYLOR, BRITISH HISTORIAN

TYPE: Weizenbock
COLOR: Golden honey
SMELL: Citrus and floral hops
TASTE: A very complex and interesting beer with flavors of wheat, hops, clove, and banana, then finishes soft with baked cracker and lemon zest.
FOOD PAIRING: Szechuan beef with broccoli
AVAILABILITY: Year round

APR

1

Beer*words*

German terms you should know before heading to the München Oktoberfest.

- *Obazda* (n.) Bavarian cheese dish made with Camembert, onion, paprika, caraway, butter, and often beer. Served in the beer tents at Oktoberfest.
- *Ogschdocha* (adj.): Tipsy.
- *Ozapfa* (v.): To tap a keg.

- *Quartl* (n.): Quarter liter of beer. If you order one of these you will be laughed at.
- *Riesnbrezn* (n.): Giant Bavarian pretzel, beloved during Oktoberfest for being gigantic.

The Brooklyn Brewery
#1 Brewers Row
79 North 11th Street
Brooklyn, NY 11211
www.brooklynbrewery.com

🍺 Morimoto Soba Ale

Sam: "What would you say to a nice beer, Normie?" Norm: "Going down?"

    —CHEERS

TYPE: Fruit beer

COLOR: Pale golden like hay with a fluffy white head

SMELL: Sweet light molasses, honey, and citrus fruit

TASTE: This is a very mild beer, meant to pair well with the delicate flavors of sushi and a traditional Japanese menu. It's light, not particularly complex, and easy to drink, showing undertones of a superb pale ale.

FOOD PAIRING: Ice cold tuna tataki—two orders.

AVAILABILITY: Year round

APR
2

*Brew*tip

Soba is the Japanese name for buckwheat. Soba is actually a fruit, a member of the rhubarb family. High in potassium, vitamin B, phosphorous, and protein, buckwheat has long been a part of Japanese cuisine due primarily to its nutritional benefits. To use it in the brewing process, the fruit of the plant is milled to separate the brown husk from the edible insides, known as groats. These groats are then roasted and used in the same fashion as grain.

Rogue Ales
2320 OSU Drive
Newport, OR 97365
www.rogue.com

🍺 Apocalypse IPA

"I try not to drink too much, because when I'm drunk, I bite."
—BETTE MIDLER, ACTRESS

TYPE: India pale ale
COLOR: Deep gold
SMELL: Fruit and citrus hops with a touch of pine
TASTE: A clean, smooth brew with flavors of toasted malt and toffee that balance out a wide range of hop flavors including grapefruit, pine, and mandarin orange.
FOOD PAIRING: Pan-roasted halibut served with curried lentils
AVAILABILITY: Year round

APR

3

Beerfact
Legally acceptable blood alcohol concentration for drivers:

Canada .08%	New Zealand .08%
Honduras .07%	Singapore .08%
Ireland .08%	United Kingdom .08%
Malaysia .08%	United States .08%
Malta .08%	Zimbabwe .08%

10 Barrel Brewing Company
20750 High Desert Lane #107
Bend, OR 97701
www.10barrel.com

🍺 O'Fallon 5 Day IPA

"Anyone who has ever walked upright has loved beer, cele-brated over it, told tales over it . . . It's what makes us human. We brew."

—ALAN EAMES, BREWER

APR

4

TYPE: India pale ale

COLOR: Golden orange

SMELL: Yeast, grapefruit, and pine

TASTE: Flavors of fresh grass, grapefruit, lemon zest, spicy hops, and notes of honey and sweet malt. As it warms, there are noticeable peach and apricot additions. It finishes clean with a subtle lemon and pine aftertaste.

FOOD PAIRING: Seared tuna with peach salsa

AVAILABILITY: Year round

Beer*words*

Irish drinking toast:

May your pockets be heavy, Your heart be light, And may good luck pursue you, Each morning and night.

O'Fallon Brewery
26 West Industrial Drive
O'Fallon, MO 63366
www.ofallonbrewery.com

🍺 Isabelle Proximus

"Give my people plenty of beer—good, cheap beer—and you will have no revolution."
—QUEEN VICTORIA

TYPE: American wild ale

COLOR: Hazy yellow orange

SMELL: Citrus and sour malt

TASTE: A light-bodied beer with a very tart aged-ale taste. There are flavors of lemon, lime, orange, and even pineapple, mixed with grapes and vanilla.

FOOD PAIRING: Room-temperature gorgonzola on wheat crackers

AVAILABILITY: Limited

APR

5

Brewtip

After taking a "research trip" to Belgium, Sam Calagione (Dogfish Head), Tomme Arthur (The Lost Abbey), Adam Avery (Avery Brewing), Rob Todd (Allagash), and Vinnie Cirulzo (Russian River Brewing) worked together to make Isabelle Proximus. Each brewery contributed several barrels of their beer and some of their house yeast to produce this sour ale. Originally released in April 2008, limited quantities are available.

🍺 Blonde Ale

"Keep your libraries, your penal institutions, your insane asylums . . . give me beer."
—HENRY MILLER

TYPE: Blonde ale

COLOR: Golden

SMELL: Tree fruit, yeast, and citrus hops

TASTE: Light, crisp beer with flavors of wheat, floral hops, and even a little pear. Very drinkable beer, the sort that makes you want to have another.

FOOD PAIRING: Spicy shrimp jambalaya with smoked ham hock and rice

AVAILABILITY: Year round

APR

6

Beer*fact*

In the United Kingdom, a homebrewer is allowed to manufacture an unlimited quantity of fermented beverages, but only for domestic use. In South Africa, brewers can manufacture as much of their favorite fermented beverage as they like, but distilling spirits, selling alcohol, or even giving it away is against the law. In Australia and New Zealand, citizens may make their own alcohol as long as they do not use a still.

New Orleans Lager and Ale Brewing Company
3001 Tchoupitoulas Street
New Orleans, LA 70130
www.nolabrewing.com

🍺 Gargamel

"Beer he drank, seven goblets. His spirit was loosened. He became hilarious. His heart was glad and his face shone."
—*THE EPIC OF GILGAMESH*, 3000 B.C.

TYPE: Belgian sour ale
COLOR: Deep translucent amber
SMELL: Vanilla, citrus, and fresh crushed berries
TASTE: Light- to medium-bodied beer with the characteristic tartness of an aged sour ale. Sour lemon, dry raspberries, and oaky spiciness.
FOOD PAIRING: Sweetcorn fritters
AVAILABILITY: Only in the Allagash retail store

APR
7

Beerfact
Aged in oak barrels for months or even years after brewing, sour ales get their flavor from the wild yeasts and acids in the wood. Brewers employ used barrels to create these ales because the residual grape essence adds a further layer of sourness to the brew. Frequently these beers are made without additional yeast, as the wild yeast already present in the wood is enough to drive the fermentation process.

Allagash Brewing Company
50 Industrial Way
Portland, ME 04103
www.allagash.com

🍺 West Coast IPA

"Merrily taking twopenny ale and cheese with a pocket knife; But these were luxuries not for him who went for the Simple Life."
—G. K. CHESTERTON

TYPE: India pale ale

COLOR: Clear dark amber

SMELL: Very hoppy with notes of citrus and pine

TASTE: Medium- to light-bodied with a hint of malt and sweet caramel behind a wave of hoppy goodness. A bitter beer with a short, pleasing finish and not much aftertaste.

FOOD PAIRING: Skewers of broiled swordfish drizzled with lemon and sprinkled with oregano

AVAILABILITY: Year round

Brewtip

Hops help balance the taste and aroma of a beer. The citrusy bitterness of the hops resins pulls the taste buds in the opposite direction of the sweet roasted malt. In addition, the light flowery scent counteracts some of the heavy mustiness produced by the union of yeast and wort.

Green Flash Brewing Company
1430 Vantage Ct.
Vista, CA 92081
www.greenflashbrew.com

🍺 Red Tail Lager

"Smithers, this beer isn't working, I don't feel any younger or funkier."
—MR. BURNS, *THE SIMPSONS*

TYPE: Pale lager
COLOR: Deep golden brown
SMELL: Caramel and floral hops
TASTE: A crisp, lighter-bodied beer with flavors of grain, toasted bread, and sweet honey mixed with both citrus and spicy hops. Finishes clean and dry with little aftertaste.
FOOD PAIRING: Five-spice marinated rack of lamb
AVAILABILITY: Year round

APR
9

Beer*fun*

Steve, Bob, and Jeff were working on a very high scaffolding one day when suddenly, Steve fell off and was killed. Bob went to tell Steve's wife and returned in a few hours with a six-pack of beer. "So did you tell her?" asked Jeff.

"Yep," replied Bob. "When she answered the door, I asked her, 'Are you Steve's widow?' 'Widow?' She said, 'No, no, you're mistaken. I'm not a widow!' So I said: 'I'll bet you a six-pack you are!'"

Medocino Brewing Company
13351 So. Highway 101
Hopland, CA 95449
www.mendobrew.com

🍺 Rustic Ale

"The souls of men have been fed with indigestibles, but the soul could make use of beer."
—HENRY MILLER

TYPE: Amber ale
COLOR: Amber
SMELL: Sweet caramel and earth
TASTE: A medium-bodied beer with notes of sweet malt, cinnamon, and spice, balanced out by just a touch of grassy hops.
FOOD PAIRING: Monte Cristo sandwich
AVAILABILITY: Year round

APR
10

Beer*fun*
Quarters
Required supplies: One quarter, one short juice glass, beer

To play: Players take turns attempting to bounce a quarter off of a table and into the juice glass. If a player is successful, he appoints another player to take a drink of beer. If he succeeds in bouncing the quarter into the cup three times in a row, the player can make a rule (for instance, players can't say the words "drink," "drank," or "drunk"; players can't say proper names). Violating a rule requires the violator to take a drink of beer. If the player is unsuccessful in bouncing the quarter into the juice glass, play passes clockwise around the table to the next player.

Capital Brewery
7734 Terrace Avenue
Middleton, WI 53562
www.capital-brewery.com

🍺 Unfiltered Wheat Beer

"I drank to drown my pain, but the damn pain learned how to swim."
—FRIDA KAHLO, ARTIST

TYPE: Hefewiezen
COLOR: Cloudy golden
SMELL: Wheat and honey
TASTE: A refreshing light- to medium-bodied beer with a smooth mouthfeel and flavors of freshly baked wheat bread and citrus.
FOOD PAIRING: Kartoffelkloesse (German potato dumplings)
AVAILABILITY: Year round

APR

11

Beerfact

It's no coincidence that the advent of beer and the beginnings of human civilization occurred at nearly the same time. The first domesticated crops were little more than nutrient-rich wild grasses. Over time, these grasses evolved into wheat and barley. The loss of the freedom of a nomadic lifestyle and the added responsibility of having to tend the crops was offset by the sense of well-being and euphoria commonly experienced after drinking a fermented malted beverage.

Boulevard Brewing Company
2501 Southwest Blvd.
Kansas City, MO 64108
www.boulevard.com

🍺 Crème Brûlée Stout

"Drink to the point of hilarity."
—ST. THOMAS AQUINAS

TYPE: Imperial stout
COLOR: Black
SMELL: Burnt sugar and vanilla
TASTE: A medium- to full-bodied beer that starts with flavors of caramel, burnt sugar, and crème. Once the sweetness fades a touch, you can pick out notes of coffee and even a little smoke.
FOOD PAIRING: Raspberry crème brûlée
AVAILABILITY: June release

APR
12

Brewtip

"Boza Beer" from Bulgaria (which uses a special yeast for fermentation) has been reputed to have one gigantic side effect—it increases women's breast size. Though the specific ingredient in the beer that produces this effect has not been isolated (nor have the claims been scientifically substantiated), it is believed that the yeast is the likely culprit.

Southern Tier Brewing Company
2051A Stoneman Circle
Lakewood, NY 14750
www.southerntierbrewing.com

🍺 Session Lager

"Do not cease to drink beer, to eat, to intoxicate thyself, to make love, and to celebrate the good days."
—EGYPTIAN PROVERB

TYPE: Pale lager
COLOR: Pale straw
SMELL: Sweet malt and citrus
TASTE: A good easy-drinking beer, perfect for a lazy summer afternoon, sitting on the deck, looking out at the Hood River. Nice smooth grain flavors with just a touch of grassy hops.
FOOD PAIRING: Bacon and Swiss burger with a big slice of tomato and a soft warm bun
AVAILABILITY: Year round

APR

13

Beerfact

The ancient Egyptians, credited as the first to brew beer, held a particular reverence for their malted beverages, going so far as to build their breweries inside temples. Wealthy Egyptians would not only have their body mummified, they would have a tiny scale replica of a brewery built to be buried with them. That way, they could enjoy their journey into the next realm, all the while sipping on a deliciously brewed beer.

Full Sail Brewery
506 Columbia Street
Hood River, OR 97031
www.fullsailbrewing.com

 Hades

Woody: "How would a beer feel, Mr. Peterson?" Norm:
"Pretty nervous if I was in the room."
   —*CHEERS*

TYPE: Belgian strong pale ale
COLOR: Golden yellow
SMELL: Yeast, banana, clove
TASTE: Light- to medium-bodied beer with flavors of sweet honey, roasted malt, yeast, and a touch of stone tree fruit, balanced out by a nice spiciness that finishes dry with just a hint of floral, earthy hops.
FOOD PAIRING: Fresh crusty bread with a smear of triple cream Brie
AVAILABILITY: Year round

APR
14

Beer*thought*

George Wendt, one of America's most famous television beer drinkers (he played Norm on the long-running show *Cheers*), has a favorite toast he uses at weddings. "Sixty-three percent of marriages end in divorce. The other thirty-seven percent end in death." Then he raises his glass and says, "I hope you die."

Great Divide Brewing Company
2201 Arapahoe Street
Denver, CO 80205
www.greatdivide.com

🍺 Bitch Creek

"Beer needs baseball, and baseball needs beer—it has always been thus."
    —PETER RICHMOND, AUTHOR

TYPE: Extra special bitter
COLOR: Rusty amber
SMELL: Floral hops
TASTE: Light- to medium-bodied beer dominated by the delicious bitterness of hops. Underneath are flavors of burnt caramel and toasted marshmallow. In the end it finishes with a smooth taste of pine and spicy citrus.
FOOD PAIRING: Morel mushrooms in a garlic butter sauce
AVAILABILITY: Year round

APR

15

Beer*fact*

ESB or extra special bitter refers to a well-balanced pale or bitter ale. Though the name suggests that these beers have a lot of hops or other bittering agents, they tend to be a combination of many flavors. The term "bitter" in England initially referred to a pale ale that had an unusually high hop content. More recently, the term has been used to categorize a much broader spectrum of beers. ESB then referred to any pale ale that is at least 4.8% ABV.

Grand Teton Brewing Company
430 Old Jackson Highway
Victor, ID 83455
www.grandtetonbrewing.com

🍺 Chimay Red, Prémiere

"It is my design to die in the brew house."
—ST. COLUMBANUS, 612 C.E.

TYPE: Dubel
COLOR: Copper
SMELL: Stone fruit and spice
TASTE: A creamy, smooth, medium-bodied beer with flavors of sweet malt, stone fruit, cocoa, cloves, and banana. A true classic.
FOOD PAIRING: Fresh baked biscuits with sliced ham and apricot preserves
AVAILABILITY: Year round

APR
16

Beerfact

Trappists, also known as the Order of the Strict Observance, are a Roman Catholic religious order. Only seven of the more than 150 Trappist monasteries in the world produce beer. Chimay, pronounced "she-may," is made by the monks of the Trappist monastery of Notre-Dame at Scourmont, in the south of Belgium. The monks there have been making their brew since the mid to late 1800s.

Bieres De Chimay S.A.
Route Charlemagne, 8
6464 Baileux (Chimay)
Belgium
www.chimay.com

🍺 Ommegeddon

*"Twas beautiful ale, and I wished to value his kindness . . .
and not to be so ill-mannered as to drink only a
thimbleful."*
—THOMAS HARDY, *FAR FROM THE MADDING CROWD*

TYPE: American wild ale

COLOR: Hazy dark gold

SMELL: Pale malt and lemon zest

TASTE: A lighter-bodied beer with flavors of sour apple, yeast, and hay followed by bitter hops, malt, and a touch of alcohol. It finishes a little warm with a sour aftertaste.

FOOD PAIRING: Monterey jack cheese

AVAILABILITY: Limited release

**APR
17**

Beer*words*

Irish drinking toast:

> May the roof above you never fall in,
> And those gathered beneath it never fall out.

Brewery Ommegang
656 County Highway 33
Cooperstown, NY 13326
www.ommegang.com

🍺 Stout

"This beer is good for you. This is draft beer."
—ERNEST HEMINGWAY, *TO HAVE AND HAVE NOT*

TYPE: Stout
COLOR: Dark reddish brown bordering on black
SMELL: Coffee, sweet malt, and a touch of alcohol
TASTE: A creamy, medium-bodied beer with flavors of roasted malt, bitter baking chocolate, and a touch of citrus hops.
FOOD PAIRING: BBQ mopped chicken
AVAILABILITY: Year round

APR

18

Beer*words*
Ways to say you're drunk (in English):

Bashed	Gonzo
Toasted	Zombied
Clobbered	Rummy
Reeked	Invincible
Decimated	Shellacked
Soaked	Jacked

Sierra Nevada Brewing Company
1075 East 20th Street
Chico, CA 95928
www.sierranevada.com

🍺 Liberty Ale

"Let no man thirst for good beer."
—SAMUEL ADAMS, BREWER

TYPE: Pale ale
COLOR: Golden amber
SMELL: Piney hops with just a touch of toasted bread
TASTE: Originally brewed in 1975 to commemorate the 200th anniversary of Paul Revere's historic ride, this beer tastes like nostalgia. For the record, nostalgia has flavors of pine and dandelion mixed with unripe stone fruit followed by a crisp, hoppy aftertaste.
FOOD PAIRING: Philadelphia cheese steak sandwich with onions
AVAILABILITY: Year round

APR

19

Beerfact

The vast majority of the world's hops are used in the production of beer. They are also present in two other beverages: Julmust, a carbonated drink similar to soda pop, which is popular in Sweden during the winter months, and Malta, a Latin American soft drink. Hops are also sometimes used as an herbal remedy for treatment of anxiety, restlessness, and insomnia. Hops contain the chemical compound dimethylvinyl carbinol, which produces a sedative effect in humans.

Anchor Brewing Company
1705 Mariposa Street
San Francisco, CA 94107
www.anchorbrewing.com

🍺 Hefeweizen

"Beer should be enjoyed with the right mixture of abandon and restraint."
—M.F.K. FISHER

TYPE: Hefeweizen
COLOR: Cloudy yellow
SMELL: Wheat and tree fruit
TASTE: A light- to medium-bodied beer with flavors of fresh wheat, apple, pear, and a touch of hops. Crisp, refreshing, and thirst quenching.
FOOD PAIRING: Sausage, pepperoni, ham, bacon, salami, and meatball pizza
AVAILABILITY: Year round

APR
20

Publore

Just one large block off the walking embankment that runs along the Huangpu River and nearly in the shadow of the Pearl Television Tower rising up from the other side of the riverbank in Pudong, the Bund Brewery is one of only two brewers of specialty beer in Shanghai.

Visit the Bund Brewery at The Custom House, 11 HanKou Road, Shanghai, China 200002PRC, *www.thebundbrewery.com.cn/#.*

Santa Cruz Ale Works
150 Dubois Street
Santa Cruz, CA 95060
www.santacruzaleworks.com

🍺 Bourbon Barrel Dopple Bock

Sam: "How about a beer, Norm?" Norm: "That's that amber sudsy stuff, right? I've heard good things about it."
—*CHEERS*

TYPE: Dopplebock
COLOR: Deep amber brown
SMELL: Sweet malt, bourbon, caramel, and a touch of hops
TASTE: A rich, creamy, boozy, full-bodied beer with flavors of caramel, oak, malt, and vanilla.
FOOD PAIRING: BBQ beef brisket
AVAILABILITY: Limited release

APR
21

Pub*lore*

If you like good BBQ and good beer, Slows Bar B Q will treat you right. They pride themselves on good food paired with the world's best beer. They have only the finest craft beers on tap and an extensive bottle list that includes favorites from England, Belgium, and beyond.

Visit Slows Bar B Q at 2138 Michigan Avenue, Detroit, MI 48216, *www.slowsbarbq.com.*

Sprecher Brewing Company
701 W. Glendale Avenue
Glendale, WI 53209
www.sprecherbrewery.com

🍺 Vertical Epic Ale 09.09.09

"When your companions get drunk and fight, take up your hat and wish them good night."
—PROVERB

APR

22

TYPE: Belgian-style imperial porter

COLOR: Deep luscious brown

SMELL: Chocolate and coffee

TASTE: A magnificent, silky smooth beer that starts off with rich milk chocolate, moves into dark-roasted coffee, then ventures somewhere in between with notes of mocha bean. It finishes with a sweetened bitterness that fades into a very subtle licorice aftertaste.

FOOD PAIRING: Vertical Epic Ale vanilla ice cream float

AVAILABILITY: Limited

Beerthought

The first time the world witnessed a Vertical Epic Ale was February second, 2002—02.02.02. The next was 03.03.03, then 04.04.04. It has happened now eight times, and will continue to happen until 12.12.12. Oh, if only I were patient enough to keep them all until then.

Stone Brewing Company
1999 Citracado Parkway
Escondido, CA 92029
www.stonebrew.com

 Sweetgrass IPA

"There's nothing wrong with sobriety in moderation."
—JOHN CIARDI, AUTHOR

TYPE: India pale ale

COLOR: Cloudy amber gold

SMELL: Lemon meringue pie followed by fresh grass and a hint of ripe apricot

TASTE: Tangerine and ruby grapefruit with a thick hop resin aftertaste that lasts and lasts

FOOD PAIRING: Kumimoto oysters with a shallot mignonette sauce

AVAILABILITY: Year round

APR
23

Pub*lore*

In 1989 Wyoming pub owners Charlie and Ernie Otto discovered an old European beverage vessel—essentially a tin pail with a lid—that was used to carry beer home from brewpubs before bottling was a common practice. This vessel was known as a "growler." Charlie and Ernie reinvented this rather inefficient device as the 64-ounce glass jug that is now commonly used in brewpubs across the nation.

Grand Teton Brewing Company
430 Old Jackson Highway
Victor, ID 83455
www.grandtetonbrewing.com

🍺 The Poet

"I think a man ought to get drunk at least twice a year just on principle, so he won't let himself get snotty about it."
—RAYMOND CHANDLER

TYPE: Oatmeal stout
COLOR: Dark brown, almost black
SMELL: Sweet dark chocolate, roasted nuts, and dark malt
TASTE: If you were to describe this beer in just two words, they would be "tart" and "roasted." A light- to medium-bodied beer with flavors of roasted coffee and roasted grain paired with the delightful tartness of grapefruit and lemon zest.
FOOD PAIRING: Burnt-end ribs
AVAILABILITY: Year round

APR
24

Pub*lore*

The self-proclaimed "Temple of Beer Worship" in East Village Manhattan, Burp Castle used to be known in the nineties as the place where the bartenders and waiters all dressed up in monks' robes and shushed you if your conversation got too loud. Though the robe wearing now only takes place on special occasions, the shushing still happens.

Visit Burp Castle NYC at 41 East 7th Street, New York, NY 10003, *www.burpcastlenyc.wordpress.com.*

New Holland Brewing Company
66 E. 8th Street
Holland, MI 49423
www.newhollandbrew.com

 Hyde Park Stout

"The brewery is the best drugstore."
—GERMAN SAYING

TYPE: Irish dry stout
COLOR: Black
SMELL: Roasted malt and earthy hops
TASTE: A smooth, thick brew with flavors of dark-roasted malt, baker's chocolate, coffee beans, and bitter hops up front that fade into sweet toffee and a citrus finish.
FOOD PAIRING: Beer-brined pork chops
AVAILABILITY: Year round

APR
25

Beerfood
BEER-BRINED PORK CHOPS

2 cups water
2 cups porter or stout
¼ cup coarse salt
3 tablespoons (packed) dark
  brown sugar
3 tablespoons light molasses

6 bone-in pork chops (1-inch thick)
1 cup ice cubes
7 cloves minced garlic
3 teaspoons black pepper
2 teaspoons salt
2 teaspoons dried sage

Combine water, beer, coarse salt, sugar, and molasses. Stir until salt and sugar dissolve. Stir in ice. Place pork chops in large sealable plastic bag with brine and refrigerate 4 to 8 hours, turning bag occasionally. Remove pork chops from beer brine and pat them dry. Mix garlic, pepper, salt, and sage, and rub both sides of chops. Grill at 375°F about 10 minutes per side to an internal temperature of 145°F to 150°F. Let rest for 5 minutes, then serve.

Augusta Brewing Company
5521 Water Street
Augusta, MO 63332
www.augustabrewing.com

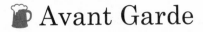 Avant Garde

"In de hemel is gee daarom drinken wij hee." ('In heaven there is no beer, so we drink it here.')
—TRAPPIST MONK PROVERB

TYPE: Bière de garde
COLOR: Cloudy amber
SMELL: Sweet malt and fruit
TASTE: A medium-bodied beer with a sweet malt backbone and a very mild hoppy finish that blends into a syrupy aftertaste.
FOOD PAIRING: Mussels and frites
AVAILABILITY: Year round

APR

26

Beer*fest*

2009 Great American Beer Festival Winners by Category

Old Ale or Strong Ale: Old Scrooge '98, Silver City Brewery, Silverdale, WA

Barley Wine–Style Ale: Old Inventory Barley Wine, Valley Brewing Co., Stockton, CA

Mid-Size Brewing Company and Mid-Size Brewing Company Brewer of the Year: Flying Dog Brewery, Frederick, MD; Robert Malone

Small Brewing Company and Small Brewing Company Brewer of the Year: Dry Dock Brewing Company, Aurora, CO; Dry Dock Brewing Team

The Lost Abbey
155 Mata Way
San Marcos, CA 92069
www.thelostabbey.com

 Maibock

"Beer. If you can't taste it, why bother?"
—ANONYMOUS

TYPE: Maibock
COLOR: Deep golden
SMELL: Sweet malts and spice with a touch of alcohol
TASTE: A medium-bodied beer with flavors of sweet malt, caramel, honey, biscuit, and spice, coupled with a mild hoppiness.
FOOD PAIRING: Honey-glazed ham
AVAILABILITY: Spring

APR
27

Publore

A German-style beer house in the middle of Moscow, Bavarius has all the trappings of Oktoberfest—large wooden communal tables, Oompah music, liter beer steins, barmaids in traditional German attire, and a menu of Bavarian specialties including knockwurst and sauerkraut. In addition, they have an outdoor beer garden where you can enjoy any of the dozen beers they have on tap.

Visit Bavarius at Saddovaya-Triumfalnaya Ulitsa 2/30, Str. 1, Moscow, 103006, *www.bavarius.ru/*.

Summit Brewing Company
910 Montreal Circle
St. Paul, MN 55102
www.summitbrewing.com

🍺 Dos Perros

Woody: "What's going down, Mr. Peterson?" Norm: "My butt cheeks on that bar stool."
—CHEERS

TYPE: Brown ale
COLOR: Clear brown
SMELL: Nutty sweet malt and spicy hops
TASTE: A light- to medium-bodied beer with a soft mouthfeel and flavors of fruit, sweet malt, nuts, fresh crusty bread, and a touch of cocoa. There are notes of spicy hops and a touch of bitterness. It ends with more nuttiness and has a dry finish.
FOOD PAIRING: Spicy black bean burrito
AVAILABILITY: Year round

**APR
28**

*Pub**lore***

Just outside of Boston is The Publick House. Each of their 200 beers is served in its appropriate glassware, and the menu will keep you entertained while you wait to get a table (it's a popular place, so be patient, it's worth it).

Visit The Publick House at 1648 Beacon Street, Brookline, MA 02445, *www.eatgoodfooddrinkbetterbeer.com/publickhouse*.

Yazoo Brewing Company
1200 Clinton Street #112
Nashville, TN 37203
www.yazoobrew.com

🍺 90 Minute Imperial IPA

"I've never been drunk, but often I've been over served."
—GEORGE GOEBEL

TYPE: Double India pale ale
COLOR: Amber
SMELL: Citrus hops and malt
TASTE: Considering how much hops are used and how long it is boiled, it's a wonder this isn't an overpoweringly hoppy monster. Instead, the hops are seamlessly blended into the perfect pairing with sweet malt and caramel flavors.
FOOD PAIRING: Molasses chicken wings
AVAILABILITY: Year round

APR
29

Brewtip
The strongest beers in the world:

> Schorschbräu Eisbock: (30.86% ABV) (Germany)
> Südstern XXL (27.6% ABV) (Germany)
> Samuel Adams Utopias (27% ABV) (United States)
> Dogfish Head 120 Minute IPA (21% ABV) (United States)

Dogfish Head Craft Brewery
6 Cannery Village Center
Milton, DE 19968
www.dogfish.com

 Scotch

"The best place to drink beer is at home. Or on a river bank, if the fish don't bother you."
—ANONYMOUS

TYPE: Scotch ale
COLOR: Dark reddish brown
SMELL: Sweet malt, grain, and dried fruit
TASTE: A medium-bodied beer with flavors of sweet malt, roasted grain, dried plum, raisin, and syrup. Goes down smooth and finishes quite dry.
FOOD PAIRING: Organic Parmesan cheese
AVAILABILITY: Year round

APR
30

Beersaint
Saint Brigid's Prayer
I'd like to give a lake of beer to God.
I'd love the Heavenly
Host to be tippling there
For all eternity.

I'd sit with the men, the women of God
There by the lake of beer
We'd be drinking good health forever
And every drop would be a prayer.

Boundary Bay Brewery
1107 Railroad Avenue
Bellingham, WA 9225
www.bbaybrewery.com

 McChouffe

"You think man needs rule, he needs beer."
—HENRY MILLER

TYPE: Belgian strong dark ale
COLOR: Dark brown
SMELL: Yeasty bread, spices, and dried fruit
TASTE: A medium-bodied beer with flavors of sweet malt, caramel, brown sugar, and toffee that give way to some pepper and a bitter apple finish.
FOOD PAIRING: Brined, smoked pork ribs with a maple syrup glaze
AVAILABILITY: Year round

MAY

1

Pub*lore*

Pig N Whistle in Seattle is a quintessential Seattle neighborhood pub. They have twelve beers on tap, maybe fourteen in bottles, a full bar, and a killer menu. The brews on tap rotate based on neighborhood tastes and lean heavily toward local microbrews.

Visit the Pig N Whistle at 8412 Greenwood Avenue North, Seattle, WA 98103, *www.pignwhistleseattle.com.*

Brasserie d'Achouffe
Rue du Village 32
Achoufee, 6666
Belgium
www.achouffe.be

🍺 Fat Tire

"In Belgium the magistrate has the dignity of a prince, but by Bacchus it is true that the brewer is king."
—EMILE VERHAEREN, AUTHOR (1855–1916)

TYPE: Amber ale
COLOR: Amber
SMELL: Sweet and malty with a touch of floral hops
TASTE: Medium-bodied and full-flavored, this beer fits in neatly at the edge of an old wooden bar. Flavors of sweet malt, fresh brown bread, and caramel balance nicely with just notes of floral hops.
FOOD PAIRING: Steak frites
AVAILABILITY: Year round

MAY

2

Brew*tip*

If you've homebrewed, you'll know that one of the best sources for good bottles is looting the recycling bins in your neighborhood. Some of the labels will slip off after a twenty-minute soak in hot water. If you find yourself with a stubborn label, add baking soda to the water before you soak the bottles. If that doesn't work, try scraping them with a straight-edge razor.

New Belgium Brewing Company
500 Linden Street
Fort Collins, CO 80524
www.newbelgium.com

🍺 King's Peak Porter

"What may seem depressing or even tragic to one person may seem like an absolute scream to another person, especially if he has had between four and seven beers."
—DAVE BARRY

TYPE: Porter
COLOR: Dark brown
SMELL: Chocolate and coffee
TASTE: A lighter-bodied beer with flavors of lightly roasted coffee, sweet chocolate, and fresh bread. Finishes with a touch of hops and a burnt-toast aftertaste.
FOOD PAIRING: Mesquite-smoked turkey served over Parmesan rice
AVAILABILITY: Year round

**MAY
3**

Beer*fact*

The Kalevala is an epic poem composed by Elias Lönnrot. The book is thought to be the most significant piece of Finnish literature ever written. The poem consists of 22,795 verses. Two hundred of them are dedicated to the creation of the world, but describing the creation of beer requires four hundred.

Uinta Brewing Company
1722 South Fremont Drive (2375 West)
Salt Lake City, UT 84104
www.uintabrewing.com

🍺 Saint Lupulin

"If four or five guys tell you that you're drunk, even though you know you haven't had a thing to drink, the least you can do is to lie down a little while."
—JOSEPH SCHENCK, MOVIE PRODUCER

MAY

4

TYPE: Pale ale

COLOR: Clear golden

SMELL: Fresh baked bread and lemon zest

TASTE: A light- to medium-bodied beer with flavors of citrus and pine hops followed by caramel, malt, and yeast. Finishes with a touch of alcohol and ends with a hop resin aftertaste.

FOOD PAIRING: Twice-baked potatoes with bacon, sour cream, and three kinds of cheese

AVAILABILITY: May through September

Beer*fun*

Old Man Murphy had worked down at the brewery for years, but one day he tripped and fell over into the beer vat and drowned. The foreman informed his widow of her husband's death. She wept and covered her face and asked, "Did he suffer?" "I don't think so," said the foreman. "He got out three times to go to the men's room."

Odell Brewing Company
800 East Lincoln Avenue
Fort Collins, CO 80524
www.odellbrewing.com

DuClaw Brewing Company

🍺 el Guapo

"Does thou think that because thou art virtuous there will be no more cakes and ale?"
—WILLIAM SHAKESPEARE

TYPE: Munich-style Helles
COLOR: Golden
SMELL: Quite malty
TASTE: Light to medium body with a smooth mouthfeel and a rich caramelized sugar backbone. Underneath, a subtle bitter hoppiness helps pull the sweetness back and balance it out on the back end.
FOOD PAIRING: Black bean, jalapeño, and pulled-pork nachos
AVAILABILITY: Brewed for Cinco de Mayo

MAY

5

Beer*words*

German terms you should know before heading to the München Oktoberfest:

- *Haud scho* (n.): Yes! Expression of success.
- *Helles* (n.): The most popular type of Bavarian beer.
- *Hoiwe* (n.): Half liter of beer.
- *Maß* (n.): One liter of beer.

- *Maßkruagstemma* (n.): A game where the players hold one maß beer with straight arms. The player who can hold the beer the longest wins.
- *Noagerl* (n.): The last swallow of beer in a glass.

DuClaw Brewing Company
901 S. Bond Street
Baltimore, MD 21231
www.duclaw.com

🍺 Chokolat Stout

"Beer and chocolate are two pleasures that should be enjoyed and savored."
—SAMUEL ADAMS, BREWER

TYPE: Imperial stout

COLOR: Opaque brown

SMELL: Chocolate

TASTE: If you closed your eyes, you might think you were drinking a love potion administered by a tribe of Amazonian warrior goddesses. Okay, so it's not really brewed by Amazons, but it tastes like it might be.

FOOD PAIRING: Chokolat stout ice cream

AVAILABILITY: November release

MAY

6

Beerfact

Things you probably didn't know about Southern Tier Brewing:

Southern Tier Brewing Company has been in business since 2004, and they now produce over 12,000 barrels of beer each year. That's just shy of the amount needed to fill 4 million twelve-ounce bottles. When they first started out, they released only three beers: an IPA and two flagship brews—Pilsner and Mild Ale. Both of their flagships flopped, but the IPA was such a success that they lived to brew another day.

Southern Tier Brewing Company
2051A Stoneman Circle
Lakewood, NY 14750
www.southerntierbrewing.com

🍺 Hefe Weiss

"Laissez la bonne biere verser." ("Let the good beer pour.")
—FRENCH SAYING

TYPE: Hefeweizen
COLOR: Cloudy pale straw
SMELL: Yeast, wheat, banana, and spice
TASTE: A smooth, creamy, medium-bodied beer with flavors of freshly cut wheat, fresh yeasty bread, banana, and clove. It finishes with lemon and grapefruit and ends crisp and dry.
FOOD PAIRING: Fresh warm bread, fontina cheese, and sliced pears
AVAILABILITY: Year round

MAY

7

Beerfact

Things you probably didn't know about Sprecher Brewing Company:

The company was founded in 1985 by Randal Sprecher. The facility they currently use was formerly an elevator car factory. In addition to beer, Sprecher also produces eight soft drinks: root beer (and lo-cal root beer), cream soda, orange soda, Raving Red (cherry, cranberry honey, and ginseng flavor), ginger ale, cherry cola, and a regular cola.

Sprecher Brewing Company
701 W. Glendale Avenue
Glendale, WI 53209
www.sprecherbrewery.com

🍺 Juju Ginger

"You foam within our glasses, you lusty golden brew.
Whoever imbibes takes fire from you."
—ANONYMOUS

TYPE: Spiced ale
COLOR: Bright golden
SMELL: Ginger and roasted corn
TASTE: Light and crisp with a distinct ginger flavor on the back end. There are notes of toasted malt and melted caramel with a nice balance of floral hops. The ginger comes out more on the aftertaste as well.
FOOD PAIRING: Pumpkin and sweet potato soup
AVAILABILITY: Year round

MAY

8

Beerfact

When the Egyptian sun god Ra grew displeased with his followers for the lackluster way in which they were worshiping him, he sent his daughter Sekhmet to teach them a lesson. Sekhmet laid waste to everything she encountered and drank the blood of her victims. One wily human gave her a red beer, hoping that she would think it was blood. The goddess drank it down, falling into a deep slumber. And that was how mankind was saved—by beer.

Left Hand Brewing Company
1265 Boston Avenue
Longmont, CO 80025
www.lefthandbrewing.com

 Orval Trappist Ale

"Drinking is the soldier's pleasure."
—JOHN DRYDEN

TYPE: Belgian pale ale
COLOR: Hazy reddish amber
SMELL: Sweet malt, banana, and citrus
TASTE: A medium-bodied beer with flavors of banana, yeast, clove, and apple. A dry, rather crisp beer that is deceptive in its drinkability. Sure you could down quite a few, but then try to get up off that bar stool.
FOOD PAIRING: Spicy lemongrass soup
AVAILABILITY: Year round

MAY

9

Beerfact

Beer has been brewed in Orval since the thirteenth century. The monastery was destroyed after the French Revolution in 1793 and reconstructed in 1926, but it wasn't until 1932 that the new brewery started its operations. Despite this long brewing history, their beer has only been considered an official Trappist product since 1980.

Brasserie D'Orval
Villers-devant-Orval, 6823
Belgium
www.orval.be

🍺 Jasperilla Old Ale

"The pub knows a lot. Almost as much as the churches."
—JOYCE CAREY, AUTHOR

TYPE: Old ale
COLOR: Golden
SMELL: Plums, raspberries, and fresh bread
TASTE: A smooth, light- to medium-bodied beer that features flavors of yeasty biscuit and sweet malt that are accentuated by dark fruit and berry notes. A nice sipping beer that finishes with just a hint of port wine flavors.
FOOD PAIRING: Tiramisu
AVAILABILITY: Brewed once a year and released after six months of aging

MAY
10

Pub*lore*

Started in a little house in Houston, the Gingerman pubs (*www.gingermanpub.com*) have spread over Texas and now have locations on the East Coast as well. These easygoing, laid-back pubs are a haven for beer drinkers with more than seventy-five beers on tap and an even bigger bottle list.

Independence Brewing Company
3913 Todd Lane #607
Austin, TX 78744
www.independencebrewing.com

🍺 Honey Brown Ale

Sam: "Beer, Norm?" Norm: "Have I gotten that predict-able? Good."
—CHEERS

TYPE: Brown ale
COLOR: Deep brown
SMELL: Roasted malt, honey, and caramel
TASTE: A light- to medium-bodied beer with initial flavors of citrus and pine that give way to a smooth pairing of honey and caramel. There are hints of roasted malt and biscuit that fade into a crisp, dry finish.
FOOD PAIRING: Szechuan beef with broccoli
AVAILABILITY: Year round

MAY

11

Publore

Café Sound Garden in the Netherlands is located near the old site of the infamous Club Roxy. Patrons can sit at communal tables in an outdoor beer garden and watch the boats and barges float slowly by. There is a lot of food to choose from in the immediate area, and the rotating beer selection at Café Sound Garden is sure to have something to match your chosen fare.

Visit Café Sound Garden at Marnixstraat 166, 1016 TG, Amsterdam, Netherlands, *www.cafesoundgarden.nl.*

Twisted Pine Brewing Company
3201 Walnut Street, Suite A
Boulder, CO 80301
www.twistedpinebrewing.com

 Porter

"No poems can live long or please that are written by water drinkers."
—HORACE

TYPE: Porter
COLOR: Dark cola brown
SMELL: Malt and dark chocolate
TASTE: Dark-roasted coffee with cola and raisin flavors mixed with mocha bean and a fruit liquor aftertaste
FOOD PAIRING: Savory wild boar ragout served over soft egg noodles
AVAILABILITY: Year round

MAY
12

Beer*fest*

Presented by the San Francisco Brewers Guild (*www.sfbrewersguild.org*), Brews on the Bay takes place in September aboard the historic World War II liberty ship SS *Jeremiah O'Brien.* The ship made seven World War II trips across the Atlantic and eleven trips across the English Channel, carrying personnel and supplies to Normandy in support of the D-Day invasion. Proceeds from the event go to benefit the care and continued restoration of the *O'Brien.*

Anchor Brewing Company
1705 Mariposa Street
San Francisco, CA 94107
www.anchorbrewing.com

🍺 Carolina Pale Ale

"The misconception is you need to learn how to taste. It's more a sense of recognition than a sense of taste."
  —JERALD O'KENNARD, BEVERAGE TESTING INSTITUTE

TYPE: Pale ale
COLOR: Golden amber
SMELL: Malt and citrus
TASTE: A medium-bodied beer with flavors of sweet malt and caramel followed by a nice bitter hoppy kick that balances things out and ends smooth.
FOOD PAIRING: Potato, rosemary, and olive oil pizza
AVAILABILITY: Year round

MAY

13

Beerfact
Legally acceptable blood alcohol concentration in drivers:

Albania 1%	Greece 2%
Armenia 0%	Mongolia 2%
Brazil 0%	Nepal 0%
Colombia 0%	Romania 0%
Czech Republic 0%	Russia 3%
Estonia 2%	Turkmenistan 3%

Carolina Brewing Company
140 Thomas Mill Road
Holly Springs, NC 27540
www.carolinabrew.com

🍺 Arrogant Bastard Ale

"I'd give my goddamned soul for just a glass of beer."
—JACK NICHOLSON, ACTOR, *THE SHINING*

TYPE: American strong ale
COLOR: Deep crimson copper
SMELL: Toast, hops, and sweet molasses cookies
TASTE: Multiple layers of citrus zest, toffee, chocolate, brown sugar, and alcohol. A real treat.
FOOD PAIRING: Alder-planked five-spice chicken
AVAILABILITY: Year round

MAY
14

Beerfact

Stone Brewing Company maintains a separate page (*www.arrogant bastard.com*) for this beer. Clicking on the link will bring up a legal page with the throbbing red word "Warning!" at the top. In addition to being at least twenty-one, the viewer must promise to hold harmless the brewer for any "insults, insecurities, and ego damages incurred by the viewing or retrieving" of the material on the actual page, and must promise to not be a "fizzy yellow beer drinking ninny."

Stone Brewing Company
1999 Citracado Parkway
Escondido, CA 92029
www.stonebrew.com

 Obsidian Stout

"Drunk is feeling sophisticated when you can't say it."
—ANONYMOUS

TYPE: Stout
COLOR: Black
SMELL: A complex aroma of mocha bean, vanilla, powdered malt, cola, and licorice
TASTE: A nice viscous, medium-bodied beer with flavors of coffee grounds, burnt toast, and dark-roasted malt with a subtle undercurrent of sour lemon and bitter citrus.
FOOD PAIRING: Coffee-rubbed beef brisket
AVAILABILITY: Year round

MAY

15

Beer*thought*

It speaks to you as you pour. Not words so much as a feeling. It's being at peace. It's the anticipation of the first sip. The whiff of something familiar. It's the thick, viscous gurgling as it slips over the edge of the glass. It's the flavors that spread out and separate as they glide over your tongue—and that feeling of release that hits moments after the first gulp. It's the message you hear so clearly as you empty the bottle, the one that compels you to raise your glass, to toast your good friends—and order another round.

Deschutes Brewery
901 SW Simpson Avenue
Bend, OR 97702
www.deschutesbrewery.com

🍺 Summer Ale

"Shoulder the sky, my lad, and drink your ale."
—A. E. HOUSMAN

TYPE: American pale ale
COLOR: Light, clear gold
SMELL: Faint grass smell with a hint of uncut wheat on a hot summer day
TASTE: Grains and malt with a little orange zest thrown in for good measure. A lighter-bodied beer that goes down smooth and refreshes. Long, pleasant finish.
FOOD PAIRING: Pan-fried noodles with chicken and oyster sauce
AVAILABILITY: April through August

MAY

16

Beer*fact*

Known also as top-fermenting beers (because the action takes place at the top of the vat or carboy), ales, and the yeasts that produce them, are fermented at warmer temperatures, usually around the typical household room temperature, or 60° to 75° Fahrenheit. The advantage to this is quicker fermentation and the creation of byproducts known as "esters," which add a floral or fruity character to the beer. Major ale styles include, pale ale, IPA, barley wine, porter, and stout.

The Shipyard Brewing Company
86 Newbury Street
Portland, ME 04101
www.shipyard.com

🍺 IPA

"You can't have a Real Country unless you have a beer and an airline—it helps if you have some kind of a football team, or some nuclear weapons, but at the very least you need a beer."
—FRANK ZAPPA

TYPE: India pale ale
COLOR: Light gold
SMELL: Lots of grain and malt with hops on the back end
TASTE: Taste of caramel malts, some stone fruit, orange peel, and a little floral earthiness. An easy beer for an easy day in the sunshine.
FOOD PAIRING: The hoppy goodness of an IPA is an ideal match for fried food—for the same reason you put lemon or vinegar on fish and chips or French fries—because it cuts through the grease
AVAILABILITY: May–September

MAY
17

Beer*thought*

The perils of international politics have often been solved over a pint of refreshing beer. After all, what better to cool the hottest of heads? Beer's resume stands on its own: It healed the wounds of a fractured nation after Prohibition. It saved us from waterborne illnesses when human civilization was in its infancy. What more could you ask for from your beverage? To refresh you on a hot summer day? Long Trail IPA will do that, too.

Long Trail Brewing Company
Route 4 and 100A
Bridgewater Corners, VT 05035
www.longtrail.com

🍺 Tannhauser Pale Ale

"Real ale fans are just like train spotters, only drunk."
—CHRISTOPHER HOWSE, AUTHOR

TYPE: Pale ale
COLOR: Cloudy amber
SMELL: Citrus and pine
TASTE: An easy drinking, light- to medium-bodied beer with flavors of pine and citrus hops, roasted malt, and just a touch of sweetness. It finishes crisp with a piney, bitter aftertaste.
FOOD PAIRING: Grilled chicken thighs marinated in coconut milk and sprinkled with crushed peanuts
AVAILABILITY: Year round

MAY
18

Beer*thought*
Irish drinking toast:
> When money's tight and hard to get, and your horse is also ran,
> When all you have is a heap of debt, a pint of plain is your only man.

Augusta Brewing Company
5521 Water Street
Augusta, MO 63332
www.augustabrewing.com

🍺 Haywire

"A little bit of beer is divine medicine."
—PARACELSUS

TYPE: Hefeweizen
COLOR: Hazy dark golden
SMELL: Wheat, yeast, and citrus
TASTE: Crisp, smooth, and light bodied, this beer exhibits flavors of fresh cut wheat, lemon, and a touch of hoppy bitterness. It would be perfect for an easy sunny afternoon on the back porch.
FOOD PAIRING: Pesto king salmon wrapped in tin foil and baked on the coals of a wood fire
AVAILABILITY: Year round

MAY

19

Beerfest

2009 Great American Beer Festival Winners by Category

American-Style Cream Ale or Lager: Milwaukee's Best, Miller Brewing Co., Golden, CO

American-Style Wheat Beer: County Seat Wheat, Blind Tiger Brewery & Restaurant, Topeka, KS

American-Style Wheat Beer with Yeast: Haywire Hefeweizen, Pyramid Breweries, Seattle, WA

Fruit Beer or Field Beer: Raspberry Creek, Breakwater Brewing Co., Oceanside, CA

Pyramid Brewing Company
91 S. Royal Brougham Way
Seattle, WA 98134
www.pyramidbrew.com

🍺 Golden State Ale

"The University of Nebraska says that elderly people that drink beer or wine at least four times a week have the highest bone density. They need it—they're the ones falling down the most."

—JAY LENO

TYPE: Belgian pale ale

COLOR: Dark gold amber

SMELL: Grain, yeast, tree fruit, and earthy hops

TASTE: A crisp, smooth, light- to medium-bodied, almost oily-feeling beer with flavors of grain, pear, green apple, yeasty bread, and lemon zest. Ends with a hint of alcohol.

FOOD PAIRING: Pastrami with green tomato relish

AVAILABILITY: Year round

Beer*fact*

If you took all the beer consumed in the United States in one year, you could fill one out of every twenty-five residential in-ground pools in the country. If you were to put that same beer in a single keg, that keg would measure 1,429 feet tall and 870 feet wide. If you were then to put it in standard twelve-ounce cans, it would amount to one can for every American over the age of twenty-one, each day of the week (except Sunday), for an entire year.

Uncommon Brewers
303 Potrero St, Suite 40-H
Santa Cruz, CA 95060
www.uncommonbrewers.com

🍺 Bare Ass Blonde

"Abstainer: a weak person who yields to the temptation of denying himself a pleasure."
—AMBROSE BIERCE

TYPE: Blonde ale
COLOR: Golden
SMELL: Earthy with notes of fruit and toasted flatbread
TASTE: Light and refreshing, there are subtle flavors of grass and citrus followed by melted marshmallow and lightly toasted bread. A very approachable beer.
FOOD PAIRING: Try this with a white fish, such as sole or halibut. The citrus notes in the beer should go well with a light squeeze of lemon over the fish.
AVAILABILITY: Year round

**MAY
21**

Brewtip
Brewing Additives

- **Epsom salts:** Adds hardness to the mash.
- **Fermax:** A yeast nutrient used primarily in low-gravity (lower alcohol content) beers and meads.
- **Gelatin:** Helps settle the yeast and suspended proteins, reducing haziness.

- **Gypsum:** Helps to harden water and clarify the final product. Most frequently used in pale ales.
- **Heading agents:** Helps give your brew a healthy head. Quite handy for low-gravity (low alcohol content) beers and those brewed with a lot of adjuncts.

DuClaw Brewing Company
901 S. Bond Street
Baltimore, MD 21231
www.duclaw.com

🍺 Steam Engine Lager

"Oh, Elizabeth! Your justice would freeze beer!"
—ARTHUR MILLER, *THE CRUCIBLE*

TYPE: Steam beer
COLOR: Dark golden orange
SMELL: Sweet malt and fresh bread
TASTE: A lighter-bodied beer with flavors of fresh baking powder biscuits, sweet malt, and citrus. Fades out sweet then balances itself with a dry, slightly hoppy finish.
FOOD PAIRING: Chili-marinated steak nachos
AVAILABILITY: Year round

MAY
22

Beer*fun*

A neutron walks into a bar. "I'd like a beer," he says. The bartender serves him a beer. "How much will that be?" asked the neutron. "For you?" replies the bartender, "no charge."

Steamworks Brewing Company
442 Wolverine Drive
Bayfield, CO 81122
www.steamworksbrewing.com

🍺 Lunar Ale

"I'm going to buy a boat . . . do a little traveling, and I'm going to be drinking beer!"
—JOHN WELSH, WINNER OF $30 MILLION LOTTERY

TYPE: Unfiltered brown ale
COLOR: Orangish brown
SMELL: Fresh wheat, sweet malt, and just a touch of fruit
TASTE: A medium-bodied beer that starts with light-roasted caramel flavors and subtly moves into biscuit and warm wheat, followed by banana and clove.
FOOD PAIRING: Stuffed pumpkin with walnut and lamb sausage
AVAILABILITY: Year round

MAY

23

Beerfest

The yearly beer guzzling celebration known as Oktoberfest originated in Germany. However, Oktoberfest was never intended to be an annual event. The sometimes month-long party began as a simple affair, meant to celebrate the marriage between Crown Prince Ludwig and Princess Teresa of Bavaria. Held for the first time on October 17, 1810, in the town of Munich, the festivities included a horse race, music, dancing, and of course, plenty of beer drinking.

Boulevard Brewing Company
2501 Southwest Blvd.
Kansas City, MO 64108
www.boulevard.com

🍺 Saison Rue

"And the bartender says to Descartes, 'Another beer?' And Descartes says, 'I think not,' and disappears."
—ANONYMOUS

TYPE: Saison
COLOR: Hazy copper
SMELL: Citrus, honey, ginger, and clove
TASTE: A medium-bodied beer with flavors of biscuit and honey that provide a backbone for a host of spice and fruit—ginger, clove, lemon zest, tangerine, and tart apricots.
FOOD PAIRING: Ginger pumpkin soup
AVAILABILITY: Year round

MAY
24

Beer*fun*

A man in New York walks into a pub and says, "Give me three pints of beer, please. I have two brothers, one on the West Coast, and one in the Midwest. We made a vow to each other that every Saturday night we'd still drink together. So right now, my brothers have three pints of beer too, and we're drinking together."

Every week the bartender sets up the guy's three beers. Then one week, the man comes in and orders only two. The bartender sadly says, "I'm sorry that one of your brothers died."

The man replies, "Oh, my brothers are fine—I just quit drinking."

The Bruery
715 Dunn Way
Placentia, CA 92870
www.thebruery.com

🍺 Sawtooth Ale

"For a quart of ale is a dish for a king."
—WILLIAM SHAKESPEARE

TYPE: Extra special bitter
COLOR: Amber
SMELL: Citrus and mild roasted malt
TASTE: Toasted nuts and caramel followed by a floral, earthy hoppiness.
FOOD PAIRING: Onion pancakes with poblano chili relish
AVAILABILITY: Year round

MAY
25

Beerfact
The hop plant was introduced to the United States from England in 1629. The first large-scale hop yard was established in 1808 in the state of New York. By the mid-1900s, Wisconsin had also become a major producer of the crop, as the cultivation of hops had spread south and further west. By the 1920s, however, downy mildew swept through New York and Wisconsin, effectively wiping out all cultivation in both states. Today, the Yakima Valley in Washington state produces nearly 75 percent of the hops grown in the United States.

Left Hand Brewing Company
1265 Boston Avenue
Longmont, CO 80025
www.lefthandbrewing.com

🍺 Bad Elmer's Porter

"Why do I drink? So I can write poetry."
—JIM MORRISON

TYPE: Porter
COLOR: Dark brown
SMELL: Molasses, sweet malt, and chocolate
TASTE: A medium-bodied beer with flavors of coffee, anise, chocolate, raisins, molasses, and toffee.
FOOD PAIRING: Chocolate mint fudge
AVAILABILITY: Year round

MAY
26

Beerfest

2009 Great American Beer Festival Winners by Category

Sweet Stout: Cow Stout, Pizza Port Carlsbad, Carlsbad, CA

Oatmeal Stout: Ernest's Silky Smoove, Pizza Port San Clemente, San Clemente, CA

Imperial Stout: Gonzo Imperial Porter, Flying Dog Brewery, Frederick, MD

Scotch Ale: Reed's Wee Heavy, Pizza Port Carlsbad, Carlsbad, CA

Upland Brewing Company
350 W. 11th Street
Bloomington, IN 47404
www.uplandbeer.com

 White

"And brought of mighty ale a large quart."
—GEOFFREY CHAUCER, *THE CANTERBURY TALES*

TYPE: Witbier
COLOR: Cloudy pale yellow
SMELL: Yeast and fresh cut wheat with a touch of lemon meringue pie
TASTE: Lots of fresh wheat and spice, with a considerable amount of lemon and smooth lime.
FOOD PAIRING: Goat cheese, grape, and walnut salad
AVAILABILITY: Year round

MAY
27

Beer*fest*

Celebrating its tenth anniversary in 2010, Brüegala is an international beer festival (*www.bruegala.com*), encompassing more than 200 brews. Occurring annually in the city of Bloomington, Illinois, during the month of September, the festival takes place over two days and includes a rousing tournament of Bags—known also as Corn Toss, Soft Horseshoes, or Indiana Horseshoes. However, the more common and passionately used name for this game is Cornhole.

Allagash Brewing Company
50 Industrial Way
Portland, ME 04103
www.allagash.com

🍺 Siamese Twin

"For drink, there was beer, which was very strong when not mingled with water, but was agreeable to those who were used to it."

—XENOPHON

TYPE: Dubbel

COLOR: Cloudy amber

SMELL: Coriander and sweet honey

TASTE: Smooth, medium-bodied beer with a myriad of flavors—coriander, banana, lemongrass, yeast, sweet roasted malt, and cream followed by a pleasant sour taste and undertones of ginger.

FOOD PAIRING: Thai lemongrass chicken marinated in coconut milk

AVAILABILITY: Year round

MAY

28

Beerfact

King Hammurabi, the ruler of Babylon from 1792 to 1750 B.C., set out the "Code of Hammurabi" that included laws dealing with everyday life. Of those, four are related to taverns. Rules in Babylon about wine or beer drinking were strict, as can be seen from the following: "If a priestess who has not remained in the sacred building shall open a tavern, or enter a tavern for drink, that woman shall be burned."

Uncommon Brewers
303 Potrero St, Suite 40-H
Santa Cruz, CA 95060
www.uncommonbrewers.com

🍺 Old Viscosity

"Payday came, and with it, beer."
—RUDYARD KIPLING

TYPE: American strong ale
COLOR: Dark brown
SMELL: Sweet malt, chocolate, and rum
TASTE: A rich, medium- to full-bodied beer with flavors of roasted malt, dried fig, bittersweet chocolate, and a touch of bitter hops.
FOOD PAIRING: Mimolette—a hard cheese of French/Dutch origin
AVAILABILITY: Year round

MAY
29

Publore

The Library Ale House sports a laid-back vibe and a come-as-you-are dress code. You'll also find more than twenty beers on tap and more than thirty in bottles, ranging from Belgians to local Southern California standards and a well-selected scattering of those ports in between.

Visit the Library Ale House at 2911 Main Street, Santa Monica, CA 90405, *www.libraryalehouse.com.*

Port Brewing Company
155 Mata Way, Suite 104
San Marcos, CA 92069
www.portbrewing.com

🍺 Hop Devil Ale

"Seven beers followed by two Scotches and a thimble of marijuana and it's funny how sleep comes all on its own."
—DAVID SEDARIS, AUTHOR

TYPE: India pale ale
COLOR: Slightly hazy amber
SMELL: Citrus and pine
TASTE: A smooth, light- to medium-bodied beer with predominate hop flavors of grapefruit, lemon zest, and pine followed by some roasted sweet malt that fades away again as it finishes bitter with a lemon and pine aftertaste.
FOOD PAIRING: Ginger-marinated grilled thresher shark
AVAILABILITY: Year round

MAY
30

Beerfact

Pennsylvania has had more breweries in its history than any other state. In 1910 alone, 119 of the state's towns had at least one licensed brewer. Pennsylvania is also the only state in which you cannot simply go to a store and buy a six-pack. Since shortly after Prohibition, people in that state have been unable to buy six-packs, half-racks, or single bottles in the beer store (yes, they have separate, special stores where you buy your beer). And beer can only be purchased in full cases.

Victory Brewing Company
420 Acorn Lane
Downingtown, PA 19335
www.victorybeer.com

🍺 Imperial Russian Stout

"If my mother was tied up and held for ransom, I might think about making a light beer."
    —GREG KOCH, CEO OF STONE BREWING

TYPE: Imperial Russian stout

COLOR: Very dark brown, like liquid baker's chocolate

SMELL: Caramel and vanilla with a touch of smoke

TASTE: A nice medium body and a very silky mouthfeel accompanied by flavors of chocolate, coffee, and alcohol, balanced by the tart pinecone hoppiness.

FOOD PAIRING: Chocolate crème truffle rolled in smoked, cured bacon bits

AVAILABILITY: Early summer

MAY

31

Beerfact

Imperial stout, also known as Russian imperial stout or imperial Russian stout, was first brewed in London in 1796 by Thrale's Brewery. It was specially created for export to the court of Catherine the Great, the Empress of Russia. The beer was sold as "Thrale's Entire Porter" until the brewery was purchased by Courage & Co. and was then renamed "Courage Imperial Russian Stout." Today Russian imperial stouts are brewed all over the world.

Stone Brewing Company
1999 Citracado Parkway
Escondido, CA 92029
www.stonebrew.com

🍺 Tandem

"Alcohol is the anesthesia by which we endure the operation of life."
—GEORGE BERNARD SHAW

TYPE: Double ale
COLOR: Chocolate
SMELL: Clove, dandelion, unbleached flour, and citrus.
TASTE: Thick and beefy, like a porter, but not as heavy. Nice malty roasted flavor with a hint of spice and stone fruit. They use coriander in the brewing process.
FOOD PAIRING: Planked Copper River salmon
AVAILABILITY: Year round

JUN
1

Brew*tip*
The term "double" or "dubbel" comes from a Trappist monk convention for naming their beers. The first dubbel was brewed at the Trappist Abbey of Westmalle, located in the Campine region of Antwerp (also known as Flanders) in Belgium. The first written record of sale of the dubbel ale, which amounted to a strong version of a brown beer, was on June 1, 1861.

The Pike Brewing Company
1415 First Avenue
Seattle, WA 98122
www.pikebrewing.com

🍺 Organic California Blonde Ale

"Praise not the day until evening has come; a sword until it is tried; ice until it has been crossed; beer until it has been drunk."
—VIKING PROVERB

TYPE: Blonde ale
COLOR: Dark golden
SMELL: Grains and floral hops
TASTE: A light- to medium-bodied beer with flavors of sweet malt and fresh bread balanced by notes of grapefruit and bitter orange hops.
FOOD PAIRING: Stewed rabbit with pomme frites
AVAILABILITY: Year round

JUN
2

Beerthought

Text on a warning placard found at the Eel River Brewing Company website:

"Warning: The consumption of alcohol may create the illusion that you are tougher, handsomer, and smarter than some really big guy named Chuck."

I don't know who this Chuck fellow thinks he is, but we can take him.

Eel River Brewing Company
1777 Alamar Way
Fortuna, CA 95540
www.eelriverbrewing.com

🍺 Lookout Stout

"O Beer! Guinness, Allsopp, Bass! Names that should be on every infant's tongue."
—C. S. CALVERLEY, POET

TYPE: Stout
COLOR: Dark brown
SMELL: Coffee and dark-roasted malt
TASTE: A medium-bodied beer with flavors of dark-roasted coffee, mocha bean, and burnt toast that are balanced by a nicely dry hoppy finish.
FOOD PAIRING: Smoked chicken drumsticks
AVAILABILITY: Year round

**JUN
3**

Beer**words**

Irish wedding toast:

Sliocht sleachta ar shliocht bhur sleachta.

May there be a generation of children on the children of your children.

Health and long life to you, land without rent to you, a child every year to you, and death in Old Ireland.

Golden City Brewery
920 12th Street
Golden, CO 80401
www.gcbrewery.com

🍺 Kentucky Ale

"When I get a chance to play golf or go on a boat with good people, take the boat out and put some lobsters on the grill, get the ice-cold beer and the cigars—that's heaven here on earth."

—BERNIE MAC

TYPE: Pale ale

COLOR: Light copper

SMELL: Grains and just a touch of hops

TASTE: A smooth, light-bodied beer with a mild malt and toasted barley character balanced by subtle floral and citrus hops.

FOOD PAIRING: Chicken-fried steak with mashed potatoes

AVAILABILITY: Year round

JUN

4

Beer*fact*

In 1970, United States federal law allowed for drivers to have no more than a blood alcohol content of 0.15. That limit has been reduced more than once and is now 0.08, which is tied as the highest in the world. In Germany, the limit is 0.05. And in the Czech Republic (along with eleven other countries), there is a zero-tolerance law. Having even a sip of beer before getting behind the wheel of a car is enough to get you thrown in jail.

Alltech's Lexington Brewing Company
401 Cross Street
Lexington, KY 40508
www.kentuckyale.com

🍺 Hopitoulas

"My rule of life prescribed as an absolutely sacred rite smoking cigars and also the drinking of alcohol before, after, and if need be, during all meals and the intervals between them."
—WINSTON CHURCHILL

TYPE: India pale ale

COLOR: Hazy golden

SMELL: Citrus and pine

TASTE: A light-bodied beer with a great blend of both pine and citrus flavors that give way to overall bitterness. This is definitely an IPA, one for the hop lover in all of us.

FOOD PAIRING: Rotisserie baby back pork ribs

AVAILABILITY: Year round

**JUN
5**

Beerfact

There is some dispute among scholars about when the first wooden barrel was invented. However, the general consensus is that the creation of the first wood barrel took place sometime between 300 B.C.E. and 1 C.E. Before then, beverages were most commonly stored in clay jugs or inside large concrete or glass vats.

New Orleans Lager and Ale Brewing Company
3001 Tchoupitoulas Street
New Orleans, LA 70130
www.nolabrewing.com

🍺 Code 24

"24 hours in a day, 24 beers in a case. Coincidence?"
—STEVEN WRIGHT, COMEDIAN

TYPE: Pale ale
COLOR: Deep gold/amber
SMELL: Dry grains and hops
TASTE: A medium-bodied beer that exhibits nice floral and fruit hop flavors and subtle citrus notes that are balanced out by a nice, smooth, roasted-malt character and a crisp, dry finish.
FOOD PAIRING: Firehouse five-bean chili
AVAILABILITY: Year round

JUN

6

Beerfact

Prior to 1970, when a fire had been put out the call would go up on the fire scanner for a "Code 24." This alerted the younger firemen that it was time for them to head to the store and pick up cases of beer (24 packs), and bring them back to the fire, as the old timers finished up. 10 Barrel Brewing's Code 24 is a salute to those brave heroes.

10 Barrel Brewing Company
20750 High Desert Lane #107
Bend, OR 97701
www.10barrel.com

BIG SKY BREWING COMPANY

🍺 Montana Trout Slayer

"Ale it is called among men, and among gods, beer."
—OLD NORSE SAYING

TYPE: Pale wheat ale
COLOR: Dark golden
SMELL: Hops and grain
TASTE: A light, easy-to-drink beer with flavors of lemon, apricots, grains, sweet honey, and tangerine followed by a dandelion aftertaste. A great beer for camping or a day out on the river.
FOOD PAIRING: Quesadillas grilled on a hot, flat stone beside a campfire
AVAILABILITY: Year round

JUN
7

Beerfun

Two fishermen were adrift. One of the men found an old lamp in the boat and rubbed it. At once, a genie appeared and told the men he could grant one wish. The man blurted out, "Make the entire ocean into beer!" The genie clapped his hands, and immediately the entire sea turned into the finest brew ever sampled by mortals.

One man looked disgustedly at the other whose wish had been granted. "Nice going idiot!" he said. "Now we're going to have to piss in the boat!"

Big Sky Brewing Company
5417 Trumpeter Way
P.O. Box 17170
Missoula, MT 59808
www.bigskybrew.com

Stillwater Vanilla Cream Ale

"The church is near, but the road is icy. The bar is far away, but I will walk carefully."
—RUSSIAN PROVERB

TYPE: American cream ale
COLOR: Golden
SMELL: Slight vanilla
TASTE: A nice, smooth, light-bodied beer that transitions from the flavors of malt and light hops into a very delightful vanilla. Nice for cooling down on a hot evening when the fan just doesn't quite do the trick.
FOOD PAIRING: Raspberry crème brûlée with shavings of white chocolate and a sprinkle of cocoa over the top
AVAILABILITY: Summer

**JUN
8**

Beer*thought*

Imagine sitting in a rocking chair on a wraparound porch. The weatherman says the high today was in the mid-eighties, but the heavy, wet air makes you feel like you've spent the entire day in a steam room. You reach down into a cooler of ice that has already half melted. Wrapping your fingers around a bottle, you pull up a Stillwater Vanilla Cream Ale, pop the top, and let the slightly sweet, frigid liquid soak into you.

Sometimes it's good to get too hot.

Thomas Creek Brewery
2054 Piedmont Highway
Greenville, SC 29605
www.thomascreekbeer.com

IPA

"I would not have thought of eating a meal without drinking a beer."
—ERNEST HEMINGWAY

TYPE: India pale ale
COLOR: Copper
SMELL: Hoppy, not overpowering, very pleasant
TASTE: Smooth, easy to drink, a hint of oak with the telltale bitterness that lingers from the hops you knew were lurking behind the bold, proud letters I, P, and A displayed on the label.
FOOD PAIRING: Rich, creamy, earthy cheese—like a Spanish Patacabra—spread over crusty bread.
AVAILABILITY: Year round

JUN

9

Beer*thought*

Inside a bottle of Lagunitas IPA is the custom of the land, the essence of life, and the very heart of what makes our spirits soar. Like all good craft beers, it clarifies our purpose here on Earth, challenges us to be better people. Twisting off the cap, with the little doggie printed on top, is nothing less than a metaphor for the separation between man and beast— the bottle a symbol of humanity, the beer the glorious nectar of potential that is inside of us all.

Lagunitas Brewing Company
1280 North McDowell Blvd.
Petaluma, CA 94954
www.lagunitas.com

🍺 Westmalle Trappist Dubbel

"This is grain, which any fool can eat but for which the Lord intended a more divine means of consumption . . . beer!"

—FRIAR TUCK, *ROBIN HOOD, PRINCE OF THIEVES*

TYPE: Dubbel
COLOR: Dark mahogany
SMELL: Caramel, dried fruit, spice, and yeast
TASTE: A medium-bodied beer with flavors of warm caramel, banana, spicy yeast, figs, currents, nutmeg, sugar crystals, and toffee that finishes with a long, sour aftertaste.
FOOD PAIRING: Baked bacon-wrapped dates
AVAILABILITY: Year round

**JUN
10**

Beer*fest*

The Montreal Beer Festival (*http://festivalmondialbiere.qc.ca/*), held in June in Montreal, Quebec, has as its mission, "To restore beer to its rightful and noble place, by offering the general public the opportunity to taste beer from five continents, while encouraging responsible consumption." The 50,000 people who attend can help in this by tasting some of the 300 beers available.

Brouwerij Westmalle
Malle, 2390
Belgium
www.trappistwestmalle.be

🍺 Fire Rock Pale Ale

"I am a firm believer in the people. If given the truth, they can be depended upon to meet any national crisis. The great point is to bring them the real facts, and beer."
—ABRAHAM LINCOLN

JUN

11

TYPE: Pale ale
COLOR: Coppery gold
SMELL: Toasted bread with just a touch of floral hops
TASTE: Lots of rich maltiness here—cereal grains with flecks of burnt toffee chips. Medium-bodied beer with a solid amount of hops to balance out the sweetness.
FOOD PAIRING: Slow-turned, open-pit whole roast pig
AVAILABILITY: Year round

Beerfact
In Japan it is illegal to brew your own beer if it has an alcohol content of higher than 1% alcohol by volume. Retailers are permitted to sell kits and distribute recipes that will yield batches of higher alcohol content, but they are required to send out a warning to their customers explaining the law. It is then up to the homebrewer to comply by either modifying the recipe or deciding not to brew.

Kona Brewing Company
7192 Kalaniana'ole Highway
Inside Hawaii Kai, waterside
Honolulu, HI 96825
www.konabrewingco.com

🍺 1856 IPA

"Nothing anyone says in a bar is true."
—MARK RUFFALO, ACTOR

TYPE: India pale ale
COLOR: Cloudy amber
SMELL: Pine and citrus hops
TASTE: A smooth, medium-bodied beer with flavors of grapefruit, grass, and lemon that step aside just long enough for some bready malt to make an appearance.
FOOD PAIRING: Braised saffron halibut
AVAILABILITY: Year round

JUN

12

Beerfolk
Saint Lawrence (born 225 C.E., died 258 C.E.)
One of the seven deacons of ancient Rome, Saint Lawrence was martyred during the persecution of Valerian, the Emperor of Rome from 253 C.E. to 260 C.E. Lawrence is the patron saint of any profession related to fire, including brewers, cooks, bakers, innkeepers, and firemen.

Augusta Brewing Company
5521 Water Street
Augusta, MO 63332
www.augustabrewing.com

🍺 Elliot Ness

"He is a wise man who invented beer."
   —PLATO

TYPE: Amber lager
COLOR: Dark amber, almost toffee color
SMELL: Crisp, light aroma of hops and cracker
TASTE: Surprising amount of malt with a nice balance of grapefruit and spicy hops. Smooth, medium body with a sweet caramel aftertaste and a nice easy finish.
FOOD PAIRING: Deep-fried catfish po' boy sandwich with coleslaw
AVAILABILITY: Year round

JUN

13

Beerfact

There is validity to the argument that some beers are better when served slightly warmer: the aromas and flavors present in the malts and hops sometimes don't adequately come out until they have warmed by a few degrees. Here's a guide to serving your favorite style of beer at its ideal temperature.

• 35–45 degrees: hefeweizen, American lager, pilsner, amber lager
• 45–55 degrees: porter, pale ale, stout, amber ale
• 56–58 degrees: IPA bock, brown ale
• 59–63 degrees: barley wine, doppelbock

Great Lakes Brewing Company
2516 Market Avenue
Cleveland, OH 44113
www.greatlakesbrewing.com

🍺 Great White

"Why should mother go without her nourishing glass of ale or stout on washing day?"
—ANTI-TEMPERANCE SLOGAN

TYPE: Witbier
COLOR: Golden with a slight haze
SMELL: Citrus and yeast
TASTE: A light-bodied beer with a silky mouthfeel and a host of interesting spices. There is a slight sweetness on the palette with flavors of coriander, banana, mandarin orange, and just a hint of pineapple.
FOOD PAIRING: Grilled swordfish drizzled with a ginger cream sauce
AVAILABILITY: Year round

JUN

14

Beerfact

In 2003, the *Journal of Nutrition* published a study about the bellies of beer drinkers, wine drinkers, spirits drinkers, and nondrinkers. In the study, each participant was weighed and measured. The study concluded that the beer drinkers in the study had no more measurable body fat than the nondrinkers.

Lost Coast Brewery
123 West Third Street
Eureka, CA 95501
www.lostcoast.com

🍺 Pollenator

"When I read about the evils of drinking, I gave up reading."
—HENNY YOUNGMAN

TYPE: Pale ale
COLOR: Vibrant gold
SMELL: Sweet honey and caramel with only a hint of floral hops
TASTE: Light bodied and nicely balanced. There's a floral spiciness that accompanies the sweet, making Pollenator a great hot-weather beer.
FOOD PAIRING: Try with a piece of gooey Camembert cheese topped with a sweet fig spread and some good crackers.
AVAILABILITY: May–September

JUN
15

Brew*tip*
Long Trail calls their brewing philosophy "EcoBrew," which includes their efforts in heat recovery, water conservation, using recycled materials, consumption reduction, and offering the over eight tons of spent mash they create every day to local dairy farmers.

Long Trail Brewing Company
Route 4 and 100A
Bridgewater Corners, VT 05035
www.longtrail.com

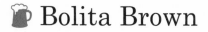 Bolita Brown

"Let ale be placed to my mouth when I am expiring, that when choirs of angels come, they may say, 'Be God propitious to this drinker.'"
—ST. COLUMBANUS, 612 C.E.

TYPE: Double nut brown ale
COLOR: Dark brown
SMELL: Dark-roasted malt and coffee
TASTE: A medium- to full-bodied beer with flavors of roasted malt, cocoa bean, and nuts followed by some grassy hops and just a touch of spice.
FOOD PAIRING: Gruyère grilled cheese sandwich
AVAILABILITY: September

JUN

16

Beerfest
2009 Great American Beer Festival Winners by Category

Wood- and Barrel-Aged Beer: Humidor Series IPA, Cigar City Brewing, Tampa, FL

Wood- and Barrel-Aged Strong Beer: Cereal Killer Barleywine, Arcadia Brewing Co., Battle Creek, MI

Wood- and Barrel-Aged Sour Beer: Bourbonic Plague, Cascade Brewery Co. LLC, Portland, OR

Aged Beer: Horn Dog Vintage 2007, Flying Dog Brewery, Frederick, MD

Cigar City Brewing
3924 West Spruce Street, Suite A
Tampa, FL 33607
www.cigarcitybeer.com

🍺 La Chouffe

"The sway of alcohol over mankind is unquestionably due to its power to stimulate the mystical faculties of human nature."

—WILLIAM JAMES

TYPE: Belgian strong pale ale

COLOR: Dark yellow orange

SMELL: Yeast, fruit, and hay

TASTE: A medium-bodied beer with touches of sweet malt, yeast, honey, cloves, and both grassy and floral hops.

FOOD PAIRING: Salmon en croûte with leeks and dill

AVAILABILITY: Year round

JUN

17

Beerfact

Brasserie d'Achouffe was founded in 1982. In 1988 they began exporting their beer, first to Quebec, then eventually expanding from there. Currently, they offer five different beers, as well as a brandy, called Esprit d'Achouffe. They have little gnomes on all their labels, which is a play on their name, Achouffe, since *chouffe* means "gnome" or "dwarf" in Walloon (a language spoken in Wallonia, Belgium).

Brasserie d'Achouffe
Rue du Village 32
Achoufee, 6666
Belgium
www.achouffe.be

 Celts Golden Ale

"I envy people who drink—at least they know what to blame everything on."
—OSCAR LEVANT

TYPE: Golden ale
COLOR: Golden
SMELL: Slightly sweet caramel malt
TASTE: Overall dry flavor with notes of orange, bitter lemon, and a touch of residual sugar. A light-bodied beer built to satisfy and quench your thirst all at the same time.
FOOD PAIRING: Tempura shrimp
AVAILABILITY: Year round

JUN

18

Beerfact

Hangover helpers:

• **Almonds:** A Native American cure claims that eating six raw almonds before you drink will help prevent intoxication and the resulting hangover.

• **Bifidus powder:** Bifidus is a bacteria found naturally in the intestinal tract that aids in digestion. Place a teaspoon or two of this powder in a large glass of water and drink it before you go to bed. In the morning you'll be glad you did.

Molyan's Brewery
15 Rowland Way
Novato, CA 94945
www.moylans.com

🍺 Holy Mackerel Mack in Black

Coach: "Can I draw you a beer, Norm?" Norm: "No, I know what they look like. Just pour me one."
—*CHEERS*

JUN
19

TYPE: American strong ale
COLOR: Coal black
SMELL: Roasted barley and ground coffee
TASTE: Dark malts and bitter chocolate up front with a little hint of heavily roasted coffee beans, ending with just a bit of pomegranate juice and vanilla. This is a unique beer in that pomegranate juice is used during the brewing process to add some spice and bitterness.
FOOD PAIRING: Asian orange chicken with ginger, green onion, and red pepper flakes
AVAILABILITY: Year round

Beerfact

Robert K. Gordash began brewing beer in his home in 1993. His first batches were heated on the kitchen stove and yielded only five gallons at a time. Not satisfied with just a carboy's worth of brew, he convinced a friend (read: bribed him with free beer) to help build a twenty-gallon fire-brewed system on his back patio. In 1997, he won the Samuel Adams World Homebrew Contest with his "Extra Special Bitter." Ten years later the Gordash Brewing Company was founded.

Gordash Brewing Company
3804 SW 30th Avenue
Fort Lauderdale, FL 33312
www.holymackerelbeers.com

🍺 Gumballhead

"Alcohol is necessary for a man so he can have a good opinion of himself—undisturbed by the facts."
—*FINLEY PETER DUNNE*

TYPE: Pale wheat ale
COLOR: Golden
SMELL: Fresh hops and caramelized sugar
TASTE: A mix of fresh wheat and roasted malt sweetness paired with a floral hoppiness
FOOD PAIRING: Wok-seared albacore tuna with coconut curry
AVAILABILITY: Summer seasonal

JUN
20

Beer*words*

- **Clarifier:** A substance used to remove suspended particles that can create a hazy-looking beer.
- **Esters:** A compound formed by joining an alcohol and an acid, which produces fruity aromas and flavors in brewed beers.
- **Finishing hops:** Hops added to the wort late in the boil, to impart a hoppy aroma rather than bitterness.
- **IBU:** International Bittering Units. A standard measure of the hop content in beer.

Three Floyds Brewery
9570 Indiana Parkway
Munster, IN 46321
www.threefloydspub.com

 Export Ale

"The first draught serveth for health, the second for plea-sure, the third for shame, the fourth for madness."
  —SIR WALTER RALEIGH

TYPE: American pale ale
COLOR: Dark golden that borders on copper or maybe even rusty
SMELL: Reminiscent of freshly mown grass or cut hay
TASTE: Not overly thick, this medium-bodied beer has a nice caramel-ized sugar flavor up front that blends into the floral, grassiness of the hops. It leaves you with the wheat and malt before disappearing entirely.
FOOD PAIRING: Duck sliders with plum sauce and wild greens
AVAILABILITY: Year round

JUN
21

Brewtip

Fermentation is the process of creating alcohol. Yeast consumes the sugars in the malt and releases alcohol and carbon dioxide. In addition to these two byproducts, yeast also creates small amounts of other compounds, which add flavor or complexity to the brew. For craft brewers, the strain of yeast is very important in achieving a particular flavor, and many will go to the extreme of creating their very own propriety style in order to create a unique taste for their beer.

The Shipyard Brewing Company
86 Newbury Street
Portland, ME 04101
www.shipyard.com

🍺 Double Trouble

"Not drunk is he who from the floor, Can rise alone and still drink more; But drunk is he, who prostrate lies, Without the power to drink or rise."
—THOMAS LOVE PEACOCK (1785–1866)

TYPE: India pale ale
COLOR: Orange copper
SMELL: Grapefruit and pine
TASTE: Initial sweet malt flavor that drifts away quite quickly as the bitter hops move in. Flavors of grapefruit and earthy grass dominate, finishing with a nice, classic hoppy bitter aftertaste. A hop lovers delight.
FOOD PAIRING: Stir-fried crab curry with white pepper and cilantro
AVAILABILITY: Seasonal

JUN 22

Beerfact

Hangover helpers:

- **Water:** Drink two to three large glasses of water and take two to three aspirin or ibuprofen before bed. The water will help rehydrate you, and the aspirin will help thin your blood and kill the pain.
- **Exercise:** Okay, so the last thing you want to do the next morning is get up for a jog, but breaking a sweat and getting your blood flowing will help rid your body of toxins and make you feel better. The first step is always the hardest.

Founders Brewing Company
235 Grandville Avenue SW
Grand Rapids, MI 49503
www.foundersbrewing.com

🍺 Wheat Monkey

"Beer will always have a definite role in the diet of an individual and can be considered a cog in the wheel of nutritional foods."

—BRUCE CARLTON, PHYSICIAN

JUN

23

TYPE: American wheat ale

COLOR: Golden and cloudy

SMELL: Strong wheat right out of the bottle with a sweet fruitiness, almost bubblegum

TASTE: After the fresh wheat flavor there is a spice of coriander and a citrus finish.

FOOD PAIRING: Aged cheddar macaroni and cheese with buttered breadcrumbs

AVAILABILITY: Year round

Pub*lore*

Lakefront Brewery owes its success to something rather unexpected—sibling rivalry. The president of the company, Russ Klisch, bought his brother, Jim, a book on homebrewing as a birthday present. Jim not only read the book, he produced a batch of really good beer. Not to be outdone, Russ got into the act, and the two began entering their brews in local homebrew contests. Several awards later, they turned their hobby, and their rivalry, into a thriving, thirst-quenching business.

Lakefront Brewery
1872 N. Commerce Street
Milwaukee, WI 53212
www.lakefrontbrewery.com

🍺 Windmill Wheat

Cliff: "Hey, Norm! What's up?" Norm: "My blood alcohol level."

—*CHEERS*

TYPE: Pale wheat ale
COLOR: Hazy golden
SMELL: Yeast, fresh wheat, honey, and citrus
TASTE: A light-bodied, refreshing beer with flavors of freshly cut wheat, yeast, and lemon. Great for a session or just cooling down on a hot day.
FOOD PAIRING: Canadian bacon and pineapple pizza
AVAILABILITY: Year round

JUN
24

Beer*fun*

A guy walks into a bar and says to the bartender, "Give me a beer, give everyone in the place a beer, and have one yourself." The bartender serves everyone a beer and draws one for himself. He asks his benefactor for money. The man tells him he has none. The bartender physically ejects him from the bar. The man picks himself up and strides back into bar. He crawls onto a stool and says to the bartender, "Give me a beer and give everyone here a beer, but none for you. You get too mean when you drink."

Millstream Brewing Company
835 48th Avenue
Amana, IA 52203
www.millstreambrewing.com

🍺 O'Fallon Smoked Porter

"If all be true that I do think, There are five reason why men should drink, Good friends, good beer, or being dry, Lest we be like to be so, bye and bye. Or any other reason why."

—ANONYMOUS

TYPE: Porter
COLOR: Dark brown, almost black
SMELL: Alder wood smoke
TASTE: A light- to medium-bodied beer with a powerful alder smoke flavor that is complemented by just a hint of bitter hops and a note of chocolate. Finishes with a wood smoke aftertaste.
FOOD PAIRING: Alder smoked Alaska salmon
AVAILABILITY: Year round

Beerfact

In 2008, a Virginia Beach man called local area police with a bomb threat on a nearby Target store. Surveying the area, the police found no bomb but arrested a very drunk man for public intoxication. Upon further questioning, they discovered he had called in the threat. It seems he wanted to get the police at the grocery store to respond to the Target store, so that he could safely rob the place of beer when they left.

O'Fallon Brewery
26 West Industrial Drive
O'Fallon, MO 63366
www.ofallonbrewery.com

🍺 Rochefort 10

"I like beer. On occasion, I will even drink beer to celebrate a major event, such as the fall of Communism or the fact that the refrigerator is still working."
—DAVE BARRY

TYPE: Quadrupel
COLOR: Dark brown
SMELL: Brown sugar, dried fruit, and alcohol
TASTE: A very complex beer that takes several swallows to completely grasp. It starts with sweet dark fruit, freshly baked bread, and a touch of brown sugar. With more investigation, there are flavors of baker's chocolate and some dry hoppy bitterness, only to end with sweet brown sugar and plum.
FOOD PAIRING: Smoked beef ribs
AVAILABILITY: Year round

**JUN
26**

Beerfact

In the centuries before the invention of the thermometer, brewers would test the temperature of their brews prior to adding yeast by sticking in their thumb. Too cold, and the yeast wouldn't grow. Too hot, and the yeast would die. From this practice, we get the phrase "rule of thumb."

At least, that sounds like the right explanation.

Brasserie de Rochefort
B – 5580 Rochefort
Belgium
www.trappistes-rochefort.com

🍺 Old Leghumper

"Beer has long been the prime lubricant in our social intercourse and the sacred throat-anointing fluid that accompanies the ritual of mateship."
—RENNIE ELLIS, PHOTOGRAPHER

TYPE: Porter
COLOR: Chocolate Labrador
SMELL: Chocolate, sweet malt, and coffee
TASTE: Creamy and smooth on the tongue, this beer follows its nose with flavors of coffee and chocolate blended with a malty backbone and a touch of sour bitterness on the finish.
FOOD PAIRING: Beef bone and barley soup
AVAILABILITY: Year round

**JUN
27**

Beer*thought*

"Let an old dog lie." Yeah, I'll lie right here. The view is just fine.

"You old dog." I've still got it.

"You can't teach an old dog new tricks." Who needs new tricks? My old ones are working just fine.

"A piece of grass a day keeps the vet away." A piece of grass, huh? A piece of something.

Thirsty Dog Brewing Company
529 Grant Street, Suite B
Akron, Ohio 44311
www.thirstydog.com

🍺 Independence Pale Ale

"Fruit rollups for Bart. Beer rollups for Homer."
—MARGE SIMPSON

TYPE: Pale ale
COLOR: Gold
SMELL: Floral and citrus hops, biscuits
TASTE: A lighter-bodied, crisp beer with flavors of sweet malt and freshly baked bread followed by citrus and floral hops that develop into more pine as it drifts to a dry finish.
FOOD PAIRING: Pan-fried, breaded oysters with lemon aioli
AVAILABILITY: Year round

JUN

28

Beer*words*
Beer toasts of the world:

Austrian: *Prost*
Belgian: *Op uw gezonheid*
Croatian: *Zivjeli*
Esperanto: *Sanon*
Frisian: *Tsjoch*

Galician: *Chinchin*
Hindi: *Apki Lambi Umar Ke Liye*
Latin: *Bene tibi*
Mandarin: *Gan bei*
Norwegian: *Skal*

Independence Brewing Company
3913 Todd Lane #607
Austin, TX 78744
www.independencebrewing.com

🍺 Samurai

"You can never buy beer. You just rent it."
—ARCHIE BUNKER, *ALL IN THE FAMILY*

TYPE: Rice ale
COLOR: Bright golden
SMELL: Fresh grain and floral hops
TASTE: A lighter-bodied beer with a very dry, clean, crisp feel and flavor. There are notes of grain, and a touch of stone fruit, and of course a bit of floral hops.
FOOD PAIRING: Suntan tuna with sesame seeds
AVAILABILITY: Year round

JUN

29

Beerwords
Beer toasts of the world:

Albanian: *Shendeti tuaj, Gezuar*
Bulgarian: *Nazdrave*
Catalan: *Salut*
Danish: *Skal*
Egyptian: *Fee sihetak*

Finnish: *Kippis*
Gaelic: *Slánte*
Hebrew: *L'chaim*
Italian: *Salute, Cin cin*
Korean: *Konbe*

Great Divide Brewing Company
2201 Arapahoe Street
Denver, CO 80205
www.greatdivide.com

 Decadent Imperial IPA

"Oh, well, of course everything looks bad if you remember it."
—HOMER SIMPSON

TYPE: Imperial IPA
COLOR: Hazy orange
SMELL: Floral hops dominate with sweet malt and a bit of alcohol detectable underneath
TASTE: Tons of floral hops right off the bat followed by powerful flavors of grapefruit and sweet caramel malt. This is a bold beer (10% ABV and 99 IBU) that starts bitter and finishes bitter.
FOOD PAIRING: Shrimp pad thai, four stars
AVAILABILITY: Year round

**JUN
30**

Beerfact

Hangover helpers:

- **Peanut butter:** An African preremedy, eating peanut butter before a night of drinking is said to help prevent the next morning blues.
- **Tomato juice:** Tangy, acidic drinks help to reduce the craving for alcohol. As a preventative, try drinking a glass of tomato juice with a little fresh lemon squeezed in for good measure.

Ska Brewing Company
225 Girard Street
Durango, CO 81301
www.skabrewing.com

🍺 Sapient Trip Ale

"At social parties no gentleman ever thought of leaving the table sober; the host would have considered it a slight on his hospitality."
—F. W. HACKWOOD, *ETIQUETTE IN 18TH CENTURY ENGLAND*

TYPE: Amber ale
COLOR: Cloudy brown and gold
SMELL: Sweet malt, mandarin orange, and coriander
TASTE: Medium bodied with flavors of warm caramel, sweet malt, and spice with just a touch of orange and grapefruit. Finishes with orange and cardamom.
FOOD PAIRING: Steamed mussels and clams in a broth of garlic, fennel, tomatoes, and orange zest
AVAILABILITY: Spring/Summer seasonal

JUL

1

Beerfood

Next time someone asks if you like your beer cold or warm, tell them you prefer it hot, in a mug. Heating beer with sugar and spices was popular up until the nineteenth century and was done to improve the taste of the relatively low quality of many beers available at that time. The typical recipes involve adding several tablespoons to half a cup of sugar to a pint of ale along with a combination of one or more of cinnamon, clove, ginger, allspice, nutmeg, and cardamom.

Dark Horse Brewing Company
511 S. Kalamazoo Avenue
Marshall, MI 49068
www.darkhorsebrewery.com

IPA

"Ale, man, ale's the stuff to drink for fellows whom it hurts to think."
—A. E. HOUSMAN

TYPE: India pale ale
COLOR: Deep gold
SMELL: Lots of floral hops with scents of pine and tangerine
TASTE: This light-bodied beer has lots of good citrus and pine hoppiness with just enough sweet roasted malt to seamlessly hold it together.
FOOD PAIRING: Angel hair pasta with prawns in a tomato cream sauce
AVAILABILITY: Year round

JUL
2

Beerfact

Hangover helpers:

- **Honey:** The next morning, take three to six teaspoons of honey every twenty to thirty minutes until you feel better. The potassium in the honey will help reduce your cravings for alcohol, and the sugar will replenish what you lost from your bloodstream during your night of drinking.
- **Lemon:** Squeeze one lemon into a cup of black coffee and drink it straight—without sugar or milk.

Marble Brewery
111 Marble Avenue NW
Albuquerque, NM 87102
www.marblebrewery.com

🍺 Hefe-Weizen

*"Here's a toast to the roast that good fellowship lends,
With the sparkle of beer and wine. May its sentiment
always be deeper, my friends, Than the foam at the top of
the stein."*
—ANONYMOUS

JUL

3

TYPE: Hefewiezen
COLOR: Cloudy yellow
SMELL: Wheat, banana, and spice
TASTE: Refreshing, light- to medium-bodied beer with flavors of fresh wheat, banana, coriander, clove, and even bubblegum.
FOOD PAIRING: Wilted spinach salad with warm bacon dressing and fresh strawberries
AVAILABILITY: Year round

Beerfact

Making your own beer is legal in Sweden as long as it's only for personal consumption. Selling your homebrew is against the law. In Singapore, homebrewing is legal as long as you are eighteen years of age or older, and all intoxicating beverage manufactured at home must be fermented, no distillation of spirits is allowed. In addition, everything you make must be for personal use only and cannot exceed 30 liters per month.

Olde Hickory Brewery
222 Union Square
Hickory, NC 28601
www.oldehickorybrewery.com

 Porter

"The road to excess leads to the palace of wisdom."
  —WILLIAM BLAKE

TYPE: Porter
COLOR: Pitch black
SMELL: Molasses, dark-roasted coffee, chocolate, and sweet malt
TASTE: A dark, delicious beer with flavors of chocolate block, coffee
  bean, and rich toffee with just a subtle hint of bittering hops.
FOOD PAIRING: Chocolate-dipped strawberries
AVAILABILITY: Year round

JUL
4

Beerfood
BEER BBQ SAUCE

1¼ cup chili sauce
¾ cup light molasses
¾ cup beer (porter works great)
2 tablespoons dijon mustard

2 tablespoons chili powder
2 teaspoons soy sauce
1½ teaspoon fresh lemon juice
½ teaspoon garlic powder

Mix all ingredients in saucepan. Bring to boil over medium heat, stirring occasionally. Reduce heat and simmer until the sauce thickens and is reduced to 2 cups (about 15 minutes). Stir frequently. Cool, then use.

Founders Brewing Company
235 Grandville Avenue SW
Grand Rapids, MI 49503
www.foundersbrewing.com

🍺 Prairie Path Golden Ale

"Paintings are like beer, only beer tastes good and it's hard to stop drinking beer."
—BILLY CARTER

TYPE: Golden ale
COLOR: Golden
SMELL: Earthy
TASTE: Light, crisp, and refreshing with just a subtle hint of hoppiness. An easy drinking beer for an easy summer afternoon.
FOOD PAIRING: Jamaican jerk pork
AVAILABILITY: Year round

JUL

5

Beerfood
Beer-Boiled Brats
Bratwurst purists will tell you that the only way to cook one of these delicious sausages is to first boil them in beer. To achieve true perfection:

- Avoid poking holes in the casing. Doing so will allow the juices to squirt out and your sausage will be dry.
- Lighter beers tend to work a little better, but darker beers can add interesting flavors. Feel free to experiment.
- Boiling beer can actually be a little rough and will sometimes destroy your sausages. Bring your beer to a nice simmer, just below boiling, to make sure the casing stays intact.
- Allow your brats to soak in the hot beer for twenty to thirty minutes.

Two Brothers Brewing Company
30W315 Calumet Avenue
Warrenville, IL 60555
www.twobrosbrew.com

🍺 Ninja Porter

"Then here's to the heartening wassail, wherever good fellows are found, be its master instead of its vassal, and order the glasses around."
—OGDEN NASH AND SUE KING

TYPE: Porter
COLOR: Black with a tan head
SMELL: Roasted malt, dark chocolate, and a touch of anise
TASTE: A medium-bodied beer with flavors of roasted malt, baker's chocolate, caramel, and sugar that finishes with mocha bean and a clean, slightly bitter aftertaste.
FOOD PAIRING: Cola-glazed ham
AVAILABILITY: Year round

JUL

6

Beer*thought*

Drinking toast:

> Here's to the guy who is never blue,
> Here's to the buddy who is ever true,
> Here's to the pal, no matter what the load,
> Who never declines, just one for the road.

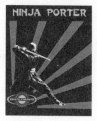

Asheville Brewing Company
675 Merrimon Avenue
Asheville, NC 28804
www.ashevillebrewing.com

🍺 Chimay Blue, Grande Réserve

"The selling of bad beer is a crime against Christian love."
—LAW RECORD, CITY OF AUGSBURG, THIRTEENTH CENTURY

TYPE: Belgian strong dark ale
COLOR: Black, almost purple
SMELL: Berries, yeast, and citrus
TASTE: A velvety smooth, medium-bodied beer with notes of fig, date, and raisin mixed with brown sugar, clove, cinnamon, and a touch of warming alcohol.
FOOD PAIRING: Chimay Grand Classic cheese
AVAILABILITY: Year round

**JUL
7**

Pub*lore*

In the heart of the Fremont neighborhood of Seattle, Washington, sits Brouwer's Café, a Belgian-centric pub. Sixty-four beers on tap. More than 300 bottles in glass-door refrigerators. More than sixty scotches, and fantastic food. It's not uncommon to wander in for a beer and a bite only to find yourself smack dab in the middle of a barleywine festival or Belgian ale salute, or some other special event.

Visit the Brouwer's Café at 400 N. 25th Street, Seattle, WA 98107, *www.brouwerscafe.com.*

Bieres De Chimay S.A.
Route Charlemagne, 8
6464 Baileux (Chimay)
Belgium
www.chimay.com

🍺 Billy's Chilies

"There are better things in life than alcohol, but alcohol makes up for not having them."
—TERRY PRACHETT

> **TYPE:** Chili beer
> **COLOR:** Cloudy golden
> **SMELL:** Spicy peppers
> **TASTE:** A light-bodied beer with a very prominent chili pepper flavor. There are other flavors present here, a touch of grain and hops, but they cave under the peppery assault.
> **FOOD PAIRING:** Thai chicken panang, five stars
> **AVAILABILITY:** Year round

JUL

8

Beerfest

2009 Great American Beer Festival Winners by Category

American-Style Brown Ale: Dirty Helen Brown Ale, Barley Island Brewing Co., Noblesville, IN

German-Style Altbier: Bismarck Altbier, Dry Dock Brewing Co., Aurora, CO

German-Style Sour Ale: Berliner Weisse, Southampton Publick House, Southampton, NY

South German-Style Hefeweizen: Top Heavy Hefeweizen, Piece Brewery, Chicago, IL

Twisted Pine Brewing Company
3201 Walnut Street, Suite A
Boulder, CO 80301
www.twistedpinebrewing.com

🍺 Hefeweizen

"Everybody is using coffee. If possible, this must be prevented. My people must drink beer."
—FREDERICK THE GREAT

TYPE: Hefeweizen
COLOR: Cloudy pale yellow
SMELL: Raw bread dough
TASTE: Light and refreshing with a clean, fresh aftertaste. Perfect patio party beer.
FOOD PAIRING: Triple cream Cambozola cheese with figs and good crackers
AVAILABILITY: Year round

JUL

9

Beerfact

In Bavaria, putting fruit in your cloudy wheat beer might be sacrilege, but not in brewpubs across the United States. And you have Widmer Brothers to thank for that. When Widmer began serving their Weizen, they served up pints with a slice of citrus. The tangy juice went so well with the bready, yeasty tastes in the beverage that when they tried their hand at an unfiltered hefe, the bartenders continued the trend, putting lemon on the edge of each frothy glass.

Widmer Brothers Brewing Company
929 N. Russell Street
Portland, OR 97227
www.widmer.com

🍺 Au Naturale

"If I had to live my life over, I'd live over a saloon."
—W. C. FIELDS

TYPE: Blonde ale
COLOR: Pale golden
SMELL: Raw wheat and oatmeal with a hint of green melon
TASTE: Light-bodied beer with an almost electric hoppiness. The acids really reach out and grab you, presenting a very nice tangy flavor, which is accompanied by an overture of freshly baked sourdough with a slightly toasty crust.
FOOD PAIRING: Khoresh fesenjan—mild Persian-style stew of crushed walnuts and pomegranate paste
AVAILABILITY: Year round

**JUL
10**

Beer*thought*

Is it the curve of her hip, or the way the fading sunlight outlines the rest of her body? Maybe it's the setting. The powerful pine trees, imposing dark stone mountains, and the warm inviting hot springs. No, that's not it. It's the beer in her hand that she sips from as she turns and sinks lower into the hot, steaming water. Well, that and the fact that she's naked.

Grand Teton Brewing Company
430 Old Jackson Highway
Victor, ID 83455
www.grandtetonbrewing.com

ESB

"Drinking beer doesn't make you fat, It makes you lean . . .
against bars, tables, chairs, and poles."
—ANONYMOUS

TYPE: Extra special bitter
COLOR: Copper
SMELL: Sweet malt, caramel, and just a touch of citrus
TASTE: Unlike the nose, there is quite a bit of bitterness to this beer, followed up with a smooth, sweet, toasted caramel flavor.
FOOD PAIRING: Towering pub burger with white cheddar cheese and a pickle wedge
AVAILABILITY: Year round

JUL

11

Beerfact

In the year 1920, the start of Prohibition, it became illegal to import, export, manufacture, sell, or even transport alcoholic beverages. Thirteen years later, when alcohol became legal again, despite the fact that major breweries and manufacturing facilities were able to produce and sell their wares, homebrewing remained illegal. It wasn't until 1979 that Congress and President Carter signed a bill that rolled back the restrictions on brewing beer at home.

Redhook Ale Brewery
14300 NE 145th Street
Woodinville, WA 98072
www.redhook.com

🍺 Red Rocket Ale

"Beauty lies in the eyes of the beerholder."
—ANONYMOUS

TYPE: Amber ale

COLOR: Root beer brown

SMELL: Hop resin, lavender, and mango sap

TASTE: A contest that starts out with the hops getting the upper hand only to let the sweet maltiness push its way back in about halfway into a good gulp. But in the end the broiled toffee flavors fade, giving way to a slight fruitness that completely succumbs to a long, hoppy grapefruit finish.

FOOD PAIRING: Oven-roasted acorn squash stuffed with chorizo, celery root, and ancho chilies

AVAILABILITY: Year round

JUL
12

Beerfact

In the United States, individual states now regulate intoxicating substances, and there are still several in which homebrewing is illegal. Often in these same states you can find thriving homebrew stores that sell all the necessary equipment and supplies. Though the laws vary, in states where it is legal to brew your own beer, you can do so if are at least twenty-one years of age and produce no more than 100 gallons a year—or 200 gallons if there is another adult over twenty-one years of age in the home.

Bear Republic Brewing Company
345 Healdsburg Avenue
Healdsburg, CA 95448
www.bearrepublic.com

🍺 Colorado Kolsch

Woody: "What's going on, Mr. Peterson?" Norm: "The question is, 'What's going in Mr. Peterson?' A beer please, Woody."
—CHEERS

TYPE: Kölsch
COLOR: Translucent yellow
SMELL: Fresh bread dough and tree fruit
TASTE: A crisp, clean, light-bodied beer with flavors of apple, pear, roasted grain, and wheat bread. Floral hops fade in after the initial flavors have stepped aside, and it finishes with notes of toasted bread.
FOOD PAIRING: Poached pears with candied pecans and crème fraîche
AVAILABILITY: Year round

JUL
13

Beer*fun*

A gorilla walks into a bar, pulls up a stool, and orders a beer. The bartender pours him a tall, frothy mug and says, "That'll be five bucks." As the gorilla is paying for his beer, the bartender adds, "You know, we don't get many gorillas in here." To which the gorilla replies, "At five bucks a beer, it's no wonder."

Steamworks Brewing Company
442 Wolverine Drive
Bayfield, CO 81122
www.steamworksbrewing.com

🍺 Monkshine

"Life, alas, is very drear. Up with the glass! Down with the beer!"
—LOUIS UNTERMEYER, AUTHOR

TYPE: Belgian pale ale
COLOR: Amber
SMELL: Citrus, pear, and stone fruit with a note of vanilla
TASTE: A medium-bodied beer with a yeasty, malty backbone followed by hints of citrus hops and allspice.
FOOD PAIRING: Roasted red and golden beet salad with blue cheese
AVAILABILITY: Year round

JUL
14

*Pub*lore

Though located in the heart of Paris, France, the overwhelming majority of the beers served at L'Académie de la Bière are from Belgium. The food ranges from French (paté on toasted bread, fine cheese) to German (sausage with pomme frites) to Belgian (Carbonnade). And since their research library includes about a dozen brews on tap, a couple ciders, and a huge list of bottled beer, all of us could study at this fine establishment of higher learning.

Visit Académie de la Bière at 99bBis, Boulevard de Port Royal, Paris, France 75005, *www.academie-biere.com.*

Four + Brewing
1722 South Fremont Drive (2375 West)
Salt Lake City, UT 84104
www.fourplusbrewing.com

🍺 Heavy Seas Red Sky at Night

"To some it's a six-pack; to me it's a support group."
—ANONYMOUS

TYPE: Saison ale
COLOR: Golden brown
SMELL: Yeast and floral hops
TASTE: Malty and spicy with quite a bit of yeast. Crisp and fairly light on the tongue with a pleasingly sour aftertaste.
FOOD PAIRING: Goat cheese in phyllo with roasted red peppers
AVAILABILITY: May to August

JUL
15

Brewtip
Brewing Additives

- **Kieselsol:** Fining agent that helps clarify your beer and prevent unwanted odors or tastes.
- **Irish Moss:** Clarifying agent. Put it in your wort for the last fifteen minutes of the boil. It will bond with the negatively charged ions, making them heavier and more likely to settle in the carboy.
- **Isinglass:** Made from shredded freeze-dried sturgeon swim bladders, isinglass helps settle yeast and clarify your brew.

Clipper City Brewing Company
4615 Hollins Ferry Road, Suite B
Baltimore, MD 21227
www.ccbeer.com

🍺 Double Bag Ale

"We old folks have to find our cushions and pillows in our tankards. Strong beer is the milk of the old."
—MARTIN LUTHER

TYPE: Strong ale

COLOR: Dark amber

SMELL: Starts out sweet with strong malt followed by a layer of citrus and a hint of hops

TASTE: At 7.2% alcohol, gulping a few of these might get away from you fast. The thick malt blends into toffee and cocoa that balances nicely with a hoppy finish. As the beer warms, more of the citrus comes out.

FOOD PAIRING: Double Bag traces its roots back to Dusseldorf, Germany, so open a bottle with a plate of grilled bratwurst, some sauerkraut, and fried potatoes.

AVAILABILITY: Year round

**JUL
16**

Beerthought

We've all heard the jokes about the double bag. Maybe you've even told them. Perhaps next time it would be wise to remember those jokes before the end of the evening. Maybe the wisdom that comes with age can count for something and we can instead turn to the sweet nectar of Long Trail's strong ale. Next time you put the moves on a double bagger, use a bottle opener.

Long Trail Brewing Company
Route 4 and 100A
Bridgewater Corners, VT 05035
www.longtrail.com

 Sleighr

"Draft beer, not people!"
—SIXTIES PEACE SLOGAN

TYPE: Altbier
COLOR: Deep reddish amber
SMELL: Sweet roasted malt and nuts
TASTE: A medium- to full-bodied beer with flavors of fresh caramel,
  mocha bean, and a touch of nuttiness.
FOOD PAIRING: Thai chicken sate with peanut dipping sauce
AVAILABILITY: Winter seasonal

JUL
17

Beer*thought*

Excerpts from The Hymn to Ninkasi, found inscribed on a nineteenth-century B.C.E. tablet:

"Ninkasi, you are the one who waters the malt, you are the one who soaks the malt in a jar.

"You are the one who spreads the cooked mash on large reed mats, You are the one who holds with both hands the great sweet wort.

"Brewing with honey and wine, when you pour out the filtered beer of the collector vat, it is the onrush of Tigris and Euphrates."

Ninkasi Brewing Company
272 Van Buren Street
Eugene, OR 97402
www.ninkasibrewing.com

🍺 Kentucky Bourbon Barrel Ale

"If you guys are going to be throwing beer bottles at us, at least make sure they're full."
—DAVE MUSTAINE, MEGADETH

TYPE: American strong ale

COLOR: Clear amber

SMELL: Vanilla, caramel, oak, and bourbon

TASTE: A smooth, medium-bodied beer with flavors of caramel, vanilla, oak, bourbon, and buttered brown bread. There are notes of warm alcohol that surface with the bourbon flavor.

FOOD PAIRING: Applewood-smoked bacon-wrapped filet mignon

AVAILABILITY: Year round

JUL
18

Beerfun
High or Low
Required supplies: Deck of cards, beer

A dealer deals a card to the player on his left. The player guesses if the next card is going to be higher or lower than the dealt card. If he is correct, he collects the card. If he fails, he takes a number of drinks equivalent to the number of cards in the pile in front of him, and all cards in the pile are discarded. After three correct guesses, the player is allowed to pass to the player on his left. Passing moves all collected cards to the next player.

Alltech's Lexington Brewing Company
401 Cross Street
Lexington, KY 40508
www.kentuckyale.com

🍺 Achel 8 Blonde

"Don't you know alcohol kills brain cells . . . any damn brain cell that can't live through a good drunk deserves to die."
—JAMES WEBB, AUTHOR

TYPE: Tripel
COLOR: Hazy golden orange
SMELL: Green apples and citrus
TASTE: A light- to medium-bodied beer with flavors of yeast, lemon zest, mandarin orange, and tart green apples. It has a creamy texture and finishes slightly alcoholic.
FOOD PAIRING: Salted bread and a hunk of white cheddar cheese
AVAILABILITY: Year round

JUL
19

Beerfact

The Trappists, or Cistercian Order of the Strict Observance, were first started in the year 1098. Today, there are seven recognized Trappist breweries, six in Belgium and one in the Netherlands: Achel, Chimay, Koningshoeven, Orval, Rochefort, Westmalle, and Westvleteren. Between the years of 1999 and 2005, one of those breweries—Koningshoeven (the Abbey of Schaapskooi in Tilburg, Netherlands)—lost its official recognition and was no longer allowed to use the "Authentic Trappist Product" logo.

Achel Brewery
Hamont-Achel, 3930
Belgium
www.achelsekluis.org

🍺 Petite Orval

"If the headache would only precede the intoxication, alcoholism would be a virtue."
—SAMUEL BUTLER

TYPE: Belgian pale ale
COLOR: Burnt umber
SMELL: Herbal hops
TASTE: A light, easy-to-drink brew with flavors of banana, cloves, and yeast. Just what the monks ordered for a nice, refreshing beer that can be drunk without getting too drunk.
FOOD PAIRING: Frogs legs with wild mushrooms
AVAILABILITY: Year round

JUL
20

Beersaint

Saint Benedict (born 480 C.E., died 547 C.E.)
Often called the founder of Western Christian monasticism, he is best known for establishing the Benedictine order and the monasteries that follow the Rule of St. Benedict. This includes the Trappist monasteries that brew beer.

Brasserie D'Orval
Villers-devant-Orval, 6823
Belgium
www.orval.be

🍺 The Wise

"I thought for a change I would give up drinking, and it was a great mistake, and although I reduced the size of my nose and improved my beauty, my stomach suffered."
—WINSLOW HOMER

JUL
21

TYPE: India pale ale

COLOR: Deep golden orange

SMELL: Pine and citrus along with bread and sweet malt

TASTE: Medium-bodied beer that starts with a grapefruit and lemon hoppiness that fades into the caramel and toasted malt flavors, only to return for a nice balanced aftertaste.

FOOD PAIRING: Fire-roasted oysters with ginger and wasabi butter

AVAILABILITY: Year round

Beerfact

Some interesting facts about beer:

- Beer is the second-most popular drink in the world (the first is tea).
- The oldest recipe is for beer.

Elysian Brewing
1221 E. Pike Street
Seattle, WA 98122
www.elysianbrewing.com

 Judgment Day

Woody: "What's the story, Mr. Peterson?" Norm: "The
Bobbsey twins go to the brewery. Let's cut to the happy
ending."
   —CHEERS

TYPE: Quadrupel
COLOR: Cloudy light brown
SMELL: Malt and cola
TASTE: A medium-bodied beer with a solid sweet core of brown sugar,
   molasses, cola, and dried fruit flavors. Notes of chocolate and roasted
   coffee come out as the beer gets closer to room temperature, finish-
   ing with a dried plum and dark cherry aftertaste.
FOOD PAIRING: Plum sorbet
AVAILABILITY: Year round

JUL
22

Beerfact

At first there was Pizza Port restaurant and brewing company—and it
was good. Then, one of the owners, Vince Marsaglia, after tasting of the
fruit of the Abbey-style beers, decreed that they must make this nectar of
the gods in their very own brewery—and it was good.

In 1997, Tomme Arthur wandered into the Port, and he decreed that
he could lead the way to the promised land, and so he was hired—and
it was good. And Tomme, with the help of Vince, brewed the nectar that
the drinking masses did so crave—and it was good.

The Lost Abbey
155 Mata Way
San Marcos, CA 92069
www.thelostabbey.com

🍺 Pale Ale

"Ah, good ol' trustworthy beer. My love for you will never die."

—HOMER SIMPSON

TYPE: Pale ale
COLOR: Light amber
SMELL: Malt and earthy hops
TASTE: An easy drinking, light- to medium-bodied beer with a fair amount of citrus and grain followed by a bitter finish and a dandelion aftertaste.
FOOD PAIRING: Polish sausage and potato pancakes
AVAILABILITY: Year round

JUL

23

Beer*words*

Polish drinking toasts:

We got together as friends to have a drink. Let's drink to getting together as friends.

I drink till I fall, fall till I rise, I rise to drink, drink to be wise.

To the drunkard: who lives half as long, but sees everything twice.

Yazoo Brewing Company
1200 Clinton Street #112
Nashville, TN 37203
www.yazoobrew.com

Che

"A tavern is a place where madness is sold by the bottle."
—JONATHAN SWIFT, AUTHOR

TYPE: Pale lager

COLOR: Clear golden

SMELL: Wheat with just a touch of hops

TASTE: A dry, light-bodied, crisp beer that starts out with roasted flavors and a little nutty then hints at mild hops before disappearing entirely.

FOOD PAIRING: Cuban roasted cayenne pepper shrimp with saffron rice

AVAILABILITY: Year round

JUL

24

Beerfact

Based out of the old Southern California Brewing company facility in Torrance, Angel City Brewing is the work of Michael Bowe, the two-time California Homebrewer of the Year. Located in Alpine Village, a self-supporting Bavarian village and the home of Oktoberfest in Los Angeles, the brewery focuses on producing consistently great beer. There is no tasting room or brewpub, just the brewing equipment and bottling line and Michael, working nearly round the clock.

Angel City Brewing
833 W. Torrance Blvd., Suite 105
Torrance, CA 90502
www.angelcitybrewing.com

🍺 Wipeout IPA

"Let us drink for the replenishment of our strength, not for our sorrow."
—CICERO

TYPE: India pale ale

COLOR: Slightly cloudy golden bronze

SMELL: Citrus and pine hops

TASTE: Nice and bitter, the way a good IPA should taste. This is a classic. It's not overpowering, won't make your lips pucker. The sweet malt taste behind the heavy hops gives it a nice balance.

FOOD PAIRING: Pizza Monterey (pepperoni, mushrooms, onions, and artichoke hearts)

AVAILABILITY: Year round

**JUL
25**

Beerfact

In 1992, Solana Beach Pizza Port proprietors Vince and Gina Marsaglia began brewing their own beer. In a very short while they started making more than they could comfortably drink on their own. Pizza and beer made a pretty good combo, so they began selling it to their regular customers.

This beer is for the unfortunate surfer who got up at the "butt crack of dawn" only to find it "4 to 6 feet and offshore" crowded with other surfers and then "blammo you wipeout." Whatever that means.

Port Brewing Company
155 Mata Way, Suite 104
San Marcos, CA 92069
www.portbrewing.com

🍺 Sunray Wheat Beer

"Oh, I have been to Ludlow fair, and left my necktie God knows where. And carried half home or near, pints and quarts of Ludlow beer."
—A. E. HOUSMAN

TYPE: Hefewiezen
COLOR: Cloudy yellow
SMELL: Banana, clove, and raw wheat
TASTE: Tastes very much like it smells. Smooth flavors of banana, freshly threshed wheat, and spice go down quite easily. In the mouth, it's smooth and silky, with a light to medium body.
FOOD PAIRING: Cow's milk blue cheese drizzled liberally with tupelo honey served with apple slices
AVAILABILITY: Year round

JUL
26

Beerfact

Started in April of 2002, Terrapin won their first award not six months after commercially producing their first beer. The American Pale Ale Gold Medal at the 2002 Great American Beer Festival was their first, but it certainly wasn't their last. A quick glance at their awards page includes no fewer than eighteen medals, at least one coming every year since their inception.

Terrapin Beer Company
265 Newton Bridge Road
Athens, GA 30607
www.terrapibeer.com

🍺 Amber Ale

"Marriage is based on the theory that when a man discovers a particular brand of beer exactly to his taste, he should at once throw up his job and go to work in a brewery."
—H. L. MENCKEN

JUL

27

TYPE: Amber ale

COLOR: Dark amber

SMELL: Sweet malt, fruit, and clove

TASTE: A smooth, sultry beer that starts out with a mild sweetness comprised of rich malt, caramel, clove, and cinnamon, followed by yeast and a bit of spicy bitterness at the end.

FOOD PAIRING: Wild boar sliders with a beer and cheese sauce

AVAILABILITY: Year round

Beer*fun*
Modified Jenga
Required supplies: One set of Jenga blocks, beer

Prior to playing the game, the owner of the Jenga blocks writes a command on the inside edge of each block (e.g., Take one drink. Make a barnyard animal noise. Make a rule. Kiss the person to your left). Stack the blocks carefully as directed by the game. If a player successfully removes a block without making the tower topple, he reads the command on the block and follows the instructions. If a player knocks over the tower during the course of gameplay, he must drink an entire beer.

Dark Horse Brewing Company
511 S. Kalamazoo Avenue
Marshall, MI 49068
www.darkhorsebrewery.com

 O'Fallon Gold

"Most men are disguised by sobriety."
—THOMAS DE QUINCY, AUTHOR

TYPE: Blonde ale
COLOR: Clear golden
SMELL: Yeasty fresh bread dough and citrus
TASTE: A light, easy-to-drink beer with flavors of honey, biscuit, and yeast complemented by just a hint of lemon, grapefruit, and spicy pepper. Finishes dry and crisp, and leaves with a honey aftertaste.
FOOD PAIRING: Five-star spicy hot wings
AVAILABILITY: Year round

JUL

28

Beersaint
Saint Florian (died 304 C.E.)

The protector of those in danger of fire and flood, Saint Florian is the patron of brewers, soap makers, chimneysweeps, and firefighters. When Nuremburg, Germany, caught fire, Florian flooded the streets with beer from the vats of a nearby brewery, ending the threat but leaving the citizens without anything to drink in celebration.

O'Fallon Brewery
26 West Industrial Drive
O'Fallon, MO 63366
www.ofallonbrewery.com

🍺 Shakespeare Stout

"Be not afraid of greatness: some are born great, some achieve greatness, and some have greatness thrust upon 'em."
—WILLIAM SHAKESPEARE

TYPE: Stout

COLOR: Ebony with a creamy tan head

SMELL: Roasted malt, baker's chocolate, and citrus fruit

TASTE: Melted bittersweet chocolate paired with roasted coffee and spicy hops. Medium- to full-bodied beer with a smooth creaminess.

FOOD PAIRING: Poured over homemade vanilla bean ice cream and served with caramel wafers.

AVAILABILITY: Year round

JUL 29

Beerfact

Shakespeare Stout's Achievements:

- 2007 Celebration of Suds—*Best Stout*
- 2006 World Beer Cup—*Gold*
- 2005 Great American Brewers Festival—*Gold*
- 2005 Great Intl. Beer Festival—*Gold*
- 2005 Intl. Beer Festival (London)—*Silver*
- 2005 World Beer Championships—*World Champ*

Rogue Ales
2320 OSU Drive
Newport, OR 97365
www.rogue.com

 Modus Hoperandi

"I've always believed that paradise will have my favorite beer on tap."
    —RUDYARD WHEATLEY, AUTHOR

TYPE: India pale ale
COLOR: Deep gold
SMELL: Pine and citrus
TASTE: Light caramel sweetness underneath a mouth-puckering barrage of citrus and pine flavors followed by a smooth finish.
FOOD PAIRING: Beer can chicken
AVAILABILITY: Year round

JUL
30

Beerfood
BEER CAN CHICKEN

1 whole frying chicken (five pounds or more—big enough to stick a beer can up inside)
1 can of beer
Salt, pepper, and smoked paprika

Drink a third to a half of the beer. Remove the top of the can with a can opener. Dust the outside of your chicken with salt, pepper, and smoked paprika. Cook the chicken over indirect heat. Place the prepared beer can on the grill, then seat the chicken on top of it. Close the lid and let it cook at 300° to 325°F. Turn every half hour. When the chicken has reached an internal temperature of 175°F, it's done.

Ska Brewing Company
225 Girard Street
Durango, CO 81301
www.skabrewing.com

🍺 Backdraft Brown

Coach: "What'll it be, Normie?" Norm: "Just the usual, Coach. I'll have a froth of beer and a snorkel."
—*CHEERS*

TYPE: Brown ale
COLOR: Dark brown
SMELL: Chocolate and roasted malt
TASTE: A surprisingly lighter-bodied beer with notes of roasted sweet malt and a touch of woodiness followed by a nice hoppy bitterness and a clean finish.
FOOD PAIRING: Oven-roasted pork tenderloin
AVAILABILITY: Year round

JUL

31

Beerfact

Tips for cooling beer fast:

- Add water to the ice in your cooler. The water will fall to just above freezing, and with the beer submerged completely in the water, it will cool faster.
- Add salt and more ice. The salt (we're talking cups, not tablespoons) will lower the freezing temperature of the water, and the extra ice will help reduce the temperature to below zero.
- Spin your beer. The spinning motion allows the beer to circulate past the ice-cold glass or metal, cooling it even faster.

Hook and Ladder Brewing Company
8113 Fenton Street
Silver Spring, MD 20910
www.hookandladderbeer.com

#9

"A herd of buffalo can only move as fast as the slowest buffalo. And when the herd is hunted, it is the slowest and weakest ones at the back that are killed first. . . . In much the same way, the human brain can only operate as fast as the slowest brain cells. Excessive intake of alcohol, as we know, kills brain cells. Regular consumption of beer eliminates the weaker brain cells . . . That's why you always feel smarter after a few beers."
—CLIFF CLAVIN, *CHEERS*

TYPE: Fruit beer
COLOR: Pale golden with just a touch of haziness
SMELL: Apricots in the forefront with a light crispness underneath
TASTE: Apricot is noticeable, though not overpoweringly sweet.
FOOD PAIRING: Brillat Savarin triple cream cow's milk uncooked cheese.
AVAILABILITY: Year round

AUG

1

Beerfact

The top five states in breweries per capita are:

1. Vermont 2. Montana 3. Oregon 4. Maine 5. Colorado

Magic Hat Brewing Company
5 Bartlett Bay Road
South Burlington, VT 05403
www.magichat.net

🍺 Tricerahops

"The hard part about being a bartender is figuring out who is drunk and who is just stupid."
—RICHARD BRAUNSTEIN

TYPE: Double India pale ale
COLOR: Hazy amber
SMELL: Lemon, mandarin, and stone fruit with a touch of pine
TASTE: Big and hoppy, this one starts out electric, then balances out with a rich, malty, caramel backbone that gives in once again to a fresh citrus finish and a long, pleasant hoppy aftertaste.
FOOD PAIRING: Spanish okra and pork medallions
AVAILABILITY: Year round

Pub*lore*

In Ho Chi Minh City, Vietnam, you can find Luong Son, an open-air beer garden and do-it-yourself barbeque. Is there a better way to enjoy a pitcher of beer than to do it while the waitstaff bring you plates of marinated beef, which you can then throw on top of your very own personal charcoal grill?

Visit Luong Son/Bo Tung Xeo at 31 Ly Tu Trong Street, District 1, Ho Chi Minh City, Vietnam.

Ninkasi Brewing Company
272 Van Buren Street
Eugene, OR 97402
www.ninkasibrewing.com

🍺 Organic Dread Brown Ale

"Drink today and drown all sorrow; You shall perhaps not do't tomorrow."
—JOHN FLETCHER, PLAYWRIGHT

TYPE: Brown ale
COLOR: Dark brown
SMELL: Sweet caramel with a touch of smoke
TASTE: Light- to medium-bodied beer with flavors of roasted malt, nuts, a touch of chocolate, and smooth smokiness, finishing with dark coffee
FOOD PAIRING: Verbena crème brûlée
AVAILABILITY: Year round

AUG

3

Publore

Created in 1589 to brew beer for the Duke of Bavaria, the Hofbräuhaus is still a working brewery. Songs and chants are common, and the whole place becomes a roaring party. Beer is brought to your table in one-liter stone or glass steins by maidens in traditional Bavarian garb. Trying to sneak out with a stein (less so for a barmaid) is a serious offense and will land you in jail faster than you can say Oktoberfest.

Visit Hofbräuhaus at 9 Platzl, 80331 Altstadt-Lehel, Munich, Germany, *www.hofbraeuhaus.de.*

Santa Cruz Mountain Brewing
402 Ingalls Street
Santa Cruz, CA 95060
www.santacruzmountainbrewing.com

🍺 Road Dog

"You can't seriously want to ban alcohol. It tastes great, makes women more attractive, and makes a woman virtually invulnerable to criticism."
—MAYOR QUIMBY, *THE SIMPSONS*

AUG

4

TYPE: Porter
COLOR: Dark-roasted coffee brown
SMELL: Floral with notes of stone fruit and even a hint of toasted sesame seeds
TASTE: Light bodied and surprisingly clean tasting, there are flavors of dark coffee and earthy iced tea along with toasted malt. Quite an easy drinker.
FOOD PAIRING: Scottish gingerbread
AVAILABILITY: Year round

Beer*thought*

By the time it has worked its way into your stomach, it's already too late. The fall is slow at first, enjoyable. Then you close your eyes, just for a second, and the whole world tilts out from under you. That gets your attention. You put your bottle down on the table to begin what you hope is a controlled drift into tomorrow's hangover. Maybe you have the good sense to take a handful of aspirin and down a couple glasses of water. That'll help.

Flying Dog Brewery
4607 Wedgewood Blvd.
Frederick, MD 21703
www.flyingdogales.com

🍺 Captain's Reserve Imperial IPA

"Nothing . . . sharpens the appetite like an India Pale Ale."
—MICHAEL JACKSON, THE BEER HUNTER

TYPE: India pale ale
COLOR: Rich yellow
SMELL: Hop resins
TASTE: Citrus, grass, and pine flavors overlay a solid core of malt sweetness. There are five different kinds of hops in this brew, and you can taste the subtle nuances after several sips.
FOOD PAIRING: You-peel-em shrimp with a spicy cocktail sauce
AVAILABILITY: Year round

AUG
5

Beer*fun*

Beer Blow

Required supplies: Beer in bottles, deck of playing cards

Place a deck of cards on top of an unopened bottle of beer. Players take turns blowing cards off the top of the deck. If an ace is uncovered during a player's turn, he or she is required to take a drink. The player who blows the last card off of the deck has to drink the beer underneath.

Captain Lawrence Brewing Company
99 Castleton Street
Pleasantville, NY 10570
www.captainlawrencebrewing.com

🍺 Scarlet Lady Ale

"Always remember that I have taken more out of alcohol than alcohol has taken out of me."
—WINSTON CHURCHILL

TYPE: Extra special bitter
COLOR: Reddish copper, like the long flowing hair of a feisty redhead
SMELL: Slight berry scent
TASTE: Sweet maltiness followed by fresh crushed cranberries and dandelions—yes, like the ones you used to eat as a kid.
FOOD PAIRING: Lasagna a la parmigiana
AVAILABILITY: Year round

AUG

6

Beerfact

Translated to English, *Reinheitsgebot* means "purity law." It is the oldest food or beverage regulation in the world still in existence today. In the fifteenth century, as the beer industry in Germany grew, unscrupulous brewers began putting cheaper ingredients in their beers to inflate their profits; thus the need to create a law. The first beer regulation was laid down in Augsburg, Bavaria, in 1490. Brewers who served bad brew were fined, and their beer was poured in the gutter.

Stoudt's Brewing Company
Route 272
2800 North Reading Road
Adamstown, PA 19501
www.stoudtsbeer.com

🍺 Circus Boy

"[I recommend] . . . bread, meat, vegetables, and beer."
—SOPHOCLES' PHILOSOPHY OF A MODERATE DIET

TYPE: Hefeweizen
COLOR: A cloudy pale yellow, the color of freshly threshed wheat
SMELL: Baked wheat bread with fresh cut lemongrass
TASTE: Fresh biscuits baked with lemon peel and a touch of banana. Brewed with actual lemongrass, you can really taste the spicy citrus, especially on the aftertaste.
FOOD PAIRING: Potato and chorizo empanadas with cilantro and sour cream
AVAILABILITY: Year round

AUG
7

Beerfact

Originally from southern Germany, hefeweizens are brewed with a significant percentage of wheat. Most beers extract fermentable sugars from malted barley (which of course are grains that have been sprouted by being soaked in water then dried quickly to halt the germination process). By German tradition, in order to be called a hefeweizen, the beer must have been brewed with at least 50 percent wheat—often being mixed fifty/fifty with malted barley—and must remain unfiltered.

Magic Hat Brewing Company
5 Bartlett Bay Road
South Burlington, VT 05403
www.magichat.net

🍺 White Hawk IPA

"Bad men live that they may eat and drink, whereas good men eat and drink that they may live."
—SOCRATES

TYPE: India pale ale

COLOR: Light amber

SMELL: Roasted malt and grapefruit

TASTE: A light- to medium-bodied beer with flavors of caramel and roasted malt followed by grapefruit and lemon zest that balance things out. It finishes with notes of alcohol and leaves with a hint of bitterness.

FOOD PAIRING: Stir-fried broccoli with walnuts

AVAILABILITY: Year round

AUG

8

Beer*fact*

You've probably heard of arachnophobia (the fear of spiders), and acrophobia (the fear of heights), and agoraphobia (the fear of open spaces), and claustrophobia (the fear of confined spaces), and mysophobia (the fear of germs), but have you heard of cenosillicaphobia? That would be the fear of an empty (beer) glass.

Medocino Brewing Company
13351 So. Highway 101
Hopland, CA 95449
www.mendobrew.com

🍺 Union Jack

"Whoever called it near beer was a poor judge of distance."
—SAYING DURING PROHIBITION

TYPE: India pale ale

COLOR: Warm golden, almost the color of honey

SMELL: Pine, citrus, and dried sweet fruit

TASTE: Thick and creamy, this one starts off with rich flavors of sweet malt, honey, toffee, and candied fruit followed by a trio of bitterness— dandelion, grapefruit, and pine. It finishes with a long citrusy aftertaste.

FOOD PAIRING: Deep-fried oysters with coleslaw and thin-cut French fries

AVAILABILITY: Year round

AUG

9

Beerfest

2009 Great American Beer Festival Winners by Category

American-Style Pale Ale: Sweetgrass IPA, Grand Teton Brewing Co., Victor, ID

American-Style Strong Pale Ale: Racer 5 IPA, Bear Republic Factory Five, Cloverdale, CA

American-Style India Pale Ale: Union Jack, Firestone Walker Brewing Co., Paso Robles, CA

Imperial India Pale Ale: Organic Ace of Spades Imperial IPA, Hopworks Urban Brewery, Portland, OR

Firestone Walker Brewing Company
1400 Ramada Drive
Paso Robles, CA 93446
www.firestonewalker.com

🍺 Lazy Boy Stout

"Now, son, you don't want to drink beer. That's for daddies and kids with fake IDs."
—HOMER SIMPSON

TYPE: Stout
COLOR: Obsidian with a tan head
SMELL: Roasted malt, coffee, and chocolate
TASTE: A light- to medium-bodied stout, with flavors of espresso, bittersweet chocolate, roasted barley, and just a touch of freshly made caramel followed up by subtle hoppy notes.
FOOD PAIRING: Oyster po'boy sandwich with sweet pickle tartar sauce
AVAILABILITY: Year round

AUG
10

Beer*fact*

Other things to do with beer:

- **Lawn maintenance:** Got brown spots in your lawn? Try watering them with beer. The fermented sugars not only kill unwanted fungus, they also provide food for the struggling lawn—stimulating further growth and bringing back the green.
- **Bubble bath:** Putting a thick, yeasty beer in your bath as you run the water will create a tub full of foamy goodness. The yeast, left on after your bath, will promote smoother, healthier skin.

Vino's Brewpub
923 West 7th Street
Little Rock, AR 72201
www.vinosbrewpub.com

🍺 Marshal Zhukov's Imperial Stout

"Nothing goes as well with seafood as a Dry Porter or Stout or accompanies chocolate like an Imperial Stout."
—MICHAEL JACKSON, THE BEER HUNTER

TYPE: Russian imperial stout
COLOR: Black
SMELL: Espresso and cocoa bean
TASTE: A silky smooth, medium-bodied brew that assaults your senses with darkly roasted malt and coffee followed by notes of chocolate and a pleasant bitterness.
FOOD PAIRING: Shredded beef in a chocolate mole sauce with fresh corn tortillas
AVAILABILITY: August

AUG
11

Beerfact

Born in 1896, Gregory Zhukov served in both the Russian Imperial army and the communist Red Army. His skill and loyalty caught the attention of Joseph Stalin, who appointed Zhukov chief of staff in 1940. During World War II, Zhukov was credited with saving Moscow from the Nazis, pushing the Germans back, and eventually scoring a Russian victory in the Battle for Berlin. His achievements earned him the rank of Marshal.

Cigar City Brewing
3924 West Spruce Street,
Suite A
Tampa, FL 33607
www.cigarcitybeer.com

🍺 Calico Amber Ale

"Beer—because one doesn't solve the world's problems over white wine."
—ANONYMOUS

TYPE: Amber ale
COLOR: Clear amber
SMELL: Rich, sweet malt and lychee fruit
TASTE: Hoppy up front that fades into burnt sugar in the middle, followed by a long, bitter dandelion finish with a tree fruit and lychee nut aftertaste.
FOOD PAIRING: Dungeness crab cakes
AVAILABILITY: Year round

AUG
12

Beerfact

Hangover helpers:

- **Scalp massage:** The gentle massaging will stimulate blood flow and help cure your headache—plus it just feels good.
- **Milk thistle:** Take two capsules of milk thistle before or while drinking. This herb protects liver cells by preventing toxins from entering, and helps remove those that have already wormed their way in.
- **Thyme:** Crush several dried thyme leaves and pour hot water over them to make a tea.

Ballast Point Brewing Company
10051 Old Grove Road, Suite B
San Diego, CA 92131
www.ballastpoint.com

🍺 Three Philosophers

"'Ere's to English women an' a quart of English beer."
—RUDYARD KIPLING

TYPE: Quadrupel
COLOR: Mahogany
SMELL: Dried dark fruit, brown sugar, and spicy yeast
TASTE: A complex, interesting beer with layers of different flavors. Full
bodied and ripe, this one starts out with dried cherries, thick honey,
toffee, and molasses, followed closely by spice and yeast. As they fade, a
warm rum seeps in, finishing with caramel and a touch of citrus.
FOOD PAIRING: Salami, prosciutto, melon, Gruyère and white cheddar
cheese
AVAILABILITY: Year round

AUG
13

Beerfood
BEER SORBET
½ cup beer
½ cup pilsner
½ cup dubbel, trippel, or quadrupel
⅓ cup agave nectar
1½ cups baker's sugar
2½ cups milk

Leave all liquids in the refrigerator until needed. Thoroughly mix all ingredients. Churn in an ice cream maker for about 45 minutes. Freeze overnight.

Brewery Ommegang
656 County Highway 33
Cooperstown, NY 13326
www.ommegang.com

🍺 Blue Sunday

"Beer does not make itself property by itself. It takes an element of mystery."
—FRITZ MAYTAG, AMERICAN BREWER

TYPE: Blended, aged ale
COLOR: Cloudy amber
SMELL: Yeast, sour cherries, citrus
TASTE: It starts out with a tart, sour cherry, almost-candy flavor that mellows and grows more fruity as a sip turns into a gulp. Underneath is a breadiness that appears as the sour begins to fade. You'll notice rich malt and dried plums emerge as the beer warms.
FOOD PAIRING: Cocoa-rubbed pork tenderloin
AVAILABILITY: Special release

Beerfact

Things you probably didn't know about New Holland Brewing Company:

New Holland Brewing Company was founded on New Year's Day 1996. The brewery was opened on New Year's Day 1997, and the first beer was made on May 1. Six years later, in 2003, they shipped nearly 3,700 barrels of beer. By 2007, they were shipping almost 8,000 barrels of beer a year.

New Holland Brewing Company
66 E. 8th Street
Holland, MI 49423
www.newhollandbrew.com

🍺 Bourbon Barrel RIPA

*"The attempt to make the consumption of beer criminal is
as silly and as futile as if you passed a law to send a man
to jail for eating cucumber salad."*
—STEPHEN LEACOCK, WRITER

TYPE: Barrel-aged blend of a red ale and an India pale ale
COLOR: Deep amber with ruby highlights
SMELL: Oak and citrus
TASTE: A smooth, full-bodied beer with sweet flavors of vanilla, caramel, and toffee with a nice balance of hoppy bitterness and notes of bourbon alcohol.
FOOD PAIRING: Pecorino Oro Antico cheese
AVAILABILITY: Special release

AUG
15

Beerfact

Beer is a cancer-fighting agent: Some scientists believe that polyphenols
can slow the growth of human cancer cells. Hops happen to be absolutely
brimming with polyphenols. Beer also makes you smarter: Moderate beer
drinking has shown to improve memory, reasoning, and problem solving,
and can help reduce age-related mental decline. Beer has shown to reduce
the chances of kidney stones by up to 40 percent.

10 Barrel Brewing Company
20750 High Desert Lane #107
Bend, OR 97701
www.10barrel.com

MASTER CRAFTSMEN OF FERMENTED BEVERAGES
10 BARREL BREWING COMPANY.
BEND OREGON // UNESTABLISHED 2006
INDEPENDENTLY HANDCRAFTED IN THE NORTHWEST

🍺 Original Orange Blossom Ale

"Beer that is not drunk has missed its vocation."
—MEYER BRESLAU

TYPE: Amber ale

COLOR: Amber

SMELL: Tangerines and orange soda

TASTE: A light- to medium-bodied beer with flavors of floral orange blossom and orange candy. It brings back nostalgic childhood memories of running through the sprinkler with your orange soda, orange Pez, and orange popsicles.

FOOD PAIRING: Baked pheasant with an orange shallot sauce

AVAILABILITY: Year round

AUG
16

Beerfood

Other drinks made with beer:

- Black and Satin: Equal parts porter and champagne.
- Trojan Horse: Equal parts stout and cola.
- Michelada: Three ounces Mexican beer, one ounce lime juice, dash Worcestershire sauce, one to two dashes hot sauce.
- Jimmy and Guinney: Drop a shot of Jameson in a Guinness and drink.

Buckbean Brewing Company
1155 S. Rock Blvd., Suite 490
Reno, NV 89502
www.buckbeanbeer.com

🍺 Commodore Perry

"It is a fair wind that blew men to the ale."
—WASHINGTON IRVING

TYPE: India pale ale
COLOR: Light golden
SMELL: Hoppy, refreshing, and light—an easy, enjoyable scent
TASTE: Clean, bitter flavor with very little aftertaste. A nice, refreshing beer with a whopping 7.5% alcohol by volume. A slight pine flavor lingers just on the edge of your tongue.
FOOD PAIRING: A pot full of steamer clams in a broth of garlic, celery, and white wine.
AVAILABILITY: Year round

AUG
17

Beer*thought*

Why do beer and boats go so well together? Is it the frothy, turned-up wake that reminds us of the thick head on top of our pint glass? Is it the hard work and sweat of hauling up an anchor or raising a sail? Is it the smooth rocking of the waves that lulls and relaxes our weary minds? Or is it something more primal—a deep thirst that grew from the moment we humans found a way to float upon the water?

Whatever it is, remember the credo of Great Lakes Brewing Commodore Perry: "Don't give up the sip."

Great Lakes Brewing Company
2516 Market Avenue
Cleveland, OH 44113
www.greatlakesbrewing.com

🍺 Kentucky Light Ale

*"Here with my beer I sit, while golden moments flit: alas!
They pass unheeded by: and as they fly, I, being dry, sit
idly sipping here my beer."*
—GEORGE ARNOLD, POET

TYPE: Kölsch
COLOR: Hazy light straw
SMELL: Citrus and fruit
TASTE: A light-bodied beer with flavors of rice, honey, barley, and yeast. A great beer for a hot day pushing a lawnmower or sitting under the shade tree.
FOOD PAIRING: Chili cheese dog
AVAILABILITY: Year round

AUG

18

Beer*words*
Beer toasts of the world:

Afrikaans: *Gesondheid*
Brazilian: *Tchim Tchim, Viva*
Czech: *Na zdravi*
Dutch: *Proost*
Farsi: *Ba'sal'a'ma'ti*

German: *Prost*
Hungarian: *Egészségedre*
Icelandic: *Santanka nu*
Japanese: *Kampai*

Alltech's Lexington Brewing Company
401 Cross Street
Lexington, KY 40508
www.kentuckyale.com

🍺 Troegenator Double Bock

"You've got yoga, honey. I've got beer. You got overpriced.
And I got weird."
—BILLY JOEL

TYPE: Dopplebock
COLOR: Bronzy brown
SMELL: Fresh bread and malt
TASTE: Flavors of sweet caramel and spice provide a backdrop for dried plums and raisins followed by a warming burst of alcohol. The dried fruit and sweet malt become more pronounced as it gets closer to room temperature.
FOOD PAIRING: New York steak and baked potato
AVAILABILITY: Year round

AUG
19

Beer*fact*

Things you probably didn't know about Tröegs Brewing Company:

Started in 1997, the company was founded by the Trogner brothers. Today, they produce eleven different beers. In addition, in their tasting room, they serve the "Scratch Beer Series"—ultra-small batch beers they make to celebrate their more than a decade of brewing beer.

Tröegs Brewing Company
800 Paxton Street
Harrisburg, PA 17104
www.troegs.com

🍺 Juggernaut

"I know I'm drinking myself to a slow death, but then I'm in no hurry."
—ROBERT BENCHLEY

TYPE: Red ale
COLOR: Clear amber
SMELL: Toasted caramel, floral hops, and a touch of nuttiness
TASTE: A medium-bodied beer with nicely balanced flavors of sweet malt and floral hops. It has a drier finish and a light lingering bitter aftertaste.
FOOD PAIRING: Pub nachos with ground beef, black olives, and a dollop of sour cream
AVAILABILITY: August to September

AUG

20

Pub*lore*

The best of both worlds, World of Beer offers both brews to drink at their establishment, and an extensive list of packaged goods to go. There are more than thirty taps behind the bar, with the menu written on a huge chalkboard that rises nearly floor to ceiling—two stories. Their bottle list includes more than 400 beers, and they run specials on mixed six-packs.

Visit World of Beer at 9524 West Linebaugh Avenue, Tampa, FL 33626, *www.wobusa.com.*

Pyramid Brewing Company
91 S. Royal Brougham Way
Seattle, WA 98134
www.pyramidbrew.com

🍺 Oak-Aged Unearthly Imperial India Pale Ale

Woody: "Pour you a beer, Mr. Peterson?" Norm: "All right, but stop me at one . . . make that thirty-one."
—CHEERS

TYPE: Double India pale ale
COLOR: Golden amber
SMELL: Grapefruit, lemon, and a hint of vanilla
TASTE: A smooth, oily, full-bodied beer with flavors of sweet vanilla, toasted oak, and toffee followed by grapefruit and pine. It finishes bitter, the hop resins clinging to your tongue for a long aftertaste.
FOOD PAIRING: Smoked beef brisket with BBQ sauce
AVAILABILITY: Limited release

AUG 21

Beer*saints*

Saint Arnold of Soissons (born 1040 C.E., died 1087 C.E.)

The patron saint of hop pickers and Belgian brewers, Saint Arnold was a solider before joining the Benedictine St. Medard's Abbey. He is credited with founding the Abbey of St. Peter, where he began to brew beer. He evangelized the benefits of drinking beer to the local peasants, teaching them of its "gifts of health."

Southern Tier Brewing Company
2051A Stoneman Circle
Lakewood, NY 14750
www.southerntierbrewing.com

🍺 Charlie Parker Pale Ale

"I'd like to have a beer holder on my guitar."
—JAMES HETFIELD, METALLICA

TYPE: Pale ale
COLOR: Clear gold
SMELL: Buttered honey rolls and sweet vanilla frosting
TASTE: A smooth, medium-bodied beer with flavors of toffee, honey butter, and roasted malt with a bitter finish that glides into a dandelion aftertaste.
FOOD PAIRING: Smoked Gouda
AVAILABILITY: Year round

AUG
22

Beer*thought*

Charlie Parker played jazz, a saxophone. He was a revolutionary. He helped bring about bebop. He was a leader of his generation, and nearly every generation of jazz musicians since. His songs influenced the hipsters of the forties, the Beatniks in the late fifties and early sixties, and brewers of the new millennium. His sound was described as "clean and penetrating, but sweet and plaintive . . ." Not unlike the pale ale that bears his name.

Angel City Brewing
833 W. Torrance Blvd., Suite 105
Torrance, CA 90502
www.angelcitybrewing.com

🍺 Hop Rod Rye

"A fine beer may be judged with only one sip, but it's better to be thoroughly sure."
—CZECH PROVERB

TYPE: India pale ale
COLOR: Amber
SMELL: Citrus and caramel
TASTE: Medium-bodied beer with a strong, solid hop flavor that sits on your palate for a few moments before the bold maltiness has an opportunity to come through and balance out the flavors.
FOOD PAIRING: Grilled Portobello mushrooms with garlic and ginger served over baked polenta
AVAILABILITY: Year round

AUG
23

Beer*thought*

By the first sip your brain registers that almost audible "ping!" like the sound an elevator makes when it reaches your chosen floor. As the flavor begins to fade you know the next experience will be just like the first, only perhaps this time hidden flavors or subtle nuances will be revealed. The aroma hits your nose. You lift the glass to your lips once again, and you wonder if it will be as good as you remember. When you pull your Hop Rod Rye away, you do it with a knowing smile. This could take all night.

Bear Republic Brewing Company
345 Healdsburg Avenue
Healdsburg, CA 95448
www.bearrepublic.com

George Washington's Tavern Porter

"I like fresh beer brewed by myself. I know what I like, and I know what I enjoy. My feeling is, the closer you are to the source, the better the beer."

—JOHN REYNOLDS, BREWER

AUG
24

TYPE: Porter

COLOR: Dark brown, almost black

SMELL: Dark molasses, sweet malt, and a hint of licorice

TASTE: A medium-bodied beer with flavors of toffee, dark chocolate, and molasses. A very smooth, silky brew with very little bitterness and no alcohol taste, which can be dangerous at 7% ABV.

FOOD PAIRING: Creamy Havarti cheese with thin, crispy crackers

AVAILABILITY: Year round, part of the Ales of Revolution series

Brew*tip*

To Make Small Beer take a large Sifter full of Bran Hops to your Taste. Boil these 3 hours. Then strain out 30 Gall. into a Cooler put in 3 Gallons Molasses while the Beer is scalding hot or rather drain the molasses into the Cooler. Strain the Beer on it while boiling hot let this stand til it is little more than Blood warm. Then put in a quart of Yeast if the weather is very cold cover it over with a Blanket. Let it work in the Cooler 24 hours then put it into the Cask. Leave the Bung open til it is almost done working. Bottle it that day Week it was Brewed.

—Recipe *from George Washington, 1757*

Yards Brewing Company
901 N. Delaware Avenue
Philadelphia, PA 19123
www.yardsbrewing.com

🍺 Reserve Special Black Bier Ale

"A pleasant apertif, as well as a good chaser for a short, quick whiskey, as well again for a fine supper drink, is beer."

—M.F.K. FISHER

TYPE: American strong ale

COLOR: Black

SMELL: Licorice and coffee

TASTE: A light- to medium-bodied beer with a powerful dark coffee taste that stretches out till the end.

FOOD PAIRING: Lemon meringue pie (seriously)

AVAILABILITY: Year round

AUG

25

Beer*fest*

2009 Great American Beer Festival Winners by Category:

Belgian-Style Lambic or Sour Ale: Duck Duck Gooze, The Lost Abbey, San Marcos, CA

Belgian-Style Abbey Ale: Signature Dubbel, Choc Beer Co., Krebs, OK

Belgian-Style Strong Specialty Ale: Revelations, Pizza Port Carlsbad, Carlsbad, CA

Brown Porter: St. Charles Porter, Blackstone Brewing Co., Nashville, TN

Dark Horse Brewing Company
511 S. Kalamazoo Avenue
Marshall, MI 49068
www.darkhorsebrewery.com

🍺 Dark Lager

"Teaching has ruined more American novels than drink."
—GORE VIDAL

TYPE: Munich dunkel lager
COLOR: Dark mahogany
SMELL: Roasted nuts and sweet malt
TASTE: A light, crisp, clean-tasting beer with flavors of cocoa, yeast, and nutty malt followed by a pleasant sour flavor and finishing with a nice hop aftertaste.
FOOD PAIRING: Roast beef sandwich on soft rye bread with smoked cheddar cheese and a little horseradish
AVAILABILITY: Year round

AUG
26

Beer*fun*

Three guys are riding in their truck, drinking beer. The driver looks in the mirror and sees the flashing lights of a police car so he pulls over. The other two are nervous, "What do we do with our beers?" "Just do this," the driver says. "Pull the label off of your beer bottle and stick it to your forehead and let me do the talking." The policeman walks up and says, "You boys were swerving down the road. Have you been drinking?" The driver says, "Oh, no, officer," and points to his forehead. "We're on the patch, trying to quit."

Durango Brewing Company
3000 Main Avenue
Durango, CO 81301
www.durangobrewing.com

🍺 Perseguidor

"History flows forward on rivers of beer"
—ANONYMOUS

TYPE: Oak-aged ale
COLOR: Bronze
SMELL: Dried fruit and oak with a hint of citrus
TASTE: Medium-bodied beer with tart fruit flavors—pie cherry, sour apple, dried plum, and raisin partially balanced out by sweet, toasted malt and aged balsamic vinegar.
FOOD PAIRING: Shitake mushroom risotto
AVAILABILITY: Special release

AUG
27

Publore

A very popular place to drink beer on a hot summer day in Prague, Letna Beer Garden is located inside Letna Park. Patrons can enjoy traditional Czechoslovakian beer while being treated to spectacular views of the city and the Vltava River.

Visit Letna Beer Garden at Letenské sady 341, 170 00 Prague 7-Holešovice, Czech Republic, *www.praguebeergarden.com.*

Jolly Pumpkin Artisan Ales
3115 Broad Street
Dexter, MI 48130
www.jollypumpkin.com

🍺 CoCoNut PorTeR

"The best beer in the world is the open bottle in your hand."
—ANONYMOUS

TYPE: Porter
COLOR: Dark cola
SMELL: Chocolate, vanilla, and a touch of coconut
TASTE: A light- to medium-bodied beer with flavors of bitter cocoa, mocha bean, roasted malt, and vanilla. The coconut doesn't come out right up front, but it's definitely there in the finish and clearly helps accentuate the other flavors.
FOOD PAIRING: Mussels steamed in coconut milk
AVAILABILITY: Year round

**AUG
28**

Beerfact

If all the beer consumed in the United States in one year were to be put into standard twelve-ounce cans, and those cans were stacked one on top of the other, they would reach the moon—twenty times over. If that stack were laid down on its side, the resulting line of beer would stretch around the earth 185 times.

Maui Brewing Company
Lahainatown
910 Honoapiilani Highway #55
Lahaina, Maui, HI 96761
www.mauibrewingco.com

 Mama's Little Yella Pils

"Beer is the fountain of happiness."
—ANONYMOUS

TYPE: Pilsner
COLOR: Light yellow
SMELL: Floral hops, a touch of malt and citrus
TASTE: A crisp, smooth, light- to medium-bodied beer with flavors of sweet malt and cereal grains followed by quite a bit of citrusy hops.
FOOD PAIRING: Lobster masala served over roasted golden beets
AVAILABILITY: Year round

AUG
29

Beerfest
2009 Great American Beer Festival Winners by Category
Bohemian-Style Pilsener: Vermont Lager, Otter Creek Brewing/Wolaver's Organic Ales, Middlebury, VT
Munich-Style Helles: Saint Arnold Summer Pils, Saint Arnold Brewing Co., Houston, TX
Dortmunder or German-Style Oktoberfest: Move Back, The SandLot, Denver, CO
American-Style Light Lager: Budweiser Select, Anheuser-Busch, Inc., Saint Louis, MO

Oskar Blues Brewery
1800 Pike Road, Unit B
Longmont, CO 80501
www.oskarblues.com

🍺 Backside Stout

"But the greatest love—the love of all loves, Even greater than that of a mother, Is the tender, passionate, undying love, Of one beer-drunken slob for another."
—ANONYMOUS

AUG
30

TYPE: Stout
COLOR: Black
SMELL: Burnt sugar and espresso
TASTE: A light- to medium-bodied beer with flavors of coffee, bitter baking chocolate, and burnt toast. It finishes with notes of sweet malt and leaves a bit of piney hop aftertaste.
FOOD PAIRING: Grilled eggplant with roasted tomatoes and yogurt
AVAILABILITY: Year round

Beer*fun*

A man walks into a bar and orders a beer. While chatting with the bartender the man says: "I have a method that will enable you to double the amount of beer you sell every day." "Really?" says the bartender, "How?" "Very simple. Just pour full glasses."

Steamworks Brewing Company
442 Wolverine Drive
Bayfield, CO 81122
www.steamworksbrewing.com

🍺 Holy Mackerel Special Golden Ale

"As he brews, so shall he drink."
—BEN JONSON

TYPE: Belgian strong pale ale
COLOR: Hazy golden
SMELL: Floral hops and tart green apple
TASTE: Lightly toasted grains that blend well with the fruits flavors of green apple and soft, ripe pear. The pairing of grain and fruit reminds me of a well-stacked Belgian waffle, only this one has a kick.
FOOD PAIRING: Braised chicken with mole negro sauce
AVAILABILITY: Summer

AUG
31

Beer*fest*

Held in September every year, the Beer Summit (a Samuel Adams event) claims to be the oldest Octoberfest in Boston. The festival itself takes place in two parts. On Friday night, there is a reception, which includes four beers, a commemorative mug, a host of table games (including the ever-popular Lederhosen Relay), and a guest speaker. Saturday night sees a ten-hour traditional German Beer Hall event, with live bands, more table games, and more than ten different styles of beer on tap. Check out *www.beersummit.com.*

Gordash Brewing Company
3804 SW 30th Avenue
Fort Lauderdale, FL 33312
www.holymackerelbeers.com

IPA

"Come tarry here and welcome be, and quaff the foaming brew; a friendly smile, a word, a song will cheer the heart of you."
—GERMAN BEER SIGN

TYPE: India pale ale
COLOR: Hazy amber
SMELL: Citrus, sweet malt, and pepper
TASTE: A medium-bodied beer with a solid backbone of sweet malt that is nearly crushed by bitter orange, grapefruit, and pine with a spicy hop finish.
FOOD PAIRING: Pan-fried catfish
AVAILABILITY: Year round

SEPT
1

Beerfact

Hangover helpers:

- **Vitamin C:** Helps stimulate your liver, aiding in the process of breaking down the alcohol. If you take vitamin C regularly, go ahead and add a few thousand extra milligrams. If you don't, then start out slowly. Too much vitamin C can give you diarrhea, and why add injury to insult.
- **Tomato juice:** Drinking the morning after, tomato juice provides your body with fructose, which aids in the metabolizing of alcohol. Add that to the Hair of the Dog theory, and you've just ordered a Bloody Mary at breakfast.

Santa Cruz Ale Works
150 Dubois Street
Santa Cruz, CA 95060
www.santacruzaleworks.com

 Avatar

"Whoever serves beer or wine watered down, he himself deserves in them to drown."
   —MEDIEVAL SAYING

TYPE: India pale ale
COLOR: Coppery amber
SMELL: Grapefruit and jasmine tea
TASTE: Nice hoppy IPA with the classic citrus notes. Elysian adds jasmine flowers to this one during the boil and the whirlpool, delivering an extra layer of subtle sweet floral flavors on top of the delicious hops.
FOOD PAIRING: Colonial rabbit served with currant jelly and sautéed mushrooms.
AVAILABILITY: Year round

SEPT

2

Beer*words*

Basic homebrew terms:

- **Malt:** Barley or other grain that has been soaked with water, allowed to sprout, and then dried.
- **Mash:** A mixture of hot water, crushed malt, and in some cases, adjuncts, in which the grain starches are converted to sugar.
- **Rack:** The process of transferring beer from one vessel to another in order to leave the sediment behind.

Elysian Brewing
1221 E. Pike Street
Seattle, WA 98122
www.elysianbrewing.com

🍺 Buckwheat Ale

"What I like about beer is you basically just drink it and order more."
—DAVE BARRY

TYPE: Pale wheat ale
COLOR: Rich golden
SMELL: Fresh wheat and floral hops
TASTE: A crisp, refreshing, light-bodied beer with flavors of wheat and citrus. A nice, easy beer to relax with after work or during a ballgame.
FOOD PAIRING: Lobster tacos
AVAILABILITY: Year round

SEPT

3

Beerfest

Though relatively young (2009 being the festival's second year), the High Country Beer Fest (*www.hcbeerfest.com*) attracts over fifty brewers. Held on Labor Day weekend in Boone, North Carolina, all proceeds for the event go to benefit the Hospitality House in Boone—the first nonprofit educational brewpub in the country. The program focuses on beer and brewing courses as well as offerings in renewable energy production and using alternate energy sources to run the brewery.

RJ Rockers Brewing Company
226-A West Main Street
Spartanburg, SC 29306
www.rjrockers.com

 Local 1

"Friends don't let friends drink light beer."
—ANONYMOUS

TYPE: Belgian strong pale ale
COLOR: Cloudy golden yellow
SMELL: Lemongrass, ginger, fresh flatbread
TASTE: One sip gives you visions of hard toffee, maple syrup, and warm fall spices. Further tastes of freshly baked yeasty white bread and inviting booze swirl in amongst lemon and crisp hops, followed by just a tiny hint of banana.
FOOD PAIRING: Braised pork belly spiced with fennel, coriander, cinnamon, and black peppercorns
AVAILABILITY: Year round

SEPT

4

Beerfest

The longest running and best-attended beer festival in New York, the Great World Beer Festival (*www.brewtopiafest.com*) features both American craft breweries and entries from across the pond. The three-day event is held on Labor Day weekend and includes tastings (of course), lectures, and a meet-and-greet with the brewers. Attendees can try the beers of more than 100 brewers.

The Brooklyn Brewery
#1 Brewers Row
79 North 11th Street
Brooklyn, NY 11211
www.brooklynbrewery.com

🍺 Organic Raven's Eye Imperial Stout

"Well I woke up this mornin' and I got myself a beer."
—JIM MORRISON, THE DOORS

TYPE: Imperial stout

COLOR: Black

SMELL: Dried fruit, chocolate malt, and molasses

TASTE: A medium-bodied beer with flavors of chocolate, black coffee, molasses, dried plum, and even a little licorice. It finishes with a touch of bitterness and a burnt aftertaste.

FOOD PAIRING: Chocolate soufflé

AVAILABILITY: Year round

SEPT

5

Beer*thought*

Text on a warning placard on the Eel River Brewing Company website:

"There is a dangerous virus going around. It is called 'Work.'

"If you receive Work from your colleagues, your boss, or anyone else via e-mail or any other means, do not touch it! The virus completely wipes out your private life completely.

"If you should come into contact with Work, put on your jacket, take two good friends and go straight to the nearest pub. Order the antidote known as 'Beer.' Take the antidote repeatedly until Work has been completely eliminated from your system."

Eel River Brewing Company
1777 Alamar Way
Fortuna, CA 95540
www.eelriverbrewing.com

 Karma

"The government will fall that raises the price of beer."
—CZECH PROVERB

TYPE: Belgian ale
COLOR: Translucent ruby orange
SMELL: Quite hoppy with substantial floral citrus
TASTE: Sweet and a little fruity with a yeasty finish and a lemon zest aftertaste. Quite easy to drink.
FOOD PAIRING: Basil-grilled tuna steak sandwich with heirloom tomatoes and a drizzle of aged balsamic vinegar
AVAILABILITY: Seasonal

SEPT

6

Beerfest

Held in Victoria, British Columbia, the Great Canadian Beer Festival, or GCBF for short, falls on the first weekend after Labor Day (or Labour Day as they say in Canada). Going strong and growing since 1993, the event boasts more than forty-five craft breweries from all over Canada, Belgium, and the Pacific Northwest of the United States. The brewers are on hand to participate in the festivities and pour suds for over 7,000 happy guests. Tickets for the event run about $25 or $30, and usually sell out. Check out *www.GCBF.com* to get tickets or volunteer.

Avery Brewing Company
5763 Arapahoe Avenue #E
Boulder, CO 80303
www.averybrewing.com

🍺 14'er ESB

"The mouth of a perfectly happy man is filled with beer."
—EGYPTIAN PROVERB

TYPE: Extra special bitter
COLOR: Golden amber with a fluffy white head
SMELL: Caramel, mixed nuts, and grapefruit
TASTE: Medium to light body with a nice balance between grapefruit zest and flavors of caramel apple.
FOOD PAIRING: Lamb shish kebabs with onion and peppers marinated in saffron and lemon
AVAILABILITY: Year round

SEPT

7

Beerfact

Beers that are meant to be enjoyed in large quantities within a set period of time are often referred to as "session beers." These beers tend to be lower in alcohol content so that a person could consume several of them within the allotted period of time without appearing to be inebriated when leaving the drinking establishment. The intent is primarily social, allowing the drinkers to have multiple beverages within the session without losing the ability to carry on a conversation or carry themselves home afterward.

Avery Brewing Company
5763 Arapahoe Avenue #E
Boulder, CO 80303
www.averybrewing.com

🍺 Bumbl'n Bubba's Buzz'n Brew

Sam: "What would you say to a beer, Norm?" Norm: "Daddy wuvs you."
—CHEERS

TYPE: Golden ale

COLOR: Light yellow

SMELL: Fresh baked bread, honey, toast, and cracker

TASTE: An easy drinker for those days you really want to put down more than just one. Light bodied with a touch of honey, sweet pear, and cracker, it finishes light and dry.

FOOD PAIRING: Oak club sandwich (turkey, bacon, and swiss)

AVAILABILITY: Year round

SEPT

8

Beer*fun*

Bizz Buzz

Required supplies: Beer

Players sit in a circle and count, one number at a time, progressing clockwise around the circle. (The first player says "one," the second, "two," and so forth.) Whenever a player is required to say a number that is divisible by 7, he says "Buzz" instead of the number. Whenever a player is required to say a number that is divisible by 11, he says "Bizz" instead of the number. Failure to follow the rules results in the player having to drink.

Northwoods Brewpub
3560 Oakwood Mall Drive
Eau Claire, WI 54701
www.northwoodsbrewpub.com

 Wilder Wheat

"I have respect for beer."
—RUSSELL CROWE

TYPE: Pale wheat ale
COLOR: Pale yellow
SMELL: Yeast and citrus hops
TASTE: A light-bodied beer with flavors of sour citrus, wheat, and malt.
FOOD PAIRING: Beer-steamed clams and muscles
AVAILABILITY: Year round

SEPT
9

Beer*food*
BEER-STEAMED CLAMS AND MUSCLES

2 pounds live clams, washed and
   bearded
1 to 2 bottles of amber or wheat ale
2 bay leaves
1 lemon, juiced

½ cup butter (1 stick)
4 cloves of garlic, crushed
½ cup onions, chopped
2 large celery stalks, minced
2 tablespoons fresh chopped parsley

Cook the onion, celery, and garlic over medium-high heat until just soft, 2 to 5 minutes. Place the clams in the pot and pour in enough beer to cover half way. Add everything else and bring to a boil. Cover and steam until the clams are open, another 3 to 5 minutes. Discard any clams that do not open and serve.

Santa Cruz Mountain Brewing
402 Ingalls Street
Santa Cruz, CA 95060
www.santacruzmountainbrewing.com

🍺 Supper Club Lager

"Whoever makes a poor beer is transferred to the dung hill."
—EDICT OF THE CITY OF DANZIG, ELEVENTH CENTURY

TYPE: Pale lager
COLOR: Dark amber
SMELL: Sweet malt
TASTE: A clean, crisp, lighter-bodied beer with flavors of mild malt and sweet grain with an aged-ale undertone.
FOOD PAIRING: Buffalo Carbonnade
AVAILABILITY: Year round

SEPT
10

Publore

There were only 1,001 Arabian Nights, but the Brickskeller in Washington, D.C., has more than 1,001 beers for you to try. Categorized by country and type, you can find more than twenty-five hefeweizens, nine beers from Japan, and Augustinebrau from Eritrea. It is a must-see when visiting the nation's capital.

Visit the Brickskeller at 1523 22nd Street NW, Washington, D.C. 20037, *www.brickskeller.org.*

Capital Brewery
7734 Terrace Avenue
Middleton, WI 53562
www.capital-brewery.com

🍺 Horn Dog

"The Edge . . . There is no honest way to explain it because the only people who really know where it is are the ones who have gone over."
—HUNTER S. THOMPSON

TYPE: Barley wine
COLOR: Deep reddish brown
SMELL: Bananas, caramel, and molasses
TASTE: Sweet light- to medium-bodied beer with flavors of burnt barley, rich malt, and a slight banana undertone that turns into a crisp hoppy aftertaste.
FOOD PAIRING: Sharp, cave-aged Irish white cheddar on really good crackers
AVAILABILITY: Year round

Beerfest

A celebration of all things Hunter S. Thompson, Gonzo Fest is held annually in September in the city of Fredrick, Maryland. Thompson, a journalist and author, became famous for his style of writing that eventually became known as "Gonzo Journalism," which often blends fact with fiction. Put on by the Flying Dog Brewery (*www.flyingdogales.com*), Gonzo Fest features beer drinking (of course) and a Hunter S. Thompson lookalike contest.

Flying Dog Brewery
4607 Wedgewood Blvd.
Frederick, MD 21703
www.flyingdogales.com

 Vienna

"Make your hobby your job. It'll ruin it for you as a hobby,
but you won't mind coming to work every day."
—MARC GOTTFRIED, BREWMASTER MORGAN STREET
BREWERY

TYPE: Viennese mild lager
COLOR: Bright coppery orange with a stark white head
SMELL: Malt and caramel up front with a slightly fainter scent of hops
TASTE: Light toffee, caramel, and malt flavors with very little bitterness
FOOD PAIRING: Shredded chicken quesadilla with mango salsa
AVAILABILITY: On tap at Morgan Street

SEPT

12

Beerfact

Morgan Street Brewery opened in September 1995 on Laclede's Landing.
The building where it resides was originally used by the Schoelhorn-
Albrecht Machine Company to manufacture capstans for Mississippi
River barges. The property was cleared in 1791 and was the site of the
freeing of the first mulatto slave, a woman by the name of Ester.

Morgan Street Brewery
721 North Second Street
Saint Louis, MO 63102
www.morganstreetbrewery.com

🍺 Damnation

"I hate to advocate drugs, alcohol, violence, or insanity to anyone, but they've always worked for me."
—HUNTER S. THOMPSON

TYPE: Golden ale
COLOR: Cloudy golden
SMELL: Scents of yeast and fresh wheat
TASTE: Sweet and mildly hoppy with flavors of dried peach and apricot fruit leather. Creamy mouthfeel for this light- to medium-bodied beer that finishes with a nice citrus hoppy aftertaste.
FOOD PAIRING: Stir-fried chicken and broccoli in black bean sauce served with black sticky rice
AVAILABILITY: Year round

SEPT
13

Beer*fest*

Held in September, the Great American Beer Festival (*www.greatamerican beerfestival.com*) judges beers in seventy-eight different style categories. Industry professionals from around the world gather to identify the top three beers in each specified style. The festival is the Guinness World Record holder for most beers tapped in one location. During the event's three days, which take place at the Colorado Convention Center in Denver, consumption will reach nearly 18,000 gallons of beer.

Russian River Brewing Company
725 4th Street
Santa Rosa, CA 95404
www.russianriverbrewing.com

🍺 Kilt Lifter

"The easiest way to spot a wanker in a pub is to look around and find who's drinking a Corona with a slice of lemon in the neck."

—WARWICK FRANKS, AUTHOR

TYPE: Scotch ale

COLOR: Ruby

SMELL: Malty and thick, you can almost feel it reach up and grab your nostrils.

TASTE: Kilt Lifter is rich and sweet with a nice smoky undertone that comes from the peaty Scotch whiskey malt they add to create the beer's extraordinary complexity.

FOOD PAIRING: Smoked ham and Brie sandwich with grilled apple slices on toasted sourdough bread

AVAILABILITY: Year round

SEPT

14

Beerfest

Held in mid-September in the city of Waterbury, Connecticut, the Brass City Brew Fest (*www.brasscitybrewfest.com*) is the biggest annual beer event in Connecticut in terms of beers available, and one of the largest in New England. The fest boasts more than 125 breweries and features over 300 beers. The one-day event has drawn close to 2,000 people from more than ninety towns in Connecticut and ten states up and down the East Coast.

The Pike Brewing Company
1415 First Avenue
Seattle, WA 98122
www.pikebrewing.com

DBA

"It is better to think of church in the ale house than to think of the ale house in church."
—MARTIN LUTHER

TYPE: Pale ale
COLOR: Deep, clear red
SMELL: Sweet malt and citrus
TASTE: A smooth, creamy beer that starts out sweet and malty with flavors of caramel and even a little vanilla, then balances out with a shot of hoppy bitterness.
FOOD PAIRING: Shrimp masala and garlic naan
AVAILABILITY: Year round

SEPT
15

Beer*fest*

More than 3,000 microbrew enthusiasts descend on Sacramento in September for the California Brewers Fest (*www.calbrewfest.org*). They'll taste 160 beers from over sixty brewers from the west. The event includes a full beer competition, which gives away awards in thirteen different categories. The competition is run by the Gold County Brewers Association.

Firestone Walker Brewing Company
1400 Ramada Drive
Paso Robles, CA 93446
www.firestonewalker.com

🍺 Le Freak

"Drink because you are happy, but never because you are miserable."
—G. K. CHESTERTON

TYPE: Belgian IPA (convergence of a Belgian trippel and an American IPA)
COLOR: Dark golden
SMELL: Caramel, alcohol, ripe fruit, and hops
TASTE: Honey and herbs followed by a citrus pepper and a long hoppy finish. Quite smooth and enjoyable, an interesting blend of different styles.
FOOD PAIRING: Hangar steak marinated bulgogi style then grilled, sliced, and served over mixed greens
AVAILABILITY: Year round

SEPT
16

Beerfest

For one day in the middle of September, 6,000 beer enthusiasts descend on San Diego for the annual Festival of Beer. Featuring more than sixty brewers and more than 150 beers, the festival was initially conceived to raise money for the fight to eradicate cancer. The first couple of years were only partially successful. But then the San Diego Professionals Against Cancer created a nonprofit organization to take over and the rest is history. Check out *www.sdbeerfest.org*.

Green Flash Brewing Company
1430 Vantage Court
Vista, CA 92081
www.greenflashbrew.com

🍺 Dirty Bastard

"Some people wanted champagne and caviar when they should have had beer and hot dogs."
—DWIGHT D. EISENHOWER

SEPT

17

> **TYPE:** Scotch ale
> **COLOR:** Deep mahogany brown
> **SMELL:** Roasted malt, coffee, and caramel
> **TASTE:** A full-bodied, full-of-life beer with flavors of roasted malt, warm caramel, bittersweet chocolate, and alder smoke. Thick and oily, it doesn't so much roll over your tongue as glide, then finishes smooth with a dry, bitter aftertaste.
> **FOOD PAIRING:** Smoked Gouda and mole salami with sourdough crackers
> **AVAILABILITY:** Year round

Beerfest

This annual September event, held in the city of Racine, Wisconsin, is also the host of the Schooner Homebrew Championship. Hopeful home-brewers deliver samples of their own concoctions to one of several locations before the festival to be judged and entered to win prizes. At the Great Lakes Brew Fest itself (*www.greatlakesbrewfest.com*), more than 100 breweries offer drinkers the chance to sample 250 craft beers and sodas.

Founders Brewing Company
235 Grandville Avenue SW
Grand Rapids, MI 49503
www.foundersbrewing.com

🍺 Irish Walker

"The man who isn't jolly after drinking is just a driveling idiot, to my thinking."
—EURIPIDES

TYPE: Barley wine
COLOR: Dark brown
SMELL: Sweet, deeply roasted malt with a hint of brown sugar
TASTE: A nice blending of dark, ripe fruit flavors, notes of tobacco and molasses, and bitter hops for a smooth, balanced beer.
FOOD PAIRING: Molasses baked beans and brown bread
AVAILABILITY: Year round

SEPT

18

Beerfest

A celebration of great beers and great music, the Brewgrass Festival (*www.brewgrassfestival.com*), hosted by the Great Smokies Craft Brewers Association, takes place in the city of Asheville, North Carolina. The event draws in more than forty brewers from across the United States and of course features live bluegrass music from both nationally known and local bands. There are close to 120 different beers to try out.

Olde Hickory Brewery
222 Union Square
Hickory, NC 28601
www.oldehickorybrewery.com

🍺 Heavy Seas Loose Cannon (Hop3 Ale)

"Good beer represents your best alcoholic beverage value."
—HUGH SISSON, CLIPPER CITY BREWING COMPANY

TYPE: India pale ale
COLOR: Clear golden orange
SMELL: Hops
TASTE: Flavors of pine and grapefruit over a nice backbone of malty sweetness
FOOD PAIRING: Sesame crusted salmon with Asian noodles
AVAILABILITY: Year round

SEPT
19

Beer*fest*

Nearly everything is better with bacon. The folks at Clipper City Brewery (*www.ccbeer.com*) understand this glorious pairing, since they are the mad geniuses behind the Beer and Bacon Fest. Tickets include all-you-can-taste beer and bacon. The event features samples of the brewery's beers, more than fifteen different kinds of bacon, and an array of bacon dishes including BLTs, "Piggy Candy," and bacon-wrapped scallops. Beer and Bacon Fest takes place on September 19, which by no accident is also Talk Like a Pirate Day.

Clipper City Brewing Company
4615 Hollins Ferry Road, Suite B
Baltimore, MD 21227
www.ccbeer.com

🍺 Oktoberfest

"If barley be wanted to make into malt, we must be content and think it no fault, for we can make liquor to sweeten our lips, of pumpkins and parsnips and walnut tree chips."
—COLONIAL AMERICAN SONG

TYPE: Märzen

COLOR: Clear copper

SMELL: Yeasty and slightly sweet

TASTE: A crisp, broad-flavored, full-bodied beer with notes of sweet malt, maple syrup, apple, pear, and bitter leaf that culminate in a coppery finish and a slightly sweet aftertaste.

FOOD PAIRING: Nurnberger Rostbratwurst with mashed potatoes

AVAILABILITY: Fall

SEPT
20

Beerfest

Why are so many Oktoberfest celebrations held in September? Well, the first Oktoberfest took place in 1810 to honor Bavarian Crown Prince Ludwig's marriage to Princess Therese von Sachsen-Hildburghausen. The six-day festival started on October 12, 1810, and ended on October 17 with a horse race. The anniversary of their marriage was again celebrated the following year, and the years after that, each time growing larger and eventually being moved forward into September, which allowed for better weather conditions.

Summit Brewing Company
910 Montreal Circle
St. Paul, MN 55102
www.summitbrewing.com

🍺 Belgian Night Train

"You've gotta keep fit to play that hard every night. Better order five more beers."
—JAMES HETFIELD, METALLICA

TYPE: Belgian-style ale
COLOR: Cloudy amber
SMELL: Spun sugar, honey, sweet malt, and bananna
TASTE: Medium-bodied beer with flavors of caramel, pumpkin, and spice followed by a slightly citrus finish and a long, sweet aftertaste.
FOOD PAIRING: Fried bananas drizzled in warm caramel with vanilla whipping cream
AVAILABILITY: Year round

SEPT
21

Pub*lore*

One of the world's legendary beer bars, Akkurat has that comfortable, dark, pub feel that somehow makes every sip of brew taste even better than the last. The best feature about Akkurat is their cellar list. Hundreds of vintage bottled beers have been painstakingly cared for and are available for you to buy—some of them over twenty-one years old!

Visit Akkurat at Hornsgatan 18, Stockholm, 118 20, Sweden, *www .akkurat.se.*

Angel City Brewing
833 W. Torrance Blvd., Suite 105
Torrance, CA 90502
www.angelcitybrewing.com

🍺 Colorfest

"Always be drunken. Nothing else matters."
—BAUDELAIRE

TYPE: Märzen
COLOR: Amber
SMELL: Fresh bread and spicy hops
TASTE: A medium-bodied, easy-to-drink beer with flavors of freshly baked bread, caramel, nutty malt, and earthy hops. Finishes with a touch of yeast and a bitter aftertaste.
FOOD PAIRING: Fresh grilled bratwurst on a soft roll with brown mustard
AVAILABILITY: Autumn seasonal

SEPT
22

Beerfact

How many different ways can you think of to package beer for transport? Let's see. We've got bottles, cans, vats, barrels, kegs, growlers, mugs/glasses/steins, maybe even tanker trucks. Well, outside shops in Qingdao, China, there are barrels of Tsingtao beer and piles of clean plastic bags. You buy the beer in bulk, putting it into a plastic bag, then pay for it by the kilogram (to avoid being swindled by a package that is sold by volume but is really half full of carbon dioxide and air).

Durango Brewing Company
3000 Main Avenue
Durango, CO 81301
www.durangobrewing.com

🍺 Flywheel

"Busy, curious, thirst fly
Drink with me, and drink as I."
—WILLIAM OLDYS, POET

TYPE: Pilsner
COLOR: Pale straw
SMELL: Very clean with a touch of grass and citrus
TASTE: A very smooth, light-bodied, drinkable beer that features the dry, clean, bready taste of a good pilsner. There are notes of lemon and grapefruit that fade away into a dry finish.
FOOD PAIRING: Taco salad
AVAILABILITY: Year round

SEPT
23

Beerfun
Beer Pot
Required supplies: One large pitcher of beer

A player begins drinking from the pitcher and can drink as much or as little as he cares to. Once a player stops drinking he must pass the pitcher to the next person. The pitcher is passed around the table until someone finishes the pitcher. The player who finishes the pitcher is the winner. The person who drank immediately before the winner is the loser and must buy the next pitcher.

Metropolitan Brewing Company
5121 N. Ravenswood Avenue
Chicago, IL 60640
www.metrobrewing.com

🍺 Dead Guy Ale

"Quaintest thoughts, queerest fancies, Come to life and fade away; Who cares how time advances? I am drinking ale today."

—EDGAR ALLAN POE

TYPE: Maibock
COLOR: Dark reddish
SMELL: Malty and yeasty with just a hint of fruitness
TASTE: A full-bodied beer with thick maltiness and a spicy hop finish. Smooth, creamy texture that coats your tongue and takes over your mouth. The aftertaste is quite nice.
FOOD PAIRING: Korean BBQ pork with a side of spicy kimchee
AVAILABILITY: Year round

SEPT

24

*Beer*fest

The Oktoberfest at Mount Angel, Oregon, has been running for more than forty years (*www.oktoberfest.org*). This quaint little town has a working community glockenspiel, Bavarian storefronts, and men in lederhosen blowing gigantic wooden alp horns. The festival features a traditional Biergarten and Weingarten, Alpine ethnic foods, and continuous live music on four stages from over thirty musical groups. The four-day event takes place annually on the second Thursday after Labor Day, when the hop harvest is in.

Rogue Ales
2320 OSU Drive
Newport, OR 97365
www.rogue.com

🍺 Live Oak HefeWeizen

"Shoulder the sky, my lad, and drink your ale."
—A. E. HOUSMAN

TYPE: Hefeweizen

COLOR: Hazy yellow

SMELL: Wheat, clove, and banana

TASTE: Flavors of freshly threshed wheat mix with banana fruitiness, spices of clove and bready yeast.

FOOD PAIRING: Spiced turkey burgers with apple jelly served on fresh ciabatta rolls

AVAILABILITY: Year round

SEPT

25

Beer*fest*

A four-day festival in mid-September, the Addison Oktoberfest, in Addison, Texas, is an event you should not miss (*www.addisontexas.net/events/Oktoberfest/*). Kick back in the Biers of the World and Weingarten to enjoy an original German Oktoberfest beer. Then head over to the carnival to experience some spinning, swirling joy on one of the amusement rides. After that, test your sleuthing skills in the Great Gemuetlichkeit Pretzel Hunt. Round out your day with a stop at the German Car Show.

Live Oak Brewing Company
3301 E. 5th Street, #B
Austin, TX 78702
www.liveoakbrewing.com

🍺 Barktoberfest

"A good prince will tax as lightly as possible those commodities which are used by the poorest members of society: grain, bread, beer, wine, clothing."
—DESIDERIUS ERASMUS

TYPE: Märzen
COLOR: Rusty amber
SMELL: Malty sweetness with aromas of dried fruit and floral hops
TASTE: Medium-bodied beer with flavors of warm caramel and freshly toasted artisan bread followed by a touch of peppery hops and a slightly sweet aftertaste.
FOOD PAIRING: Pork and garlic sausages served on a soft roll with honey mustard and caramelized onions
AVAILABILITY: Year round

SEPT
26

Publore

The oldest pub in Bruges, Belgium, Café Vlissinghe has been open for business since 1515. The warm, wooden bar and antique furniture will make you ponder just how many interesting historical figures sat at this very same place and had one too many. In the back is a spacious, well-worn, stone-walled garden where you can play a game of boccie.

Visit Café Vlissinghe at Blekersstraat 2, 8000 Brugge, *www.cafe vlissinghe.be*.

Thirsty Dog Brewing Company
529 Grant Street, Suite B
Akron, Ohio 44311
www.thirstydog.com

🍺 Black Noddy Lager

"Beer is the reason I get out of bed every afternoon."
—ANONYMOUS

TYPE: Schwarzbier
COLOR: Dark brown
SMELL: Coffee
TASTE: A smooth, silky, medium-bodied beer that starts off with flavors of coffee, burnt sugar, caramel, and mocha bean with a crisp, rather dry finish and just a touch of a sour aftertaste.
FOOD PAIRING: Schwarzbier cheese fondue
AVAILABILITY: Year round

SEPT
27

Beerwords
How to say you're drunk (in English):

Blitzed   Rocked
Stewed   Juiced
Ripped   Gone
Blasted   Sloshed
Smashed

Buckbean Brewing Company
1155 S. Rock Blvd., Suite 490
Reno, NV 89502
www.buckbeanbeer.com

🍺 Titan IPA

"Make sure that the beer—four pints a week—goes to the troops under fire before any of the parties in the rear get a drop."

—WINSTON CHURCHILL TO HIS SECRETARY OF WAR, 1944

TYPE: India pale ale
COLOR: Golden copper
SMELL: Citrus and pine with just a touch of malt
TASTE: A light- to medium-bodied beer with a great blending of pine, grapefruit, and lemon hop flavors overlaid on a sweet malt backbone.
FOOD PAIRING: Grilled halibut marinated in ginger, garlic, and cilantro
AVAILABILITY: Year round

SEPT
28

Beerfun
Century Club
Required supplies: Stopwatch, a shot glass for each player, about a half a case of beer per player

Each player fills a shot glass full of beer. Start the stopwatch. Players drink a shot of beer each minute, on the minute, for 100 minutes. Using one-ounce shot glasses, this amounts to just shy of nine twelve-ounce beers in just over an hour and a half. Not all players will make it to 100.

Great Divide Brewing Company
2201 Arapahoe Street
Denver, CO 80205
www.greatdivide.com

🍺 Hoppe Imperial Extra Pale Ale

"I am not a heavy drinker. I can sometimes go for hours without touching a drop."
—NOEL COWARD

TYPE: Double India pale ale

COLOR: Rusty orange

SMELL: Toasted malt with pine, citrus, and floral hops

TASTE: A medium-bodied beer with a sweet malt backbone that holds through a string of interesting hoppy flavors—grapefruit, grass, pine, and floral. Finishes with a pinch of bitter then ends clean.

FOOD PAIRING: Baseball-cut filet mignon with mashed potatoes and steamed asparagus

AVAILABILITY: Year round

Beer*words*

Drinking toast:

For every wound, a balm. For every sorrow, cheer. For every storm, a calm. For every thirst, a beer.

Southern Tier Brewing Company
2051A Stoneman Circle
Lakewood, NY 14750
www.southerntierbrewing.com

🍺 Okto

"From man's sweat and God's love, beer came into the world."
—SAINT ARNOLD OF METZ

TYPE: Altbier
COLOR: Medium amber
SMELL: Sweet malt and vanilla
TASTE: Malty and smooth with flavors of burnt caramel, warm brown sugar, and a hint of vanilla
FOOD PAIRING: Pumpkin and goat cheese ravioli with a brown butter sauce
AVAILABILITY: August to October

SEPT
30

Beer*fest*

Held in Fremont, Washington, the Fremont Oktoberfest (*www.fremont oktoberfest.com*) is held annually at the end of September and goes for three full days. Highlights include more than thirty-five breweries on hand with over seventy-five beers to sample (including Widmer Okto), a 5K race (for those who want to work off their beer before they start drinking), multiple beer gardens, and a host of local bands.

Widmer Brothers Brewing Company
929 N. Russell Street
Portland, OR 97227
www.widmer.com

🍺 Wahoo Wheat

"While I sat still and drank beer with Philip in Hahns-dorf, God dealt the papacy a mighty blow."
—MARTIN LUTHER

TYPE: Witbier

COLOR: Cloudy yellow, the color of melted butter

SMELL: Raw wheat and yeast

TASTE: A soft, velvety, medium-bodied beer with flavors of wheat, banana, and cream. Very smooth and easy to drink.

FOOD PAIRING: Cucumber, onion, and tomato salad with tahini lemon juice dressing

AVAILABILITY: Year round

OCT

1

Beer*fest*

2009 Great American Beer Festival Winners by Category

Specialty Honey Beer: Countdown Honey Brown, Thunder Canyon Brewery, Tucson, AZ

Session Beer: KinderPils, Triumph Brewing Co. of Philadelphia, Philadelphia, PA

Other Strong Beer: Cardiff, Glenwood Canyon Brewing Co., Glenwood Springs, CO

Experimental Beer: TPS Report, Trinity Brewing Co., Colorado Springs, CO

Ballast Point Brewing Company
10051 Old Grove Road, Suite B
San Diego, CA 92131
www.ballastpoint.com

🍺 Lucky Kat

"A beer in hand is worth two in the fridge."
—FOUND PRINTED ON THE INSIDE OF MAGIC HAT BEER
BOTTLE CAPS

TYPE: India pale ale
COLOR: Hazy orange like a well-lit jack-o'-lantern on a dark night
SMELL: Lots of floral hops and pine, followed by the sweet, stalking sweetness of roasted malt
TASTE: Light- to medium-bodied beer with a rich, nutty malt backbone and a fair amount of pine-flavored hops
FOOD PAIRING: Phad thai with crushed red chili flakes and sautéed king prawns
AVAILABILITY: Year round

OCT

2

Beerfact

Among the most famous fictional beers is Duff, the favorite beverage of Homer Simpson. Many episodes of *The Simpsons* have turned on Homer's love affair with Duff, often featuring Duffman (voiced by actor Hank Azaria). Duffman is based on Budweiser's former mascot, Bud Man.

Magic Hat Brewing Company
5 Bartlett Bay Road
South Burlington, VT 05403
www.magichat.net

🍺 Dragonstooth

"Wine is but single cloth. Ale is meat, drink, and cloth."
—ENGLISH PROVERB

TYPE: Stout
COLOR: Deep brown black
SMELL: Roasted grain, sweet malt, bitter chocolate, and coffee
TASTE: Sweet thick coffee with baker's chocolate melted throughout. Roasted malts, a little earthy leather, light smokiness, and some bitter hops to finish it all off.
FOOD PAIRING: Homemade Madagascar vanilla bean ice cream
AVAILABILITY: Year round

OCT

3

Beer**words**
German terms you should know before heading to the München Oktoberfest:

- *Fackl* (n.): A young pig, used to describe a jerk.
- *Fetznrausch* (n.): Totally drunk
- *Fingahackln* (n.): A Bavarian sport where two people hook their middle fingers and try to pull the opponent over the table. Very popular at Oktoberfest.
- *Gamsbart* (n.): Traditional Bavarian hat adornment
- *Gneedl* (n.): Dumpling.

Elysian Brewing
1221 E. Pike Street
Seattle, WA 98122
www.elysianbrewing.com

 Pennant Ale '55

"There is only one game at the heart of America, and that is baseball, and only one beverage to be found sloshing at the depths of our national soul, and that is beer."
—PETE RICHMOND

TYPE: Pale ale
COLOR: Dark amber
SMELL: Roasted malt
TASTE: Nicely balanced beer with flavors of rich, sweet malt in proportion to the subtle hoppy bitterness. A very drinkable, easy-to-enjoy beer.
FOOD PAIRING: Baseball stadium hotdog with plenty of mustard
AVAILABILITY: Year round

OCT
4

Beerfact

Other things to do with beer:

- **Shampoo:** Place one cup of beer into a saucepan and bring to a boil. Reduce the heat and let simmer until the beer has been reduced by more than half. Cool, then mix the de-alcoholized beer with a cup of your favorite shampoo. Wash your hair with the mixture as you would with any regular shampoo. The beer in this potent combination will add shine and smoothness to your flat, dry, boring hair.

- **Rust dissolver:** Got a stuck bolt? Try pouring a little beer over it. The carbonation and acids will dissolve the rust after a short while, unsticking the bolt.

The Brooklyn Brewery
#1 Brewers Row
79 North 11th Street
Brooklyn, NY 11211
www.brooklynbrewery.com

🍺 Late Harvest Autumn Ale

"Always do sober what you said you'd do drunk. That will teach you to keep your mouth shut."
— ERNEST HEMINGWAY

TYPE: Amber ale
COLOR: Pale amber
SMELL: Citrus and stone fruit
TASTE: Flavors of ripe apricot and dried peach round out the malty sweetness, accompanied closely by the pleasing citrus of hops that cruises in slowly to finish off the sip.
FOOD PAIRING: Spicy Buffalo chicken wings with celery and blue cheese dressing
AVAILABILITY: August through October

OCT

5

Beerfact

In the year 1880 in the United Kingdom, the Inland Revenue Act required that homebrewers apply for and acquire a five-shilling license in order to legally be allowed to pursue their hobby. The law was changed in 1963, no longer requiring the license or the fee.

Redhook Ale Brewery
14300 NE 145th Street
Woodinville, WA 98072
www.redhook.com

🍺 Two Hearted Ale

"I work until beer o'clock."
—STEPHEN KING

TYPE: India pale ale

COLOR: Hazy light amber

SMELL: Tangerine zest and honeysuckle

TASTE: Flavors of lavender, jasmine, Clementine oranges, and just a touch of sweet malt blend effortlessly with soft bitter lemon. A long, smooth finish of floral and citrus hops lingers in your mouth, growing more bitter as the beer warms.

FOOD PAIRING: Persian eggplant and red tomato stew served over lentils and saffron basmati rice

AVAILABILITY: Year round

OCT

6

Beerwords

German terms you should know before heading to the München Oktoberfest:

- *Biafuizl* (n.): A beer mat, often used by a waitress or waiter as a note pad where dashes indicate the quantity of beers ordered.
- *Bierdimpfe* (n.): A notorious beer drinker or "tavern potato."
- *Breimoaster* (n.): Master brewer
- *Ditschi* (n.): Bavarian-style hat with a dent in the middle
- *Eihebn* (n.): The state of being dizzy because of too much beer, requiring you to cling to the nearest person, light pole, or police horse.

Bell's Brewery
8938 Krum Avenue
Galesburg, MI 49053
www.bellsbeer.com

🍺 Triple Exultation

Sam: "What's new, Normie?" Norm: "Terrorists, Sam. They've taken over my stomach, and they're demanding beer."

—*CHEERS*

TYPE: Old ale

COLOR: Muddy brown

SMELL: Thick, sweet fruit syrup and pine

TASTE: Known by those at the brewery as the "Ozzy Osbourne" of old ales. Flavors of sweet malt and bittersweet chocolate pair with a touch of yeast and subtle but still clearly present hop notes.

FOOD PAIRING: Baked sweet potato

AVAILABILITY: Year round

OCT

7

Beerfest

2009 Great American Beer Festival Winners by Category

Herb and Spice or Chocolate Beer: Stillwater Rye, Montana Brewing Co., Billings, MT

Coffee-Flavored Beer: Dude! Where's My Vespa?, Rock Bottom Brewery, Arlington, VA

Specialty Beer: Chateau Jiahu, Dogfish Head Brewery, Milton, DE

Rye Beer: Crazy Jackass Ale, Great American Restaurants, Centreville, VA

Eel River Brewing Company
1777 Alamar Way
Fortuna, CA 95540
www.eelriverbrewing.com

TWO BROTHERS BREWING COMPANY

🍺 Cane and Ebel

"Eat, drink, and be merry, for tomorrow we die."
—ECCLESIASTES

TYPE: Red rye
COLOR: Dark red, amber
SMELL: Floral hops and sweet malt
TASTE: A medium-bodied beer with a smooth mouthfeel. Flavors of cola and bitter dandelion move into a lavender and floral-hop finish. Thai palm sugar gives the sweet elements a unique flavor profile.
FOOD PAIRING: Jamaican jerk pork
AVAILABILITY: Year round

OCT

8

Beer*words*

German terms you should know before heading to the München Oktoberfest

- *Schachtschüssl* (n.): A big meal comprised mostly of sausages and other meats.
- *Schnaggler* (n.): A hiccup.
- *Suri* (adj.): Tipsiness.
- *Träwan* (n.): Malt remaining in the beer when brewed.
- *Waagscheitl* (n.): The wobbling movement of the draw bar on a horse carriage, often used to describe a drunkard.
- *Wampn* (n.): Beer belly
- *Weißbia* (n.): Wheat beer served only in the smaller beer tents at Oktoberfest.
- *Weißwurscht* (n.): White sausage eaten with sweet mustard. Do not eat the skin.

Two Brothers Brewing Company
30W315 Calumet Avenue
Warrenville, IL 60555
www.twobrosbrew.com

🍺 Pliny the Elder

"Beer . . . a high and mighty liquor."
—JULIUS CAESAR

TYPE: Imperial IPA
COLOR: Clear gold
SMELL: Piney hops
TASTE: Light- to medium-bodied beer that you'll want to drink down in one beautifully hoppy mouthful after another. Very refreshing with pleasing citrus notes and a nice pine resin aftertaste. A true pleasure.
FOOD PAIRING: Stuffed grape leaves and tzaziki with warm pita triangles
AVAILABILITY: Year round

OCT
9

Beerfact

Pliny the Elder was a Roman naturalist, scholar, historian, traveler, officer, and writer. He and his contemporaries created the botanical name for hops, *Lupus salictarius*, meaning "wolf among scrubs." Hops at that time grew wild among willows, much like a wolf in the forest. Later the current botanical name, *Humulus lupulus*, was adopted. Pliny died in 79 C.E. while observing the eruption of Mount Vesuvius. He was immortalized by his nephew, Pliny the Younger, who continued his uncle's legacy by documenting much of what he observed during the eruption of Mount Vesuvius.

—From the description of Pliny the Elder at *Russianriverbrewing.com*

Russian River Brewing Company
725 4th Street
Santa Rosa, CA 95404
www.russianriverbrewing.com

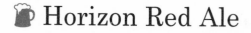 Horizon Red Ale

"Your beer drinker tends to be a straightforward, decent, friendly, down-to-earth person, whereas your serious wine fancier tends to be an insufferable snot."
—DAVE BARRY

TYPE: Red ale
COLOR: Dark amber
SMELL: Hop resins and pine needles
TASTE: Hoppy and delicious, this one starts with flavors of pine and citrus that linger as the roasted malt backbone appears then delivers slight coffee notes that fade into a long bitter, pine finish.
FOOD PAIRING: Totten Virginica oysters on the half shell
AVAILABILITY: Year round

OCT
10

Beerfest

Admission is free for Oktoberfest on the Minneapolis River Front, held on the banks of the Mississippi River in Minneapolis, Minnesota (*www.minneapolisoktoberfest.com*). If you're the strong, silent type, enter the Hammer-Schlagen, or "Striking Hammer" competition. Nails are placed around the circumference of a large cross section of a tree. Each participant gets his or her own nail and only one swing to drive the nail completely into the wood. There is a catch. Participants can only use the narrow end of the hammer!

Summit Brewing Company
910 Montreal Circle
St. Paul, MN 55102
www.summitbrewing.com

🍺 La Roja

"I have fed purely upon ale; I have eat my ale, drank my ale, and I always sleep upon ale."
—GEORGE FARQUHAR, POET

TYPE: Amber ale
COLOR: Deep amber
SMELL: Earthy with notes of dry cherries
TASTE: A medium- to full-bodied beer with flavors of caramel, dried plums, vanilla, oak, and bourbon mixed in with a sourness and floral notes with a spicy finish.
FOOD PAIRING: Apple and ginger-glazed chicken
AVAILABILITY: Year round

OCT

11

Beerfact

Hangover helpers:

- **Lime:** Put two teaspoons of fresh lime juice in an eight-ounce glass of water and sweeten with a teaspoon of sugar. Drink slowly. This concoction will help replenish your lost blood sugar.
- **Peppermint:** Chew on the fresh leaves of the peppermint plant or make peppermint tea with dried leaves. Chewing the leaves will relax your intestines, relieving stomach cramps and allowing you to get back to your normal "flow."

Jolly Pumpkin Artisan Ales
3115 Broad Street
Dexter, MI 48130
www.jollypumpkin.com

🍺 Rock Hopera

"If die I must, let me die drinking in an inn."
—WALTER MAP, AUTHOR

TYPE: Imperial IPA
COLOR: Dark mahogany
SMELL: Big pine and grapefruit
TASTE: This one starts out bold with flavors of citrus and pine. The malty backbone creeps up, creating a precarious balancing act that in the end tips in the favor of bitterness and alcohol.
FOOD PAIRING: A large margherita pizza with extra basil
AVAILABILITY: Year round

OCT

12

Brewtip

How to prepare a yeast starter:

Fill an old spaghetti sauce jar three-quarters full with water and mix in about 5 tablespoons of malt extract. Fill a stockpot with about three inches of water. Place the jar in the stockpot with the lid on top but not screwed down tight. Bring the water in the stockpot to a boil, then reduce it to a simmer and cover. After thirty minutes, remove it from the heat, pull the jar out, tighten the lid, and let it cool. When it has reached room temperature, shake the jar to aerate the liquid, then add your yeast and shake again. Loosen the lid and place in a clean, dry, warm place. It is ready when a head of thick foamy yeast has developed on top.

Vino's Brewpub
923 West 7th Street
Little Rock, AR 72201
www.vinosbrewpub.com

🍺 Roxy Rolles

"Beer. Helping ugly people have sex since 3000 B.C."
—ANONYMOUS

TYPE: Amber ale
COLOR: Very dark copper
SMELL: Sweet with the familiar scent of floral hops
TASTE: Medium body and a silky mouthfeel around flavors of deep roasted malt and just enough hops—comforting flavors as warm and comfortable as the changing color of autumn leaves
FOOD PAIRING: Grilled gruyere panini with roasted red peppers and arugula
AVAILABILITY: Fall

OCT

13

Brewtip

If you've never tried it before, homebrewing can be a really rewarding—and delicious—hobby. For about $100, you should be able to aquire all the items you'll need to brew your first batch. Here's a list:

- 5-gallon glass carboy
- A cap or rubber cork with a hole in it
- An airlock
- A length of tube for siphoning
- Racking cane
- Bottle filler
- Funnel
- A thick brush
- Priming bucket
- 50 bottle caps
- 50 beer bottles (Pop top not screw top)
- A prepackaged beer kit for the first-time brew
- Corn sugar for priming

Magic Hat Brewing Company
5 Bartlett Bay Road
South Burlington, VT 05403
www.magichat.net

🍺 Pale Ale

Sam: "What would you say to a beer, Normie?" Norm: "Hiya, sailor. New in town?"
— *CHEERS*

TYPE: Pale ale

COLOR: Golden amber

SMELL: Citrus and a hint of malt

TASTE: A light- to medium-bodied beer that starts with flavors of grapefruit and Valencia orange then gives way to pine hoppiness and a sweet, almost nutty malt. It exhibits a crisp, dry finish with nearly no aftertaste.

FOOD PAIRING: Rotisserie game hens with roasted new potatoes

AVAILABILITY: Year round

OCT

14

Beer*fest*

The original Oktoberfest, held in Munich, Germany, is the largest public festival in the world. Entry to the festival is free, but getting into the "tents" requires some preplanning. Booking seats in advance is a good idea, and arrive as early as possible. Larger groups, in particular, will have a hard time getting in, due to the popularity of the event. Anyone is free to wander into a tent and wait for a spot to open up, but only those patrons with seats will be served beer and food.

Santa Cruz Ale Works
150 Dubois Street
Santa Cruz, CA 95060
www.santacruzaleworks.com

🍺 Heavy Seas Winter Storm "Category 5" Ale

"A hangover is when you open your eyes in the morning and wish you hadn't."
—ANONYMOUS

TYPE: Extra special bitter
COLOR: Copper
SMELL: Light caramel and hops
TASTE: Biscuits and caramel up front with piney and floral hops. Dry aftertaste with citrus notes.
FOOD PAIRING: Grilled spice-rubbed chicken breast with black pepper vinegar sauce
AVAILABILITY: October to February

OCT

15

Beer*fact*

Hangover helpers:

- **Apples:** After a night of drinking eat them first thing when you get up. This should help ease or even remove your hangover.
- **Banana, milk, and honey:** Blend all three together and drink it down. The milk will sooth your stomach and rehydrate you. The honey will replenish lost sugars, and the banana will replace a bunch of electrolytes and minerals that are depleted when you drink.

Clipper City Brewing Company
4615 Hollins Ferry Road, Suite B
Baltimore, MD 21227
www.ccbeer.com

STONE BREWING COMPANY

Ruination IPA

"I drink to make other people interesting."
—GEORGE JEAN NATHAN

TYPE: India pale ale
COLOR: Cloudy golden orange with a pale tan head
SMELL: Like a fresh bouquet of hop flowers
TASTE: The name says it all. If you think you can taste anything after the International Bitterness Army commanded by General Hop Head himself marches across your tongue, more power to you. In this case, defeat never tasted so sweet, or, well, deliciously bitter.
FOOD PAIRING: Pepperoni, sausage, and extra cheese pizza
AVAILABILITY: Year round

OCT
16

Beerfact
All fifty states (and the District of Columbia) have at least one brewery. Ten states have forty or more. They are:

1. California: 221
2. Colorado: 103
3. Washington State: 100
4. Oregon: 93
5. Pennsylvania: 75

6. Michigan: 70
7. Wisconsin: 66
8. New York: 56
9. Ohio: 42
10. Illinois: 41

Stone Brewing Company
1999 Citracado Parkway
Escondido, CA 92029
www.stonebrew.com

🍺 Woodie Gold

"The roots and herbs beaten and put into new ale or beer and daily drunk, cleareth, strengthen, and quicken the sight of the eyes."
—NICHOLAS CULPEPPER

TYPE: Pilsner
COLOR: Golden
SMELL: Warm flour
TASTE: Like drinking liquid bread—lots of milled grain and yeast, followed by clean, crisp hops and a very dry finish. A classic thirst-quenching beer.
FOOD PAIRING: Roasted okra and tomatoes stewed in pimento served over basmati rice with buttered flat bread
AVAILABILITY: Year round

OCT
17

Beerfact

On Oct. 17, 1814, a ruptured tank at the Meux and Company Brewery unleashed more than 3,500 barrels of beer onto the streets of London, creating a wave of beer that knocked down walls, flooded basements, and demolished houses. Eight people drowned. A ninth died of alcohol poisoning, after attempting to stop the flood by drinking the beer.

Karl Strauss Brewing Company
5985 Santa Fe Street
San Diego, CA 92109
www.karlstrauss.com

 Brawler

"Mmmmm. Donuts. Beer. Erotic cakes."
—HOMER SIMPSON

TYPE: Brown ale
COLOR: Light brown
SMELL: Toasted grain and coffee
TASTE: A light- to medium-bodied beer with flavors of sweet toasted malt, mocha bean, caramelized sugar, and ground coffee. It finishes with notes of roasted grain and leaves with a sweet malt aftertaste.
FOOD PAIRING: Kansas City–style smoky ribs
AVAILABILITY: Year round

OCT
18

Beerfact

Sales for the United States beer industry rank thirty-fifth on the global Gross Domestic Product list (meaning that our beer industry makes more money annually than every country on Earth except thirty-four of them). Those same sales roughly equate to the annual cost of the war in Iraq.

Yards Brewing Company
901 N. Delaware Avenue
Philadelphia, PA 19123
www.yardsbrewing.com

HARPOON BREWERY

UFO

"They speak of my drinking but never of my thirst."
—SCOTTISH PROVERB

TYPE: Hefewiezen
COLOR: Cloudy golden
SMELL: Wheat and citrus
TASTE: A soft mouthfeel and a light body, UFO is identified by its yeasty, tart citrus profile. There are notes of light hops that finish clean and refreshing.
FOOD PAIRING: Kosher hot dog with yellow mustard, pickle relish, sport peppers, and a dollop of sauerkraut
AVAILABILITY: Year round

OCT
19

Beerfest
The five beer festivals of Harpoon Brewery:
- **St. Patrick's Day Festival:** First weekend in March.
- **Summer Session:** Outdoor beer drinking and live music. Early June in Boston.
- **Championship of New England BBQ:** End of July at their Windsor, Vermont, brewery.
- **Oktoberfest Boston:** First weekend in October.
- **Oktoberfest Vermont:** Second weekend in October.

Harpoon Brewery
306 Northern Avenue
Boston, MA 02210
www.harpoonbrewery.com

🍺 Barley Wine

Sam: "What's the story, Norm?" Norm: "Boy meets beer.
Boy drinks beer. Boy meets another beer."
  —*CHEERS*

TYPE: Barley wine
COLOR: Deep amber, orange
SMELL: Fruit, malt, and port wine
TASTE: Flavors of sweet dark fruit, rum, and port wine intermingle with roasted barely and chocolate. A touch of bitterness helps balance out what is a primarily sweet beer. It finishes with some vanilla and ends drier than you might expect.
FOOD PAIRING: Roasted walnuts and candied orange peel
AVAILABILITY: Limited release

OCT
20

Beerfact

John Shakespeare, William's father, was appointed as the chief ale tester for the borough of Stratford-upon-Avon in 1556. During the Elizabethan Era (which began shortly after John Shakespeare took his office), at least one of the tests administered to ale included pouring a sample of the beer on top of a small wooden stool. The ale tester would then sit upon the stool while wearing leather pants. If the stool stuck to his rump, then it meant too much sugar had been added to the ale. A stuck seat meant that the landlord would lose his license to brew and sell beer.

Sprecher Brewing Company
701 W. Glendale Avenue
Glendale, WI 53209
www.sprecherbrewery.com

IPA

"They drank this beer with a reed out of the vessel that held the beer, upon which they saw the barley swim."
—XENOPHON

TYPE: India pale ale

COLOR: Deep orange copper

SMELL: Sweet malt, honey, and grapefruit

TASTE: A medium-bodied beer with flavors of sweet malt and caramel up front followed by grapefruit, lemon zest, and pine. Finishes clean and dry with less bitter aftertaste than you might expect.

FOOD PAIRING: Tuna and salmon sashimi set

AVAILABILITY: Year round

OCT

21

Pub*lore*

The little pink elephant is the brand mascot for Delirium Tremens beer brewed by Huyghe Brewery, and he has several pubs that bear his likeness, the original being in Belgium. The Delerium Café in Brussels offers over 2,000 beers from all over the world, a wide selection of gin (including fruit gins), and of course Belgian chocolates.

Visit Delirium Café, Impasse de la Fidelite 4A, 1000 Bruxelles, Brussels, Belgium, *www.deliriumcafe.be/*.

Yards Brewing Company
901 N. Delaware Avenue
Philadelphia, PA 19123
www.yardsbrewing.com

🍺 Anchor Steam Beer

"Of beer, an enthusiast said that it could never be bad but that some brands might be better than others."
   —A. A. MILNE

TYPE: Steam beer

COLOR: Golden amber leaning toward bronze

SMELL: Floral bitterness and maple syrup

TASTE: Crisp, light, and very dry with a pleasantly bitter undertone. A good thirst-quenching summer cooler, this is a quintessential, classic American beer.

FOOD PAIRING: Ham and Camembert sandwich on a French baguette served with ice-cold fruit salad

AVAILABILITY: Year round

**OCT
22**

Brewtip

Lagers are brewed with bottom-fermenting yeast (meaning they do their work near the bottom of the carboy) and work at lower temperatures than ale yeast. This colder fermentation requires strains of yeast that do not die or go dormant at lower temperatures. Many of the most popular styles of lager yeast produce elevated levels of sulfur, which requires that the beer be stored for extended periods in cooler temperatures, known as lagering, in order to help smooth those compounds into a pleasing, crisp flavor. "Steam Beer" was a nineteenth-century nickname for lagers produced on the West Coast without the benefit of ice to help keep the brew cool during fermentation.

Anchor Brewing Company
1705 Mariposa Street
San Francisco, CA 94107
www.anchorbrewing.com

🍺 Victorian IPA

"He is not deserving the name of Englishman who speaketh against ale, that is good ale."
—GEORGE BORROW, AUTHOR

TYPE: India pale ale
COLOR: Dark copper
SMELL: Pine, citrus, and faint cracker
TASTE: A light- to medium-bodied beer with flavors of warm biscuit, pine, citrus, and peppery hops followed by sweet malt.
FOOD PAIRING: Spicy pineapple chicken wings
AVAILABILITY: Year round

OCT
23

Beerthought

Beer coming out of a bottle has been trapped inside a cramped space for who knows how long. Leave your glass on the table and pour your beer straight in. Sure, it's going to foam up. But if you're willing to be patient, you'll get yourself a much denser, creamier head full of delicious, hearty little bubbles. The end result will be a beer that's much closer to one poured off a tap.

Sonoran Brewing Company
10426 East Jomax Road
Scottsdale, AZ 85255
www.sonoranbrewing.com

🍺 Red's Rye PA

"We should look for someone to eat and drink with before looking for something to eat and drink, for dining alone is leading the life of a lion or wolf."
—EPICURUS

TYPE: Rye beer

COLOR: Deep red

SMELL: Citrus and fruity with notes of mango and grapefruit

TASTE: It tastes very similar to its smell, though more complex and sophisticated. Flavors of grapefruit and bitter lemon swirl around notes of sour, spicy rye and sweet malt. There are spikes of fruit at the beginning of each sip, only to be overtaken by the hops in the end.

FOOD PAIRING: Grilled pastrami on swirled rye with sauerkraut and Swiss cheese

AVAILABILITY: Year round

OCT

24

Beerfact

Mike Stevens and Dave Engbers graduated from college and entered the workforce, but dreamed of opening their own brewery. The two started at the old Wolverine Brassworks Building in Grand Rapids, Michigan. It took them nearly a year to get their operation up and going. It's been nearly twenty years since the inception of Founders Brewing, and today they brew more than a dozen tasty beers.

Founders Brewing Company
235 Grandville Avenue SW
Grand Rapids, MI 49503
www.foundersbrewing.com

🍺 O'Brien's Harvest Ale

"I've figured out an alternative to giving up my beer. Basically, we become a family of traveling acrobats."
—HOMER SIMPSON

TYPE: Pale ale
COLOR: Amber
SMELL: Citrus, pine, sweet malt, and yeast
TASTE: A medium- to full-bodied beer with flavors of honey, malt, and freshly baked bread followed by citrus and spicy hops ending with just a touch of bitterness. It rolls smoothly over your tongue and sticks a little to the roof of your mouth.
FOOD PAIRING: Sesame noodles with grilled prawns
AVAILABILITY: Fall seasonal

OCT

25

Beer*words*

Irish drinking toast:

> Here's to the land of the shamrock so green,
> Here's to each lad and his darlin' colleen,
> Here's to the ones we love dearest and most.
> May God bless old Ireland, that's this Irishman's toast!

Hale's Ales
4301 Leary Way NW
Seattle, WA 98107
www.halesbrewery.com

🍺 Buffalo Butt

"Remember, 'i' before 'e' except in Budweiser."
—ANONYMOUS

TYPE: Amber ale
COLOR: Amber
SMELL: Biscuit, caramel, and grassy hops
TASTE: A light- to medium-bodied beer with flavors of sweet malt and toast, followed by pepper and citrus hops and a slightly bitter aftertaste.
FOOD PAIRING: Chicken salad sandwich with thick salt-and-pepper potato chips
AVAILABILITY: Year round

OCT
26

Beerfact

Although wines are generally stored lying on their side, beer should generally be stored upright. This minimizes oxidation, as well as lessening possible contamination from the cap. The exception is if you're lucky enough to have special release beers with cork stoppers. This should be stored on its side.

Rahr And Son's Brewing Company
701 Galveston Avenue
Fort Worth, TX 76104
www.rahrbrewery.com

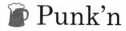 Punk'n

"If beer and women aren't the answer, then you're asking the wrong questions."
—ANONYMOUS

TYPE: Fruit beer

COLOR: Amber

SMELL: Pumpkin, yeast, and spice

TASTE: A light- to medium-bodied beer with flavors of rich caramel, fresh pumpkin, and the spices you'd expect in a pumpkin pie—allspice, cloves, cinnamon, and nutmeg.

FOOD PAIRING: Roast chicken breast and buttered spaghetti squash

AVAILABILITY: Seasonal

OCT

27

Beerfest

2009 Great American Beer Festival Winners by Category

American-Style Lager or Premium Lager: Coors Banquet, Coors Brewing Co., Golden, CO

American-Style Specialty Lager: Keystone Ice, Coors Brewing Co., Golden, CO

Vienna-Style Lager: Vienna Lager, Chuckanut Brewery, Bellingham, WA

German-Style Märzen: Dogtoberfest, Flying Dog Brewery, Frederick, MD

Four + Brewing
1722 South Freemont Drive (2375 West)
Salt Lake City, UT 84104
www.fourplusbrewing.com

🍺 Doppelbock

"There is nothing which has yet been contrived by man by which so much happiness is produced as by a good tavern or inn."
—SAMUEL JOHNSON

TYPE: Bock
COLOR: Dark, rich brown
SMELL: Malt with earthy aromas
TASTE: A robust, powerful beer with little or no taste of hops. Finishes with faint coffee flavor.
FOOD PAIRING: Beef Stroganoff with a salad
AVAILABILITY: Year round

OCT
28

Beerwords

Brewpub: A restaurant-brewery that sells 25 percent or more of its beer on site. The beer is brewed primarily for sale in the restaurant and bar. The beer is often dispensed directly from the brewery's storage tanks. Where allowed by law, brewpubs often sell beer "to go" and /or distribute to off-site accounts. Note: BA re-categorizes a company as a microbrewery if its off-site (distributed) beer sales exceed 75 percent.

—Beertown.org (The Brewer's Association website)

Morgan Street Brewery
721 North Second Street
Saint Louis, MO 63102
www.morganstreetbrewery.com

🍺 Bob's 47 Oktoberfest

"I'm gaining weight the right way: I'm drinking beer."
—JOHNNY DAMON, BASEBALL PLAYER

TYPE: Munich-style lager

COLOR: Dark amber

SMELL: Toasted caramel and spice with a touch of hops

TASTE: Smooth mouthfeel with flavors of toffee butter, toasted malt, risen yeast bread, and a slight nuttiness followed by herbal, floral hop notes and a vanilla finish.

FOOD PAIRING: Roasted lamb with apricot glaze

AVAILABILITY: September to October

OCT

29

Brewtip

Boulevard Brewing Company sold its first keg to a local restaurant in 1989. With no fleet of delivery vehicles, that keg was hand delivered in the back of a pickup truck by the founder of the brewery, John McDonald. Today the company offers six year-round beers and five rotating seasonals. In addition, they produce a small number of limited-edition beers for their "Smokestack Series." All of their beers are bottle conditioned, meaning they add a small amount of yeast to the brew as it is being bottled. They are then held in a temperature-controlled warehouse for an extra two weeks to allow secondary fermentation.

Boulevard Brewing Company
2501 Southwest Blvd.
Kansas City, MO 64108
www.boulevard.com

🍺 Rahr's Red

"Without question, the greatest invention in the history of mankind is beer. Oh, I grant you that the wheel was also a fine invention, but the wheel does not go nearly as well with pizza."
—DAVE BARRY

TYPE: Amber lager
COLOR: Amber
SMELL: Sweet malt and hops
TASTE: A highly drinkable light- to medium-bodied beer with flavors of sweet malt and fresh bread, followed by citrus and grassy hops and a biscuit and cracker aftertaste.
FOOD PAIRING: Grilled sourdough pizza with shredded pepperoni and sunflower seeds
AVAILABILITY: Year round

OCT
30

Beerfact

From the time the first universities were founded in Europe in the twelfth century down to the 1700s, it was common for institutions of higher learning to have their own breweries. Harvard, for example, had its own brewhouse in the seventeenth century. This may go a long way to explain why another feature of early university life was student riots.

Rahr and Son's Brewing Company
701 Galveston Avenue
Fort Worth, TX 76104
www.rahrbrewery.com

 Nosferatu

"I would kill everyone in this room for a drop of sweet beer."

—HOMER SIMPSON

TYPE: Strong red ale

COLOR: Deep crimson with a creamy, bronze head

SMELL: Caramel and sweetness, you can really smell the malted barley in this one.

TASTE: Heavy and rich with a smooth, thick mouthfeel, the bitter hops come out first but are quickly replaced by the sweetness of roasted malt. There are undertones of citrus (grapefruit and orange) and behind it all the taste of toffee.

FOOD PAIRING: Blood-rare steak or an old-world blue-veined cheese.

AVAILABILITY: September through October

OCT
31

Beerthought

The first sip is moist, a little thick. It takes some getting used to. The next draws you in. It's a match, the right type. With the third and forth, the reddish liquid flows freely over your lips. Careful not to take it so quickly that it runs from the sides of your mouth. That's right. Slowly. You have all of eternity to enjoy this sweet ambrosia.

Great Lakes Brewing Company
2516 Market Avenue
Cleveland, OH 44113
www.greatlakesbrewing.com

🍺 Hopsickle Imperial IPA

"Not drunk is he who from the floor,
Can rise alone and still drink more."
—THOMAS LOVE PEACOCK

TYPE: Imperial IPA
COLOR: Orangey gold
SMELL: Both citrus and floral hops
TASTE: A hophead's tonic. There is a thick backbone of rich, syrupy malt that stands strong as wave after wave of pine, citrus, and floral hops crash down on your taste buds. Over 100 IBU.
FOOD PAIRING: Cranberry and almond–stuffed pork loin
AVAILABILITY: Year round

NOV

1

Beerfact

During Prohibition, speakeasies were often referred to as a Blind Tiger because of their practice of charging patrons a fee to come inside and see the "blind tiger." Once inside, guests would receive a complimentary cocktail—thus circumnavigating the laws about selling alcoholic beverages. Eventually, it became common practice for speakeasies to place a stuffed tiger in their front windows, notifying their customer base that they had a fresh shipment of alcohol and were open for business.

Molyan's Brewery
15 Rowland Way
Novato, CA 94945
www.moylans.com

🍺 L'il Bandit Brown

"Drink is the feast of reason and the flow of soul."
—ALEXANDER POPE

TYPE: Brown ale

COLOR: Dark amber

SMELL: Butter toast and sweet malt

TASTE: A light-bodied beer that's hoppy and clean with notes of honey and warm bread followed by a burnt toffee aftertaste.

FOOD PAIRING: Hot-and-sour soup

AVAILABILITY: Year round

NOV

2

Beerfest

2009 Great American Beer Festival Winners by Category

Robust Porter: Pt. Reyes Porter, Marin Brewing Co., Larkspur, CA

Classic Irish-Style Dry Stout: Dark Starr Stout, Starr Hill Brewery, Crozet, VA

Foreign-Style Stout: Space Stout, Laurelwood Brewing Co., Portland, OR

American-Style Stout: Liberty Stout, Gella's Diner and Lb. Brewing Co., Hays, KS

Northwoods Brewpub
3560 Oakwood Mall Drive
Eau Claire, WI 54701
www.northwoodsbrewpub.com

 Siberian Night

"I usually need a can of beer to prime me."
—NORMAN MAILER

TYPE: Imperial stout
COLOR: Black
SMELL: Sweet malt and dark fruit with a whiff of chocolate and caramel
TASTE: Flavors of dark-roasted coffee, baking chocolate, freshly made caramel, hard toffee, spun sugar, and even oatmeal. The finish is a little bitter and crisp leaving a dry, slightly alcoholic finish.
FOOD PAIRING: Grilled, buttered corn
AVAILABILITY: Year round

NOV

3

Brew*tip*

Popular hop varieties and their primary use in brewing beer:

Hallertau: (Both) 4–6% alpha acids
Liberty: (Finishing) 4–5% alpha acids
Lublin: (Finishing) 3–5% alpha acids
Mt. Hood: (Finishing) 4–6% alpha acids
Northdown: (Both) 8–11% alpha acids

Thirsty Dog Brewing Company
529 Grant Street, Suite B
Akron, OH 44311
www.thirstydog.com

🍺 Drifter

"When we drink, we get drunk. When we get drunk, we fall asleep. When we fall asleep, we commit no sin. When we commit no sin, we go to heaven. Sooooo, let's all get drunk and go to heaven!"
—BRIAN O'ROURKE

NOV

4

TYPE: Pale ale

COLOR: Amber

SMELL: Clove, unbleached flour, dandelion, and citrus

TASTE: This light-bodied beer has a number of fruit esters that are easy to taste. Flavors of ripe apricots and pureed nectarines blend well with just a touch of baked cracker.

FOOD PAIRING: Cracked black peppercorn–rubbed flank steak fajitas

AVAILABILITY: Year round

Beerfact

According to Guinness World Records, the largest useable beer vessel measures 17 feet 8 inches tall and has a circumference of 27 feet 6 inches. It was on display in 2007 in Poznan, Poland, at the entrance to a newly renovated nineteenth-century brewery. Made entirely out of bronze, during its unveiling the tankard was fitted with taps and filled with 8,000 liters of Lech, which was served to those who came to the opening celebration.

Widmer Brothers Brewing Company
929 N. Russell Street
Portland, OR 97227
www.widmer.com

🍺 Tire Bite Golden Ale

"Of all meat in the world, drink goes down the best."
—PROVERB

TYPE: Kölsch
COLOR: Golden
SMELL: Yeast, apricot, and subtle hops
TASTE: Light bodied, easy to drink with flavors of fresh stone fruit.
FOOD PAIRING: Cornbread hushpuppies
AVAILABILITY: Year round

Beer*thought*

While mountain climbing in Tibet, a couple of ranchers stopped in a local bar for a drink. One of them noticed "a painting in the Flashman Hotel of a Flying Dog hanging on the wall that had been drawn by a local artist. Now, we all know dogs don't fly, but nobody told this particular dog it couldn't fly, just like no one had told George and his friends they couldn't make this extraordinary journey."
—from Flyingdogales.com

Flying Dog Brewery
4607 Wedgewood Blvd.
Frederick, MD 21703
www.flyingdogales.com

🍺 Ouachita ESB

"Beer. Now there's a temporary solution."
—HOMER SIMPSON

TYPE: Extra special bitter

COLOR: Reddish amber

SMELL: Mild fruit notes along with the sweet scent of caramel malt and just a touch of bitter hops

TASTE: This medium-bodied beer starts out with the sweet flavors of caramel and toffee malt only to be followed in a split second by a huge wave of earthy, grassy, spicy hops.

FOOD PAIRING: Grilled pork apple bratwurst served with salted sweet potato fries

AVAILABILITY: Year round

NOV

6

Beerthought

Clicking through the website for Vino's Brewpub, one might encounter their "Brief Overview of the History of Beer":

"Before civilization some lucky caveman (or woman, more than likely) discovered a bowl of grain mush that had been sitting out for a few days after a rain, drank the frothy liquid, enjoyed the ensuing euphoria and beer brewing was born."

Vino's Brewpub
923 West 7th Street
Little Rock, AR 72201
www.vinosbrewpub.com

🍺 Vienna Lager

Woody: "Hey, Mr. Peterson. Jack Frost nipping at your nose?" Norm: "Yep. Now let's get Joe Beer nipping at my liver."

—CHEERS

TYPE: Amber lager

COLOR: Amber

SMELL: Sweet malt and just a hint of citrus

TASTE: Medium bodied and quite easy to drink, this one leads with a host of roasted sweet malt that fades slowly into a crisp, clean finish of fresh, artisanal bread and dried fruit.

FOOD PAIRING: Beer-battered fish and chips with vinegar and salt

AVAILABILITY: Year round on draft

NOV

7

Beerfood
MICROBREW BEER BATTER

¾ cup flour

¾ cup cornstarch

½ teaspoon baking soda

1 tablespoon powdered sugar

2 teaspoons salt

½ teaspoon white pepper

½ teaspoon garlic powder

¼ teaspoon dry dill

½ teaspoon lemon zest

½ teaspoon red chili flakes

¾ cup amber lager

½ cup water

Mix all dry ingredients. Add beer then water and mix until smooth. If necessary, add more beer or water in small quantities until you reach a batter consistency that clings to your finger but doesn't cake on.

River City Brewing Company
545 Downtown Plaza, Suite 1115
Sacramento, CA 95814
www.rivercitybrewing.net

🍺 Tule Duck Red Ale

"Prohibition makes you want to cry into your beer and denies you the beer to cry into."
—DON MARQUIS, AUTHOR

TYPE: Red ale
COLOR: Red/amber
SMELL: Oranges and limes
TASTE: A clean, crisp, light-bodied, easy-to-drink beer with citrus flavors and an undercurrent of sour apple.
FOOD PAIRING: Bacon-wrapped scallops
AVAILABILITY: Year round

NOV

8

Beerfact

Buckbean Brewing Company takes its name from the buckbean plant, an herb that grows in mountain bogs throughout North America, Europe, and Asia. The leaves of this plant have been used throughout the centuries as a remedy for scurvy, a treatment for stomach ailments, and also as a replacement for hops in brewing beer.

Buckbean Brewing Company
1155 S. Rock Blvd., Suite 490
Reno, NV 89502
www.buckbeanbeer.com

🍺 Bellingham Blonde

"When the hour is nigh me, let me in a tavern die, with tankard by me."
—ANONYMOUS

TYPE: Blonde
COLOR: Hazy dark yellow
SMELL: Sweet malt, floral hops, and spice
TASTE: A light-bodied, easy-drinking beer for those few days in Washington when the sun actually shines. There are flavors of grapefruit, grain, and grass (a Bellingham staple), and it finishes with a touch of apple.
FOOD PAIRING: African peanut soup
AVAILABILITY: Year round

NOV
9

Beerfact

There is in fact no federal law limiting the sale and possession of alcohol to those over the age of twenty-one. Each state has the right and responsibility to set its own limit. The states are, however, being coerced by the National Minimum Drinking Age Act, which was passed in 1984. The act recognizes the state's authority to set their own limits but provides for a 10 percent decrease in federally supplied highway funding to those states that do not set that limit at twenty-one years of age.

Boundary Bay Brewery
1107 Railroad Avenue
Bellingham, WA 9225
www.bbaybrewery.com

🍺 Edmund Fitzgerald

*"And later that night when his lights went out of sight,
Came the wreck of the Edmund Fitzgerald."*
    —GORDON LIGHTFOOT

TYPE: Porter
COLOR: Dark, dark brown, like a French press full of perfectly roasted coffee
SMELL: Rich and oily with a fair amount of malt
TASTE: Strong with a bittersweet chocolate flavor that drifts into a long coffee aftertaste
FOOD PAIRING: Applewood-smoked pork chops
AVAILABILITY: Year round

NOV
10

Beer*thought*

The legend lives on from the border towns on down,
Of the big beer they call Great Lakes Porter.
The beer it was said never goes to your head,
When you've lost track of how many you've ordered.

Take a few extra sips, and wet up your lips,
Then sit back and rest on your barrel.
'Cause later that night, when you've turned out the lights,
You'll be cravin' more Edmund Fitzgerald!

Great Lakes Brewing Company
2516 Market Avenue
Cleveland, OH 44113
www.greatlakesbrewing.com

🍺 Amber Ale

"You can only drink thirty or forty glasses of beer a day, no matter how rich you are."
—COLONEL ADOLPHUS BUSCH

TYPE: Amber ale

COLOR: Cloudy rusty red

SMELL: Yeast and sweet malt, floral hops, and lavender

TASTE: A terrific mixture of orange and sweet citrus flavors blended together with bitter flower, balanced out in the end by sweet honey and malt.

FOOD PAIRING: Sweet-and-sour orange honey chicken with sesame seeds

AVAILABILITY: Year round

NOV
11

Brewtip

The oldest craft brewer east of Boulder, Colorado, Bell's Brewery was founded as the Kalamazoo Brewing Company in 1983, originally a homebrewing supply shop. Then in 1985, using a fifteen-gallon soup kettle as the cornerstone of its brewing operation, Bell's sold its first beer. The following year, its operation having expanded, it produced 135 barrels of delicious fermented malt beverage. Growing steadily, the brewery pushed onward, and by 2007 it was producing more than 90,000 barrels a year. Today, its brewing facilities can put out a whopping 140,000 barrels per annum.

Bell's Brewery
8938 Krum Avenue
Galesburg, MI 49053
www.bellsbeer.com

🍺 Yeti Imperial Stout

"Ah, the college road trip. What better way to spread beer-fueled mayhem?"
—HOMER SIMPSON

TYPE: Russian imperial stout
COLOR: Black
SMELL: Chocolate and coffee
TASTE: It comes on strong with flavors of smooth, melted sweet milk chocolate, bitter baking chocolate, molasses, and dark roasted malt.
FOOD PAIRING: Cubed steak grilled on rosemary skewers
AVAILABILITY: Year round

NOV
12

Beerfood
BEER AND SWEET POTATO WAFFLES

1½ cups flour
1 tablespoon baking powder
½ teaspoon salt
3 eggs, separated
½ cup milk
½ cup Stout

2 tablespoons bourbon
1 cup mashed sweet potato
2 tablespoons melted butter
Pinch each of nutmeg, ginger, and cinnamon

Sift together flour, baking powder, and salt. Beat the egg yolks and mix with milk, stout, bourbon, sweet potatoes, melted butter, and remaining spices. Mix with dry ingredients. Beat egg whites until soft peaks form, and fold into batter. Cook in a waffle iron.

Great Divide Brewing Company
2201 Arapahoe Street
Denver, CO 80205
www.greatdivide.com

🍺 Live Oak Pilz

"Drink moderately, for drunkenness neither keeps a secret nor observes a promise."
—MIGUEL DE CERVANTES

TYPE: Pilsner
COLOR: Golden
SMELL: Floral, piney hop resins with a hint of pepper
TASTE: This light- to medium-bodied beer starts off with flavors of biscuit and cracker, sweet malt, and yeast, followed by spicy, bitter hops that grow into tart citrus and dandelion.
FOOD PAIRING: Lamb carpaccio with a scallion ginger sauce
AVAILABILITY: Year round

NOV
13

Brewtip

The founders of Live Oak Brewing stick to a brewing style employed extensively throughout Germany and the Czech Republic. They use a decoction mash, which involves boiling part of the mash in a separate vessel and then adding it back in to raise the temperature of the entire batch, thus bringing out flavors normally unachievable with different mashing methods. Additionally, they use open fermentation and secondary lagering to get the rich maltiness, fuller development of tastes, and unique flavor profiles found in central European beers.

Live Oak Brewing Company
3301 E. 5th Street #B
Austin, TX 78702
www.liveoakbrewing.com

🍺 Perkulator

"Of doctors and medicines we have in plenty more than enough . . . For the Love of God, send us some large quantity of beer."
—DISPATCH FROM THE COLONY OF NEW SOUTH WALES, AUSTRALIA, 1854

NOV

14

TYPE: Dopplebock
COLOR: Dark murky brown
SMELL: Coffee and earthy hops
TASTE: Soft and smooth, medium bodied with flavors of coffee, toasted malts, and caramel. Overall a rather crisp beer that showcases the coffee it is brewed with quite nicely.
FOOD PAIRING: Lemongrass chicken
AVAILABILITY: Fall

Publore

Claiming to be the last original remaining beer garden in New York City, the Bohemian Hall and Beer Garden is now under the care of the Bohemian Citizens Benevolent Society. The building itself is huge, with plenty of hallways and rooms to explore after you've had one too many. There is an ample outdoor garden for leisurely enjoying your stein of beer or for catching the occasional Czech concert or festival.

Visit the Bohemian Hall and Beer Garden at 29-19 24th Avenue, Queens, NY 11102, *www.bohemianhall.com.*

Dark Horse Brewing Company
511 S. Kalamazoo Avenue
Marshall, MI 49068
www.darkhorsebrewery.com

🍺 Dale's Pale Ale

"In wine there is wisdom. In beer there is strength. In water there is bacteria."
—GERMAN SAYING

TYPE: Pale ale

COLOR: Rich amber

SMELL: Floral hops and fresh bread

TASTE: Medium bodied with nice citrus hops that build to a crescendo then gently, ever so slowly, fade. Underneath there are flavors of heavily roasted rich malt and caramel that appear but are quickly swept away by the hoppy goodness.

FOOD PAIRING: Kobe beef burger with caramelized onions and Swiss cheese

AVAILABILITY: Year round

NOV
15

Brewtip

In 2002 Oskar Blues became the first microbrewery to can their own beer. Their first canning line (really a small tabletop machine) allowed them to fill and can only two cans at a time. Today they can put out 160 cans per minute. Modern cans are coated with a special water-based polymer, completely separating the beer from the metal so no reaction or taste degradation can take place. The metal doesn't let in any damaging light, which can change the flavor of the hops to something similar to sucking on a skunk. And cans are lighter and easier to ship, which means a smaller carbon footprint.

Oskar Blues Brewery
1800 Pike Road, Unit B
Longmont, CO 80501
www.oskarblues.com

🍺 Bigfoot Barleywine Style Ale

"Religions change. Beer and wine remain."
—HERVEY ALLEN, AUTHOR

NOV
16

TYPE: Barley wine
COLOR: Cloudy brown with a touch of red
SMELL: Caramel, toffee, and dried fruit
TASTE: A medium-bodied beer with flavors of toffee chips and warm butterscotch, followed by dried pineapple and grapefruit hops.
FOOD PAIRING: Humboldt Fog goat's milk cheese
AVAILABILITY: Special release

Beerfact

Things you probably didn't know about Sierra Nevada:

After studying chemistry and physics in college, Sierra Nevada founder Ken Grossman began on his road to brewing fame by opening a retail store called The Home Brew Shop in Chico, California. The company is named for Ken's favorite backpacking spot—the Sierra Nevada Mountains. The brewery was started in 1979, and the first batch of beer, Sierra Nevada Pale Ale, was brewed on November 15, 1980.

Sierra Nevada Brewing Company
1075 East 20th Street
Chico, CA 95928
www.sierranevada.com

 Perseus

"When I die, I want to decompose in a barrel of porter and have it served in all the pubs in Dublin."
—J. P. DONLEAVY, AUTHOR

TYPE: Porter
COLOR: Dark, dark brown, almost black
SMELL: Cocoa powder and roasted malt
TASTE: Medium- to full-bodied beer with lots of chocolate and coffee flavors. There are notes of smoke and dried cherry fruit leather along with just a touch of citrusy hops. Very smooth aftertaste.
FOOD PAIRING: Maple-cured ham steaks with grilled apple
AVAILABILITY: Year round

NOV
17

Beerfact

Porters are dark, rich beers first produced in England. They get their name from their reputed popularity among the men who would transport goods from ships arriving in port to their final destinations. These thick, hearty beers not only kept them warm on blustery winter days, but they also provided a quick boost of sugar to their system, allowing them to carry their heavy loads across the city. Particularly thick or potent versions of this beer were often called "Extra" or "Stout" porters. Eventually these heavier versions took on a life of their own.

Elysian Brewing
1221 E. Pike Street
Seattle, WA 98122
www.elysianbrewing.com

🍺 Centurion Barleywine

"Lord, let me be virtuous. But not just yet."
    —ST. AUGUSTINE

TYPE: Barley wine

COLOR: Cloudy amber brown

SMELL: Caramel, chocolate, molasses, and a touch of tobacco

TASTE: A medium-bodied beer with flavors of sweet malt, caramel, roasted nuts, dried cherries and raisins followed by a rummy finish and a bitter aftertaste.

FOOD PAIRING: Smoked ham and Gruyère sandwich on soft brown bread

AVAILABILITY: Limited release—once a year

NOV

18

Beersaint

Augustine of Hippo (born November 13, 354 c.e., died August 28, 430 c.e.)

The Bishop of Hippo Regius was a Berber theologian and philosopher. Though he did not practice Christianity until later life, he is credited with coming up with the now canonical concepts of "original sin" and "just war." More importantly, however, he was known for his wild living and alcoholic beverage consumption prior to his conversion, and his change to a moderation-driven lifestyle afterward contributed to his becoming a patron saint of brewers.

Golden City Brewery
920 12th Street
Golden, CO 80401
www.gcbrewery.com

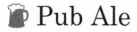 Pub Ale

"Homer no function beer well without."
—HOMER SIMPSON

TYPE: Brown ale
COLOR: Translucent deep brown
SMELL: Toasted fresh bread and dark fruit
TASTE: A lighter-bodied beer with flavors of toasted bread, caramel, and nutty sweet malt. It's balanced by notes of citrus and grass, ending with a crisp sweetness.
FOOD PAIRING: Beef sliders with vinegar and salt potato chips
AVAILABILITY: Year round

**NOV
19**

Beerwords

English drinking song from the 18th century:

> Let us sing our own treasures, Old England's good cheer,
> To the profits and pleasures of stout British beer;
> Your wine-tippling, dram-sipping fellows retreat,
> But your beer-drinking Britons can never be beat.

Sprecher Brewing Company
701 W. Glendale Avenue
Glendale, WI 53209
www.sprecherbrewery.com

🍺 Naughty Nellie

"They who drink beer will think beer."
—WASHINGTON IRVING

TYPE: Golden artisan ale
COLOR: Golden copper
SMELL: Citrus and hops
TASTE: Primarily malt with citrus peel, Nellie is well balanced and quite refreshing. The light fruitiness makes it crisp and easy to drink. Not a challenging beer, but one for a relaxing afternoon with friends.
FOOD PAIRING: Turkey, bacon, black olives, and jack cheese Cobb salad
AVAILABILITY: Year round

Beerfact

Named for Nellie Curtis, a businesswoman and madam who started her operations in Seattle in 1933—the same year beer became legalized after Prohibition—Naughty Nellie is a nod to the history of the building where Pike Brewing stands today. In 1942, Nellie opened the LaSalle Hotel, just a stone's throw from the already famous Pike Place Market. Pike Brewing was founded in the LaSalle building in 1989 (long after the brothel had become defunct).

The Pike Brewing Company
1415 First Avenue
Seattle, WA 98122
www.pikebrewing.com

🍺 Bam Bière

"St George he was for England, And before he killed the dragon, He drank a pint of English ale, Out of an English flagon."
—G. K. CHESTERTON

TYPE: Farmhouse ale
COLOR: Cloudy orange
SMELL: Yeast, lemon zest, and spice
TASTE: Loads of flavors ranging from crabapple to cinnamon and clove to bitter citrus and grass with an earthy, yeasty undertone and notes of bitter floral hops.
FOOD PAIRING: Fresh diver scallops sautéed in butter and lemon served with black pepper risotto
AVAILABILITY: Year round

NOV
21

Brew*tip*
Popular hop varieties and their primary use in brewing beer:

Bramling Cross: (Finishing) 5–7% alpha acids
British Columbia Goldings: (Finishing) 4–6% alpha acids
Centennial: (Both) 9–11% alpha acids
Chinook: (Bittering) 11–14% alpha acids
Columbus: (Both) 12–16% alpha acids
Eroica: (Both) 10–14% alpha acids

Jolly Pumpkin Artisan Ales
3115 Broad Street
Dexter, MI 48130
www.jollypumpkin.com

🍺 Oatis Oatmeal Stout

"There is nothing for a case of nerves like a case of beer."
—JOAN GOLDSTEIN, AUTHOR

TYPE: Oatmeal stout
COLOR: Deep brown
SMELL: Chocolate, coffee, and a touch of alcohol
TASTE: Silky smooth, almost oily, this beer features a rich chocolate flavor accented by deep-roasted coffee and melted caramel. Hints of butterscotch and hops make an appearance before disappearing into a mocha aftertaste.
FOOD PAIRING: Smoked turkey leg and sage stuffing
AVAILABILITY: Year round

NOV

22

Beerfest
2009 Great American Beer Festival Winners by Category
American-Style Amber Lager: Durango Colorfest, Durango Brewing Co., Durango, CO
European-Style Dunkel: Dunkel, Chuckanut Brewery, Bellingham, WA
American-Style Dark Lager: Session Black Premium Lager, Full Sail Brewing at Riverplace, Portland, OR
German-Style Schwarzbier: Schwarzbier, Iron Hill Brewery & Restaurant, Wilmington, DE

Ninkasi Brewing Company
272 Van Buren Street
Eugene, OR 97402
www.ninkasibrewing.com

 Dark

"People who drink light 'beer' don't like the taste of beer; they just like to pee a lot."
—CAPITAL BREWERY

TYPE: Munich dunkel
COLOR: Brown amber
SMELL: Sweet malt, yeast, and a hint of chocolate
TASTE: A complex blend of rich malt, brown sugar, and spicy hops that finishes dry and clean on a bitter, hoppy note.
FOOD PAIRING: Lobster bisque
AVAILABILITY: Year round

NOV
23

Beerfact
Legally acceptable blood alcohol concentration in drivers:

Argentina .05%	Israel .05%
Australia .05%	Krygystan .05%
Belarus .05%	Latvia .05%
Belgium .05%	Mauritius .05%
Cambodia .05%	Philippines .05%
Denmark .05%	South Korea .05%
El Salvador .05%	Thailand .05%
Finland .05%	Uganda .05%
Iceland .05%	

Capital Brewery
7734 Terrace Avenue
Middleton, WI 53562
www.capital-brewery.com

🍺 Old Thumper

"I fear the man who drinks water and so remembers this morning what the rest of us said last night."
—GREEK PROVERB

TYPE: Extra special bitter
COLOR: Burnt orange
SMELL: An undercurrent of vanilla after bready malt and light floral hops
TASTE: Pronounced yeast with an almost brown sugar malt, like liquid toffee and thick roasted malt. There are hints of citrus that come out as the toffee fades into butterscotch.
FOOD PAIRING: BBQ baby back pork ribs smothered in a rich, spicy, smoky sauce
AVAILABILITY: Year round

NOV

24

Beer*fact*

Founded in 1992 by master brewer Alan Pugsley, Shipyard Brewery is Maine's largest brewery and now ships over a million cases of beer a year. That's almost 82,000 barrels, but the facility they are in today has the capacity to put out a whopping 140,000 barrels of beer a year. That's 4.34 million gallons, or almost enough to fill seven Olympic-size swimming pools.

The Shipyard Brewing Company
86 Newbury Street
Portland, ME 04101
www.shipyard.com

🍺 Moloko Milk Stout

"Prohibition has divided our people into factions almost as bitterly hostile to each other as the factions that existed before the Civil War."
—WILLIAM RANDOLPH HEARST

TYPE: Milk stout
COLOR: Obsidian
SMELL: Coffee and sweet tree fruit
TASTE: Smooth, thick beer with flavors of toasted cocoa bean and dark coffee. The milk added to this beer during the brewing process adds sweet sugars that blend nicely with the other dark, roasted flavors.
FOOD PAIRING: Chocolate tiramisu
AVAILABILITY: Seasonal

**NOV
25**

Beerfact

The Great Depression, though not so named because it occurred in the middle of Prohibition, did in fact play a part in the repeal of the Eighteenth Amendment. The temperance movement that had been the main motivation behind the restricting of the manufacture and sale of alcohol lost much of its momentum as people struggled to get by and looked for ways to forget their troubles. As a result, on March 23, 1933, President Franklin Roosevelt signed into law the Cullen-Harrison Act, which allowed the legal manufacture and sale of alcohol in the United States.

Three Floyds Brewery
9570 Indiana Parkway
Munster, IN 46321
www.threefloydspub.com

🍺 Red Trolley Ale

"May your glass ever be full. May the roof over your head be always strong. And may you be in heaven half an hour before the devil knows you're dead."

—IRISH PROVERB

TYPE: Amber ale

COLOR: Copper

SMELL: Caramel and rising bread dough

TASTE: A solid, medium-bodied beer with a lot of toffee maltiness and a slightly sweet finish.

FOOD PAIRING: Spicy jambalaya with smoked chicken sausage

AVAILABILITY: Year round

NOV
26

Beer*fact*

The first metal beverage cans were made out of steel and had no pull-tab. Instead, you made two holes with a can piercer (known often as a church key), one large one for drinking out of and one smaller one to allow in air. In 1956, steel cans gave way to lighter, less expensive aluminum versions, but it wasn't until 1962 that Ermal Cleon Fraze of Dayton, Ohio, invented the pull-tab version, which could be opened without a separate device. In 1975, Daniel F. Cudzik of Reynolds Metal developed the version common today.

Karl Strauss Brewing Company
5985 Santa Fe Street
San Diego, CA 92109
www.karlstrauss.com

🍺 Anniversary Barley Wine

"I'd rather have a bottle in front of me than a frontal lobotomy."
—TOM WAITS, MUSICIAN

TYPE: Barley wine
COLOR: Mahogany
SMELL: Caramel, sweet malt, pine, and earth
TASTE: A medium- to full-bodied beer with flavors of citrus and pine hops followed by a warm caramel, baked apple, and brown sugar. It finishes with a touch of alcoholic warmth and a faint bitter aftertaste.
FOOD PAIRING: Baked chicken breast stuffed with apple, bacon, and goat cheese
AVAILABILITY: Year round

NOV
27

Beerfact

Uinta Brewing company is one of the fifty largest craft brewers in the United States, brewing and packaging over 20,000 barrels of beer a year. Small batches of the Anniversary Barley Wine were first brewed to commemorate the brewery's fifth year of producing fermented beverages. That was 1998, and the call for more of this thick, rich, delicious beer has gone up every year since.

Uinta Brewing Company
1722 South Fremont Drive (2375 West)
Salt Lake City, UT 84104
www.uintabrewing.com

🍺 Spruce Goose

"I want to be an old man with a beer belly sitting on a porch, looking at a lake or something."
—JOHNNY DEPP

NOV
28

TYPE: American strong ale

COLOR: Ruby orange

SMELL: Juniper, spruce, and spice

TASTE: Brewed from an old Viking recipe that incorporates spruce and pine. It starts out with a wall of sweet malt laced with vanilla that fades into a nice sour bite. The spruce flavor becomes more noticeable in the finish and when the beer warms a bit.

FOOD PAIRING: Fresh strawberries and peaches

AVAILABILITY: November through January

Beerfact

Why not train to become a brewer? Here are several very prestigious brewers schools:

- American Brewers Guild, Vermont, USA (*www.abgbrew.com*)
- Master Brewers Association of America, Minnesota, USA (*www .mbaa.com*)
- Siebel Institute of Technology, Illinois, USA (*www.siebelinstitute.com*)
- University of California-Davis, California, USA (*www.extension .ucdavis.edu/brewing*)

Steamworks Brewing Company
442 Wolverine Drive
Bayfield, CO 81122
www.steamworksbrewing.com

🍺 Cordillera Blanca

Norm: "Women. Can't live with 'em. Pass the beer nuts."
—CHEERS

TYPE: Fruit beer
COLOR: Dark yellow, golden
SMELL: Chocolate
TASTE: A light-bodied, easy-drinking beer that features flavors of chocolate, hazelnut, and vanilla against a light grain sweetness.
FOOD PAIRING: White-chocolate dipped rice crispy bar on a stick
AVAILABILITY: Year round

NOV
29

Publore

In the heart of Beijing, China, under a series of beer tents, sits an interesting comingling of old-world beer garden and new-world Asian economy. Wudaokou Beer Garden is a hangout for local students and explorers alike.

Visit the Wudaokou Beer Garden, Chengfu Lu, Wudaokou, west of the Wudaokou subway stop, Bejing, China.

Sonoran Brewing Company
10426 East Jomax Road
Scottsdale, AZ 85255
www.sonoranbrewing.com

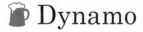 Dynamo

"Gimme a pigsfoot and a bottle of beer."
—JANIS JOPLIN

TYPE: Copper lager
COLOR: Copper
SMELL: Sweet caramel and yeast
TASTE: A medium-bodied beer with a creamy mouthfeel and flavors of caramel, sweet malt, and grain that are balanced out nicely in the end by a smooth hoppy bitterness. An enjoyable, easy-to-drink beer.
FOOD PAIRING: Hot buttered corn on the cob
AVAILABILITY: Year round

NOV
30

Beer*words*
Beer toasts of the world:

Arabic: *Shucram*
Bengali: *Joy*
Costa Rican: *Pura Vida*
Estonian: *Tei terviseks*
French: *A votre santé*

Greek: *Eis igian*
Hawaiian: *Hipahipa*
Lithuanian: *I Sveikata*
Malaysian: *Minum*
Polish: *Na zdrowie*

Metropolitan Brewing Company
5121 N. Ravenswood Avenue
Chicago, IL 60640
www.metrobrewing.com

🍺 Heavy Seas Below Decks

"Embrace your inner pyrate!"
—MOTTO OF CLIPPER CITY BEER

TYPE: Barley wine
COLOR: Amber
SMELL: Malt, yeast, and caramel
TASTE: A medium-bodied beer with a smooth and creamy mouthfeel. There are flavors of dark fruit, thick, rich malt, and freshly baked brown bread with just a touch of alcohol as well.
FOOD PAIRING: Chocolate bread pudding with walnuts and brandied raisins
AVAILABILITY: December only

DEC

1

Beerfest

Locals in Munich will fondly refer to Oktoberfest as "die Wiesen" because of its location, Theresienwiese, which was named after Therese von Sachsen-Hildburghausen *(www.oktoberfest.de/en/)*. The big highlight of the Wiesen events is the Oktoberfest Costume and Riflemen's Parade, which occurs on the first Sunday of the festival. Other important events include the Parade of Oktoberfest Landlords and Breweries, the Official Tapping of the Keg, the Oktoberfest Mass, and Böllerschießen (hand-held canon salute).

Clipper City Brewing Company
4615 Hollins Ferry Road, Suite B
Baltimore, MD 21227
www.ccbeer.com

🍺 Smooth Hoperator

*"If you ever reach total enlightenment while drinking beer,
I bet it makes beer shoot out your nose."*
—JACK HANDY, DEEP THOUGHT

TYPE: Dopplebock
COLOR: Clear red amber color with a thick tan head
SMELL: Bready and yeasty, with a light pine smell over the top
TASTE: Sweet, subtle malt taste. A flood of spun burnt sugar that accents the nice hoppy bitterness.
FOOD PAIRING: Muscles steamed in garlic, celery, and beer, then finished with cream. Sop up the juice with a crusty French bread.
AVAILABILITY: Seasonal

DEC

2

Brew*tip*

Called an "American Dopplebock," Ed Stoudt belives this beer to be the very first high-gravity lager brewed with German malts and American hops. At 7.2% ABV and 50 IBU, this beer packs a punch of both flavor and intoxicating goodness. And like all of Stoudt's beers, Hoperator is made with the soft, slightly acidic water the flows from the nearby aquifer in the Pennsylvania hills behind the brewery.

Stoudt's Brewing Company
Route 272
2800 North Reading Road
Adamstown, PA 19501
www.stoudtsbeer.com

 Rochefort 6

"Things don't make me nearly as happy as talking and having a beer with my friends."
—DREW CAREY

TYPE: Belgian strong dark ale
COLOR: Golden-tinged amber
SMELL: Dried cherries, caramel, and earthy hops
TASTE: A medium-bodied beer with flavors of yeast, sweet malt, tart apple, and citrus. Finishes dry with just a touch of sourness.
FOOD PAIRING: Greek gyros with tzaziki sauce
AVAILABILITY: Year round

DEC

3

Beerfact

The monks at the Abbay Notre-Dame de Saint-Remy, which houses the Brasserie de Rochefort, have been brewing beers since 1899. Rochefort 6, originally called Middel, was started in 1953. Rochefort 10, originally known as Merveille, was created the same year. And Rochefort 8 or Spécial, which first appeared in 1955, is today the largest of their production, weighing in at 60% of their total output.

Brasserie de Rochefort
B–5580 Rochefort
Belgium
www.trappistes-rochefort.com

🍺 Red Ale

"For he by geometric scale, Could take the size of pots of ale."
—SAMUEL BUTLER

TYPE: Amber ale

COLOR: Dark red

SMELL: Lots of dry hops

TASTE: Fruit flavors and melted caramel mix well with the spice and grapefruit that comes from the resin-heavy hops. There is a long, balanced aftertaste of both hops and lingering roasted malt.

FOOD PAIRING: Lamb stew with orange zest and cracked black pepper

AVAILABILITY: Year round

Brewtip

Brewing additives:

- **Ascorbic acid:** Ascorbic acid reduces oxidization but can add a citrusy flavor if too much is used.
- **Calcium carbonate:** Adding this to your beer will raise the pH level.
- **Citric acid:** Clarifies or reduces the haze in your beer. Also helps bring the pH levels into balance.

Marble Brewery
111 Marble Avenue NW
Albuquerque, NM 87102
www.marblebrewery.com

🍺 Pale 31

"I believe this would be a good time for a beer."
—FRANKLIN ROOSEVELT, ON SIGNING THE TWENTY-FIRST
AMENDMENT, WHICH REPEALED PROHIBITION

TYPE: Pale ale
COLOR: Golden
SMELL: Citrus hops and honey
TASTE: A nicely balanced beer with flavors of mandarin orange and
grapefruit, paired against warm caramel and sweet malt. Smooth to
drink with a medium body, it finishes with a hint of freshly baked bread
and a smooth citrus aftertaste.
FOOD PAIRING: Tandoori chicken and potato pancakes
AVAILABILITY: Year round

DEC

5

Brewtip

Created out of a desire by English brewers to offer alternatives to the
darker, thicker, more heavily roasted beers that dominated the pubs of
the day, pale ales were really only made possible by an advance in grain-
roasting technology. Once it was discovered that certain processed coals
would not only burn clean but also produce a steady temperature, it then
became possible to roast barley to a light color—which produced a
lighter, or pale-looking, brew.

Firestone Walker Brewing Company
1400 Ramada Drive
Paso Robles, CA 93446
www.firestonewalker.com

🍺 Ten Fidy

"A good local pub has much in common with a church, except that a pub is warmer and there's more conversation."
—WILLIAM BLAKE, POET

TYPE: Imperial stout
COLOR: Oily black
SMELL: Molasses, brown sugar, and a touch of alcohol
TASTE: A thick, viscous, full-bodied beer with flavors of brown sugar, roasted malt, bitter cocoa, coffee, caramel, even notes of bourbon and dried plum.
FOOD PAIRING: Handmade gnocchi served in a brown butter sauce
AVAILABILITY: Winter seasonal

DEC

6

Publore

Formerly known as the Thatched House, the Flask Tavern in Hampstead, England, also doubled as a water-bottling facility in the eighteenth century. Fresh water was collected from the nearby springs and bottled to be sold at the taverns and coffee houses of London. In addition, the Flask is said to be haunted. Drunken patrons have reported lights inexplicably swaying back and forth, glasses moving on their own, and cold chills running down their spines.

Visit the Flask Tavern at 14 Flask Walk, Hampstead, London NW3 1HE.

Oskar Blues Brewery
1800 Pike Road, Unit B
Longmont, CO 80501
www.oskarblues.com

🍺 Dragon's Milk

"They worked their will upon John Barleycorn, But he lives to tell the tale. We pour him into an old brown jug, And we call him home-brewed ale."
—OLD ENGLISH SONG

TYPE: American strong ale
COLOR: Dark brown with red highlights
SMELL: Chocolate and cream
TASTE: Smooth and sweet, it starts with milk chocolate then fades into notes of dried cherries followed by raisins and alcohol. It finishes with a distinctly rummy flavor and leaves with a chocolate and light coffee aftertaste. As it warms, the chocolate and coffee flavors fade, leaving more raisin and rum.
FOOD PAIRING: Triple coconut cream pie
AVAILABILITY: Year round, part of the high-gravity series

DEC

7

Beerfact

Monks in medieval Europe were often brewers of beer. There were several practical reasons for this. There was no water filtration, and the brewing process (boiling) along with the resultant alcohol in beer would kill anything "unwanted," making it safer to drink. Also, during fasting, monks were allowed to consume liquids, and their thick beer provided enough sustenance to keep them healthy until their next meal.

New Holland Brewing Company
66 E. 8th Street
Holland, MI 49423
www.newhollandbrew.com

🍺 Snow Cap

"Or merry swains who quaff the nut-brown ale and sing enamoured of the nut-brown maid."
—JAMES BEATTIE, POET AND PHILOSOPHER

TYPE: Winter warmer

COLOR: Mahogany

SMELL: Toasted malt with hints of dried fruit

TASTE: A medium-bodied beer with a very smooth texture exhibiting flavors of dark-roasted malt, chocolate, toffee, dried plum, and grapefruit. A hoppy presence mixes well with the beer's thick, sweet backbone and notes of spice.

FOOD PAIRING: Skewered grilled prawns with drawn butter

AVAILABILITY: October to January

**DEC
8**

Beer*thought*

The soul, rubbed raw by the daily grind, tortured and tormented at every turn. Does it not have but one salve that can soothe the sting of rules, laws, and taxes? Is there not a remedy for the agony of airport lines, holiday family gatherings, and in-laws? Have not the great minds and civilizations of this world developed a simple tonic that can tame the wild beast and calm an ill temper? But of course.

Save your soul. Drink beer.

Pyramid Brewing Company
91 S. Royal Brougham Way
Seattle, WA 98134
www.pyramidbrew.com

ESA

Woody: *"Can I pour you a beer, Mr. Peterson?"* Norm: *"A little early, isn't it, Woody?"* Woody: *"For a beer?"* Norm: *"No, for stupid questions."*
—CHEERS

TYPE: Extra special bitter
COLOR: Amber
SMELL: Molasses, grass, and floral hops
TASTE: A medium-bodied beer with flavors of molasses, sweet malt, and caramel followed by citrus hops and some floral notes. Finishes clean and dry with a slightly herbal, bitter aftertaste.
FOOD PAIRING: Mushroom, grilled onion, and Swiss burger
AVAILABILITY: Year round

DEC

9

Beerwords

Irish drinking toast:

May neighbors respect you, Trouble neglect you, The angels protect you, And heaven accept you.

Yards Brewing Company
901 N. Delaware Avenue
Philadelphia, PA 19123
www.yardsbrewing.com

🍺 Grand Cru

"If your sorority has to sell jam to buy beer, you've been drinking too much."
    —HANK, *KING OF THE HILL*

DEC
10

TYPE: Belgian strong ale

COLOR: Deep reddish brown

SMELL: Dried fruit and roasted malt with a touch of spice and a fair amount of alcohol

TASTE: Smooth, medium-bodied beer that comes across mostly sweet with just a flash of bitterness. There are flavors of banana and cloves swirling around between the sultry tastes of brown sugar and warm caramel.

FOOD PAIRING: Roasted vegetable stew with baking-powder dumplings

AVAILABILITY: Year round

Beerfact

When talking about wine, the term Grand Cru is a French designation given to vineyards with particularly noteworthy or favorable reputations. When used to describe a beer, however, the term Grand Cru generally refers to a Belgian beer, of no particular style, often given to strong seasonal beers.

Green Flash Brewing Company
1430 Vantage Court
Vista, CA 92081
www.greenflashbrew.com

Angler's Pale Ale

"Why diet if you can't have beer?"
—ANONYMOUS

TYPE: Pale ale
COLOR: Copper
SMELL: Citrus
TASTE: A medium-bodied beer that leads with rich, sweet malts and caramel followed by a blast of lemon and grapefruit hops. Finishes with flavors of yeast and sweet toffee and a soft bitter aftertaste.
FOOD PAIRING: Poached salmon with dill and hollandaise
AVAILABILITY: Year round

DEC
11

Beerfact

In December 2002, six people were crushed to death when a band of wild elephants rampaged through their village near Guwahati, India, after the elephants got drunk on rice beer. According to a source in a report from the news agency Reuters, "They smashed huts and plundered granaries and broke open casks to drink rice beer. The herd then went berserk, killing six persons."

Uinta Brewing Company
1722 South Fremont Drive (2375 West)
Salt Lake City, UT 84104
www.uintabrewing.com

🍺 Rochefort 8

"I never drink water. That's the stuff that rusts pipes."
　　—W.C. FIELDS

TYPE: Belgian strong dark ale
COLOR: Dark brown
SMELL: Brown sugar, dried fruit, and alcohol
TASTE: A medium- to full-bodied beer with flavors of sweet malt, brandy, oak, spice, ripe fruit, and bitter hops. A complex brew that finishes sweet with a bitter aftertaste.
FOOD PAIRING: Pork chops with spiced apples and stewed cabbage
AVAILABILITY: Year round

DEC

12

Beerfact

Four rules must be followed for a beer to be designated "Authentic Trappist Beer":

• The beer must have been made within the walls of a Trappist abbey or in the immediate vicinity.
• The production equipment must be maintained by the monastery.
• The beer must be made by or under the supervision of the monastery community.
• The largest part of the profit must be spent on social work.

Brasserie de Rochefort
B – 5580 Rochefort
Belgium
www.trappistes-rochefort.com

 Racer 5 IPA

"God has a brown voice, as soft and full as beer."
—ANNE SEXTON

TYPE: India pale ale
COLOR: Golden orange
SMELL: Hop resin and more hop resin—a delightful aroma
TASTE: Medium bodied with a terrific punch of spicy, piney, citrusy hops. A classic example of how good an IPA can be.
FOOD PAIRING: Lobster tail grilled until the shell just begins to burn, served with clarified butter and crusty bread
AVAILABILITY: Year round

DEC
13

Beerfact

India pale ale, otherwise known as IPA, is characterized by a very bitter taste (created by using a large amount of hops both during the brewing process and after—a process known as dry hopping) and often a higher alcohol content than other beers. Hops, the leaves of which give beer its bitter flavor and also impart aroma, is also known to be a natural preservative. Some argue that the first batches were made with extra hops to allow them to survive the long trip aboard ships sailing from England to India. Incidentally, this same argument is used to explain the usually higher alcohol content as well.

Bear Republic Brewing Company
345 Healdsburg Avenue
Healdsburg, CA 95448
www.bearrepublic.com

🍺 Mad Elf Ale

"He who will not give himself leisure to be thirsty can never find the true pleasure of drinking."
— MICHEL DE MONTAIGNE, AUTHOR

TYPE: Belgian strong dark ale

COLOR: Dark red

SMELL: Cherries, oak, and spices

TASTE: A large, complex brew that starts with lots of sweet malt and yeast then gives way to honey, crystalline sugar, holiday spices, and cherries. There is a warmth that goes well with the season, and a rather dry, fruity finish.

FOOD PAIRING: Lemon zest goat cheese and dried cherries

AVAILABILITY: October to December

DEC
14

Beersaints

Nicholas of Myra (lived sometime during the fourth century C.E.)

The modern-day reinterpretation of him as Santa Claus is due to his reputation of giving gifts in secret. There is a legend about three travelers who were slain by an unscrupulous butcher. The butcher cut up his victims and cured their bodied in salt, with the intention of selling them to his customers as ham. Saint Nicholas discovered what the butcher had done and resurrected the travelers by praying for them. It is this story that earned him the role of protector and saint of travelers and brewers.

Tröegs Brewing Company
800 Paxton Street
Harrisburg, PA 17104
www.troegs.com

🍺 Golden Ale

"Beer is not a good cocktail drink, especially in a home where you don't know where the bathroom is."
—BILLY CARTER

TYPE: Golden ale

COLOR: Deep golden

SMELL: Hops and a touch of malt

TASTE: A medium-bodied beer with just a touch of malty sweetness balanced by grapefruit and orange flavors, finishing with a subtle hoppy aftertaste.

FOOD PAIRING: Soft Brie with dried apricots

AVAILABILITY: Year round

**DEC
15**

Beerfact

Their first batch brewed in the kitchen of volunteer firefighter Rich Fliescher in 1994, Hook and Ladder are now one of the fastest growing craft brewers in the country, now distributed in 27 states and affiliated with 110 distribution partners. The brewery donates a penny from every pint and a quarter from every case to help burn treatment centers in local communities. Since 2005, Hook and Ladder has donated over $60,000 to help burned firefighters and burn survivors.

Hook and Ladder Brewing Company
8113 Fenton Street
Silver Spring, MD 20910
www.hookandladderbeer.com

🍺 Cerberus

"Beer drinkin' don't do half the harm of love makin'."
—ANONYMOUS

TYPE: Trippel
COLOR: Amber
SMELL: Banana and tree fruit with just a slight hint of hops
TASTE: Spicy and sweet, there are notes of fresh yeast, candied orange slices, and sweet, intoxicating alcohol.
FOOD PAIRING: Beer and bacon stew
AVAILABILITY: Year round

DEC

16

Beerfood

In ancient Babylonia, the father of the bride gave his son-in-law all the honey beer he could drink for a month after the wedding. This is the origin of the word "honeymoon."

Thirsty Dog Brewing Company
529 Grant Street, Suite B
Akron, Ohio 44311
www.thirstydog.com

🍺 Rahsaan Roland Kirk Stritch Stout

"But leave me to my beer!"
—GEORGE ARNOLD

TYPE: Imperial stout
COLOR: Dark brown
SMELL: Yeast and mild citrus
TASTE: Light- to medium-bodied beer with flavors of bitter melon, burnt coffee, cocoa bean, blackened toast, leather, and moist earth.
FOOD PAIRING: Grilled flank steak and fingerling potatoes
AVAILABILITY: Year round

DEC
17

Beer*fest*

2009 Great American Beer Festival Winners by Category

Kellerbier/Zwickelbier: Hell In Keller, Uncle Billy's Brew & Que, Austin, TX

Smoked Beer: Smokejumper, Left Hand Brewing Co., Longmont, CO

International-Style Pilsener: Gold Leaf Lager, Devil's Backbone Brewing Co., Roseland, VA

German-Style Pilsener: 106 Pilsner, Rock Bottom Brewery, Milwaukee, Milwaukee, WI

Angel City Brewing
833 W. Torrance Blvd., Suite 105
Torrance, CA 90502
www.angelcitybrewing.com

🍺 Achel 8 Bruin

"Whiskey's too rough, champagne costs too much. Vodka puts my mouth in gear. I hope this refrain will help me explain as a matter of fact, I like beer."
—TOM T. HALL, MUSICIAN

TYPE: Dubbel
COLOR: Translucent hazy brown
SMELL: Caramel, dried plum, and spice
TASTE: A creamy, medium-bodied beer with substantial flavors of molasses, fresh toast, brown sugar, and chocolate, complemented at various stages by lemon, bitter orange, white pepper, dark fruit and cloves.
FOOD PAIRING: Chicken and dumplings
AVAILABILITY: Year round

DEC
18

Beerfact

The Achel brewery, smallest of the seven Trappist breweries, began production in the year 1850 at the Abbey of Saint Benedict in the Belgian region of Achel, but their facilities were destroyed in 1914 during World War I. Between the destruction and 1999, the monks made three attempts to have their beer brewed by contract brewers: De Kluis (1976–1985), Sterkens (1987–1990), and De Teut 't Paterke (1991–1995). In 1999 they returned to producing their own beer.

Achel Brewery
Hamont-Achel, 3930
Belgium
www.achelsekluis.org

🍺 Devout Stout

"People who don't drink are afraid of revealing themselves."
—HUMPHREY BOGART

TYPE: Stout
COLOR: Dark brown
SMELL: Roasted malt and chocolate
TASTE: A medium-bodied beer with flavors of dried dark cherries, chocolate, rich malt, roasted coffee, and toasted brown bread with notes of sour lemon and a touch of bitter melon.
FOOD PAIRING: Roasted vegetable pasta with triple-crème cheese
AVAILABILITY: Year round

**DEC
19**

Beerfact

Hangover helpers:

• **Prickly pear cactus:** The extract of the prickly pear cactus has been found to relieve nausea and dry mouth. Additionally, it is known to reduce inflammation, which can be a major cause of discomfort for hangover sufferers. You need to know you're going into a heavy night to use this remedy as you need to take the extract five hours before drinking.

• **Raw cabbage:** Chewing on some raw cabbage the morning after can help reduce or relieve your hangover-related headache.

Santa Cruz Mountain Brewing
402 Ingalls Street
Santa Cruz, CA 95060
www.santacruzmountainbrewing.com

🍺 Dragonfly IPA

"In the Bowling Alley of Tomorrow, there will even be machines that wear rental shoes and throw the ball for you. Your sole function will be to drink beer."
—DAVE BARRY

TYPE: India pale ale

COLOR: Clear amber

SMELL: Pine and citrus hops

TASTE: A light- to medium-bodied beer with flavors of biscuit and malt balanced nicely with grapefruit zest and pine. It finishes crisp and dry with a subtle hoppy aftertaste.

FOOD PAIRING: Spicy cashew chicken with basil served over jasmine rice

AVAILABILITY: Year round

**DEC
20**

Beerfact

Things you probably didn't know about Upland Brewing Company:

They are the largest microbrewery in Indiana. Every month they brew five different styles of beer: Wheat, Rad Red Amber, Helios Pale, Dragonfly IPA, and Bad Elmer's Porter. In addition to their other equipment they have two huge sixty-barrel fermenters. Their names? King and Kong.

Upland Brewing Company
350 W. 11th Street
Bloomington, IN 47404
www.uplandbeer.com

🍺 Wyld

"I'm off for a quiet pint—followed by fifteen noisy ones."
—GARETH CHILCOTT, ATHLETE

TYPE: Pale ale
COLOR: Hazy golden
SMELL: Hoppy
TASTE: A light- to medium-bodied beer with nice sweet malt and notes of citrus and piney hops. This is a crisp, clean beer with a dry, somewhat hoppy finish.
FOOD PAIRING: Grilled salmon served cold on a toasted bagel with cream cheese, capers, and a squeeze of lemon
AVAILABILITY: Year round

DEC
21

Beerfact

Four + Brewing is the brainchild of Uinta Brewery. Created as a way to explore new, interesting brews with a bit of panache, it is something totally separate and its own outside of the already established brands. The name is a reference to the four ingredients allowed by the Bavarian Purity law or Reinheitsgebot—water, barley, hops, and later yeast. It's meant as an exploration of what can happen when established simplicity meets modern creativity.

Four + Brewing
1722 South Fremont Drive (2375 West)
Salt Lake City, UT 84104
www.fourplusbrewing.com

🍺 Wildflower Wheat

"Get up and dance, get up and smile, get up and drink to the days that are gone in the shortest while."
—SIMON FOWLER, MUSICIAN

TYPE: Wheat

COLOR: Hazy golden like fresh honey

SMELL: Floral hops, sweet honey, and fresh baked bread

TASTE: A clean, crisp beer with no trace of bitterness. The honey this beer is brewed with makes for a smooth mouthfeel with an underlying sweetness that pairs perfectly with the flavors of fresh raw wheat.

FOOD PAIRING: A nice chunk of Crozier Blue smeared on fresh baked French bread and drizzled with honey, served with slices of apple or pear

AVAILABILITY: Year round

DEC

22

Beerfact

Marble is New Mexico's newest brewery, having opened its doors in April 2008. They make ten different styles of beer, seven of which are always available and three rotating "brewer's choice" seasonals. Currently, only three of their beers are available in bottles, but the rest can be enjoyed at their pub and tasting room located at the brewery itself.

Marble Brewery
111 Marble Avenue NW
Albuquerque, NM 87102
www.marblebrewery.com

🍺 Christmas Jam

Woody: "Would you like a beer, Mr. Peterson?" Norm: "No, I'd like a dead cat in a glass."

TYPE: Witbier

COLOR: Pale yellow

SMELL: Fresh wheat, coriander, and citrus

TASTE: A crisp, smooth beer with flavors of creamy wheat and honey followed by Mandarin and Clementine oranges and spice.

FOOD PAIRING: Baking powder biscuits piled with hand-sliced ham and apricot preserves

AVAILABILITY: Limited release

DEC

23

Brew*fest*

Every year in December, for more than twenty years, in Asheville, North Carolina, a concert known as Christmas Jam attracts some of the biggest names in the music business. The goal is to raise money for Habitat for Humanity—an international nonprofit organization that helps provide housing for the homeless and impoverished. In 2009, Christmas Jam partnered with Asheville Brewing Company to create its namesake beer. Christmas Jam is available at select locations in Asheville and mail order nationally. All proceeds from the sale of the beer go to Habitat for Humanity.

Asheville Brewing Company
675 Merrimon Avenue
Asheville, NC 28804
www.ashevillebrewing.com

🍺 Christmas Ale

"Wisselton, wasselton, who lives here. We've come to taste your Christmas beer."
—ENGLISH VERSE

DEC
24

TYPE: Winter warmer
COLOR: Deep cola brown
SMELL: Pumpkin pie spices
TASTE: Flavors of nutmeg, brown sugar, cinnamon sticks, roasted malt, a touch of coffee, and a splash of cola. It tastes like Christmas Eve night, bundled up beside a fire, looking down at all the presents under the tree and wondering what Santa would be bringing you.
FOOD PAIRING: Roast beef, oven-roasted turkey, mashed potatoes, candied yams, steamed and buttered broccoli, mushroom gravy, and cranberry sauce
AVAILABILITY: November to January

Beerfact

Since 1975, Anchor Brewing Company has been producing their Christmas Ale. Each year, the recipe changes, so too does the tree on the label—a symbol of the Winter Solstice. Available in 12-ounce bottles, magnums, and on tap in select watering holes, Anchor's Christmas Ale is only around between November and January.

Anchor Brewing Company
1705 Mariposa Street
San Francisco, CA 94107
www.anchorbrewing.com

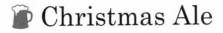 Christmas Ale

*"There's nothing like a cold beer on a hot Christmas
morning."*
  —HOMER SIMPSON

TYPE: Winter warmer
COLOR: Copper
SMELL: Ginger, cinnamon, and citrus
TASTE: Flavors of honey and bitter orange surround spices of cinnamon,
clove, and zesty ginger. It's a delightful beer that will put you in the holi-
day spirit.
FOOD PAIRING: Spiced baked apples with walnuts and raisins
AVAILABILITY: Seasonal

**DEC
25**

Brewtip
Other things to do with beer:
- **Metal polish:** The acids in the beer will easily remove oxidization
  from copper surfaces. If you have copper pots, simply let them soak
  in a beer, then wipe off the unwanted tarnish with a dry rag.
- **Foot salve:** Pour two ice-cold beers into a bucket just large enough to
  soak both of your tired feet. The carbonation will sooth the aching
  while the chill temperature will help reduce swelling.

Olde Hickory Brewery
222 Union Square
Hickory, NC 28601
www.oldehickorybrewery.com

🍺 Two Turtle Doves

Homer: "Oh, I'll never drink another beer in my life." Vendor: "Beer here! I got beer!" Homer: "Oooo! I'll take ten!"
—*THE SIMPSONS*

TYPE: Belgian strong dark ale

COLOR: Black

SMELL: Cocoa, roasted nuts, dried fruit, and yeast

TASTE: A full-bodied beer with flavors of cocoa, candied fruit, almonds, caramel, and yeast. It finishes with an alcoholic warmth and leaves with burnt toffee aftertaste.

FOOD PAIRING: Aged prime rib, grilled zucchini, and shoestring French fries

AVAILABILITY: Limited release winter seasonal

DEC
26

Beerfact

Two Turtle Doves is the second in the series of new winter releases from The Bruery. Following the lyrics to the traditional "Twelve Days of Christmas," they plan to release a new, unique seasonal every year, each named after a different line from the song. Each will be a different style, and each will be available only for a short time. Partridge in a Pear Tree, the first in the series, was released in 2008, and Twelve Drummers Drumming (the presumptive final brew in the line) is due out in 2019.

The Bruery
715 Dunn Way
Placentia, CA 92870
www.thebruery.com

🍺 Old Blarney Barleywine

"The best research for playing a drunk is being a British actor for twenty years."
—MICHAEL CAINE

TYPE: Barley wine
COLOR: Deep coppery brown
SMELL: Caramel malt, toffee, and pine
TASTE: Flavors of thick brown sugar syrup, warm caramel, rich toffee, and cocoa powder balance out nicely with spruce, pine, and bitter dandelion.
FOOD PAIRING: Venison and mushroom stew
AVAILABILITY: Year round

DEC
27

Brew*tip*

Many beers, like many wines, can be held for some time—growing more subtle and interesting as they age. Most beers are best served right out of the brewery. Here are some good guidelines on how long you can store your favorite styles:

  American strong ale—8 to 9% ABV, 1 to 5 years
  Imperial ales—7 to 10% ABV, 1 to 6 years
  Strong dark ales—8 to 11% ABV, 2 to 10 years
  Barleywine and stout—8 to 12% ABV, 3 to 15 years

Moylan's Brewery
15 Rowland Way
Novato, CA 94945
www.moylans.com

🍺 Legendary Red Ale

"Show me a nation whose national beverage is beer and I'll show you an advanced toilet technology."
—MARK HAWKINS, JOURNALIST

TYPE: Altbier

COLOR: Dark amber

SMELL: Sweet malt and cola

TASTE: A medium-bodied beer with flavors of roasted malt, sweet butter, honey, and cola. A very drinkable beer with a nice malty finish.

FOOD PAIRING: Cheese fondue served with cubes of French bread and slices of apple

AVAILABILITY: Year round

DEC

28

*Beer*food
CHEESE FONDUE WITH BEER

¾ pound white Cheddar cheese, shredded

½ pound Gruyère cheese, shredded

1 tbsp flour

1½ tbsp dry mustard

Dash cayenne

¾ cup red ale

2 tbsp Worcestershire sauce

Mix cheese, flour, mustard, and cayenne. In fondue pot, combine beer and Worcestershire sauce. Set temperature at 375°F and heat until bubbling. Gradually add cheese mixture and stir constantly until cheese melts and mixture is smooth, about 5 minutes. Reduce temperature to 200°F and serve.

Golden City Brewery
920 12th Street
Golden, CO 80401
www.gcbrewery.com

🍺 Hefeweizen

"We had this marvelous potion we took after practice. It was called beer."
—DICK ANDERSON, BASEBALL PLAYER

TYPE: Hefeweizen
COLOR: Hazy yellow
SMELL: Lemon zest, banana, yeast, and sweet malt
TASTE: A light-bodied beer with flavors of grapefruit and lemon, followed by ripe bananas and spun sugar. It finishes with tart citrus and ends clean and rather dry.
FOOD PAIRING: Sausage and jack cheese omelet
AVAILABILITY: Year round

DEC
29

Beerfact

According to Queensland Brain Institute director Professor Perry Bartlett, drinking alcohol does not kill brain cells. He found that the human brain replenishes cells every day, and that there is no evidence that consuming alcohol negatively impacts this regular cycle or leads to damage on its own. Instead, when taken in moderation, alcohol has been shown to have a positive impact on brain function.

Yazoo Brewing Company
1200 Clinton Street #112
Nashville, TN 37203
www.yazoobrew.com

🍺 Winterhook

"It only takes one drink to get me drunk. The trouble is, I can't remember if it's the thirteenth or the fourteenth."
—GEORGE BURNS

TYPE: Winter warmer

COLOR: Deep amber

SMELL: Lots of pine mixed with toasted bread

TASTE: Strong hop flavor with notes of chocolate truffle and drizzled caramel. The 2009 release had a new recipe and a higher alcohol content than before—now 6% ABV.

FOOD PAIRING: Shredded smoked duck served in soft Chinese buns and plum sauce

AVAILABILITY: October through December

DEC
30

Beerfact

When Redhook Ale Brewery was founded in 1981, the Pacific Northwest consumed more draft beer than any other region in the nation. Initially, Redhook's beer met with critical acclaim, but only amongst a very small, almost cultlike group of beer drinkers. Known affectionately as "banana beer" because of its distinctly banana flavor, the unusual brew was the talk of the town. From their humble beginnings selling fewer than 1,000 barrels, Redhook has grown to be a nationally recognized brewery, with facilities on both coasts.

Redhook Ale Brewery
14300 NE 145th Street
Woodinville, WA 98072
www.redhook.com

 True Blonde Ale

"Beer. It's the best damn drink in the world."
—JACK NICHOLSON, ACTOR

TYPE: Blonde ale
COLOR: Golden
SMELL: Yeast and honey
TASTE: A light-bodied, crisp blonde ale, with flavors of fresh baked bread, sweet honey, and raw wheat with the citrus twang of bitter hops to finish.
FOOD PAIRING: Crab cakes with chipotle lime sauce
AVAILABILITY: Year round

DEC
31

Beer*thought*

Imagine a world in which children frolic through fountains on a hot summer day while Mommy and Daddy sidle up to the long wooden bar just within earshot. They order a beer for each hand and clink glasses as they lean back and watch junior play with all the other happy children. When the children are tired, they come to sit by their parents, each ordering a root beer or craft-brewed cola. And as a family, they lift their sudsy glasses and drink deeply. I'll drink to that.

Ska Brewing Company
225 Girard Street
Durango, CO 81301
www.skabrewing.com

Beers by Type

Altbier
Golden City Legendary Red Ale
Ninkasi Sleighr
Widmer Brothers Okto

Amber / Red Ale
Alaskan Amber Ale
Ballast Point Calico Amber Ale
Bear Republic Red Rocket Ale
Bells Amber Ale
Buckbean Original Orange Blossom Ale
Buckbean Tule Duck Red Ale
Capital Rustic Ale
Dark Horse Amber Ale
Dark Horse Sapient Trip Ale
Deschute Green Lakes Organic Ale
Full Sail Amber Ale
Great Lakes Nosferatu
Independence Austin Amber Beer
Jolly Pumpkin La Roja
Karl Strauss Red Trolly Ale
Lagunitas "Censored" Rich Copper Ale
Magic Hat Roxy Rolles
Marble Red Ale
Mendocino Red Tail Ale

New Belgium Fat Tire Ale
Ninkasi Believer Double Red
Port Shark Attack Double Red Ale
Pyramid Juggernaut
Rahr and Sons Buffalo Butt
Red Hook Late Harvest Autumn Ale
RJ Rockers Honey Amber Ale
River City Woodenhead Ale
Summit Horizon Red Ale
Thirsty Dog Hoppus Maximus
Tröeg's Hopback Amber

American Cream Ale
Thomas Creek Stillwater Vanilla Cream Ale

American Strong Ale
Alltech's Lexington Kentucky Bourbon Barrel Ale
Dark Horse Reserve Special Black Bier Ale
Gordash Holy Mackerel Mack in Black
Lagunitas Hairy Eyeball
New Holland Dragon's Milk
Port Old Viscosity
Steamworks Spruce Goose

Stone Arrogant Bastard Ale

Yards Thomas Jefferson's Tavern Ale

Green Flash Grand Cru

New Belgium 1554

Troeg's Mad Elf Ale

American Wild Ale
Ommegang Omegeddon

Russian River Beatification

Biere de Guarde
The Lost Abbey Avant Garde

Two Brothers Domaine du Page

Barley Wine
Anchor Old Foghorn

Clipper City Heavy Seas Below Decks

Flying Dog Horn Dog

Golden City Centurion Barley Wine

Great Divide Old Ruffian

Maylon's Old Blarney Barley Wine

Olde Hickory Irish Walker

Pike Old Bawdy Barley Wine

Sierra Nevada Bigfoot Barley Wine Style Ale

Sprecher Barley Wine

Uinta Anniversary Barley Wine

Belgian Ale
Angel City Belgian Night Train

Avery Karma

Bieres de Chimay Chimay Blu Grande Reserve

Brasserie d'Achouffe McChouffe

Brooklyn Local 1

The Bruery Autumn Maple

The Bruery Two Turtle Doves

Dogfish Head Raison d'Etre

Blonde Ale
Boundary Bay Bellingham Blonde

DuClaw Bare Ass Blonde

Eel River Organic California Blonde Ale

Grand Teton Au Naturale

NOLA Blonde Ale

O'Fallon Gold

Ska True Blonde Ale

Steamworks Ale Diablo

Bocks
Brooklyn Brewery Brooklyner-Schneider Hopfen-Weisse

Dark Horse Perkulator

Full Sail LTD 01

Morgan Street Doppelbock

Rogues Dead Guy Ale

Sprecher Bourbon Barrel Dopplebock

Stoudt's Smooth Hoperator

Summit Maibock

Thomas Creek Deep Water Dopplebock

Troegs Troegenator Double Bock

Brown Ale

Big Sky Moose Drool

Boulevard Lunar Ale

Cigar City Bolita Brown

Hook and Ladder Backdraft Brown

Lost Coast Downtown Brown

NOLA Brown Ale

Northwoods Li'l Bandit Brown

Santa Cruz Mountain Organic Dread Brown

Sprecher Pub Ale

Twisted Pine Honey Brown Ale

Yards Brawler

Yazoo Dos Perros

Chili Beer

Twisted Pine's Billy's Chilies

Dubbel

Bières de Chimay Red Prémiere

Brouwerij de Achelse Kluis Achel 8 Bruin

Brouwerij Westmalle Trappist Dubbel

Pike Tandem

Uncommon Siamese Twin

Dunkel

Capital Dark

Durango Dark Lager

Harpoon Munich Dark

Extra Special Bitter

Avery 14'er ESB

Clipper City Heavy Seas Winter Storm "Category 5" Ale

Grand Teton Bitch Creek

Left Hand Sawtooth Ale

Red Hook ESB

Shipyard Old Thumper

Stoudt's Scarlet Lady Ale

Vino's Ouachita ESB

Yards ESA

Farmhouse Ale

Jolly Pumpkin Bam Bière

Fruit Beer

Four + Punk'n

Magic Hat #9

Rogues Ale Morimoto Soba Ale

Sonoran Cordillera Blanca

Gluten Free

Lakefront New Grist

Golden Ale

Hook and Ladder Golden Ale

Moylan's Celts Golden Ale

Northwoods Bumbl'n Bubba's Buzz'n Brew

Pike Naughty Nellie

Russian River Damnation

Two Brothers Prairie Path Golden Ale

Hefeweizen

Boulevard Unfiltered Wheat Beer

Harpoon UFO

Lake Front Wheat Monkey

Live Oak Hefeweizen

Magic Hat Circus Boy

Millstream Windmill Wheat

Olde Hickory Hefeweizen

Pyramid Haywire

Santa Cruz Mountain
Hefeweizen

Sprecher Hefe Weisse

Terrapin Sunray Wheat Beer

Three Floyd's Gumball

Uinta Golden Spike

Widmer Brothers Hefeweizen

Yazoo Hefeweizen

India Pale Ale

10 Barrel Brewing Apocalypse IPA

10 Barrel Brewing Bourbon
Barrel RIPA

Asheville Shiva

Augusta 1856 IPA

Bear Republic Hop Rod IPA

Bear Republic Racer 5 IPA

Bell's Two Hearted Ale

Boulevard Smokestack Series
Double-Wide IPA

Captain Lawrence Captain's
Reserve Imperial IPA

Clipper City Heavy Seas Loose
Cannon

Dark Horse Double Crooked Tree

Dogfish Head 90 Minute
Imperial IPA

Durango Derail Ale

Elysian Avatar

Elysian The Wise

Firestone Walker Union Jack

Founders Double Trouble

Founders Red's Rye IPA

Grand Teton Sweetgrass IPA

Great Divide Titan IPA

Great Lakes Commodore Perry

Green Flash Le Freak

Green Flash West Coast IPA

Hale's Supergoose IPA

Harpoon IPA

Karl Strauss Tower 10 IPA

Lagunitas IPA

Long Trail IPA

Magic Hat Lucky Kat

Marble IPA

Maui Big Swell IPA

Mendocino White Hawk IPA

Moylan's Hopsickle Imperial IPA

New Holland Mad Hatter

Ninkasi Total Domination IPA

Ninkasi Tricerahops

NOLA Hopitoulas

O'Fallon 5 Day IPA

Port Wipeout IPA

Russian River Pliny the Elder

Santa Cruz Ale Works IPA

Sierra Nevada Celebration Ale

Ska Decadent Imperial IPA

Ska Modus Hoperandi

Sonoran Victorian IPA

Southern Tier Hoppe Imperial
Extra Pale Ale

Southern Tier Oak-Aged
Unearthly Imperial IPA

Stone IPA

Stone Ruination IPA

Terrapin Hop Karma Brown IPA

Thomas Creek Up the Creek
Extreme IPA

Upland Dragonfly IPA

Victory Hop Devil Ale

Vino's Rock Hopera

Yards IPA

Kölsch

Alltech's Lexington Kentucky
Light Ale

Ballast Point Yellowtail Pale

Flying Dog Tire Bite Golden Ale

Metropolitan Krank Shaft

Steamworks Colorado Kolsch

Lagers

Angel City Che

Boulevard Bob's 47 Oktoberfest

Capital Supper Club Lager

DuClaw el Guapo

Full Sail LTD 02

Full Sail Session Lager

Great Lakes Elliot Ness

Kona Longboard Island Lager

Live Oak Big Bark Amber Lager

Maui Bikini Blonde

Mendocino Red Tail Lager

Metropolitan Dynamo

Morgan Street Vienna

Rahr and Son Rahr's Red

River City Vienna Lager

Märzen

Durango Colorest

Summit Oktoberfest

Thirsty Dog Barktoberfest

Oak Aged Ale

Jolly Pumpkin Perseguidor

Old Ale

Eel River Tripel Exultation

Independence Jasperilla Old Ale

Pale Ale

10 Barrel Code 24

Alltech's Lexington Kentucky Ale

Anchor Liberty Ale

Angel City Charlie Parker Pale Ale

Augusta Tannhauser Pale Ale

Big Sky Montana Trout Slayer

Brasserie d'Achouffe Chouffe
Houblon

Brasserie d'Achouffe La Chouffe

Brasserie d'Orval Petite Orval

Brasserie d'Orval Trappist Ale

Brooklyn Pennant Ale '55

Carolina Pale Ale

DuClaw Venom Pale Ale

Firestone Walker DBA

Firestone Walker Pale 31

Four + Brewing Monkshine

Four + Wyld

Gordash Holy Mackerel Special Golden Ale

Great Divide Hades

Hale's O'Brien's Harvest Ale

Independence Pale Ale

Kona Fire Rock Pale Ale

Long Trail Pollinator

Millstream Iowa Pale Ale

Odell Saint Lupulin

Oskar Blues Dale's Pale Ale

RJ Rockers Buckwheat Ale

RJ Rockers Patriot Pale Ale

River City Cap City Pale

Santa Cruz Ale Works Pale Ale

Santa Cruz Mountain Wilder Wheat

Shipyard Export Ale

Shipyard Summer Ale

Sonoran Burning Bird

Southern Tier Phin and Matt's

Stoudt's American Pale Ale

The Lost Abbey Inferno

Uinta Angler's Pale Ale

Uncommon Golden State Ale

Widmer Brothers Drifter

Yazoo Pale Ale

Pilsner

Karl Strauss Woodie Gold

Live Oak Pilz

Metropolitan Flywheel

Northwoods Walter's Premium Pilsner

Oskar Blues Mamma's Little Yella Pils

Victory Brewing Prima Pils

Porter

Alaskan Smoked Porter

Anchor Porter

Asheville Ninja Porter

Elysian Perseus

Flying Dog Road Dog

Founders Porter

Great Lakes Edmund Fitzgerald

Kona Pipeline Porter

Maui CoCoNut PorTeR

O'Fallon Smoked Porter

Stone Vertical Epic Ale 09.09.09

Summit Great Northern Porter

Thirsty Dog Old Leghumper

Twisted Pine Pearl Street Porter

Uinta King's Peak Porter

Uncommon Brewers Baltic Porter

Upland Bad Elmer's Porter

Yards George Washington's Tavern Porter

Quadrupel

Ommegang Three Philosophers

The Lost Abbey Judgment Day

Red Rye Ale

Two Brothers Cane and Ebel

Rice Ale

Great Divide Samurai

Saison

Clipper City Heavy Seas Red Sky at Night

The Bruery Saison Rue

Schwarzbier

10 Barrel S1N1STOR

Buckbean Black Noddy Lager

Sprecher Black Bavarian

Scotch Ale

Boundary Bay Scotch Ale

Founders Dirty Bastard

Odell 90 Shilling Ale

Pike Kilt Lifter

Sour Ale

Allagash Gargamel

New Holland Blue Sunday

Spiced Ale

Left Hand Juju

Steam Beer

Anchor Steam Beer

Lakefront Riverwest Steam Beer

Morgan Street Cobblestone Steam Lager

Steamworks Steam Engine Lager

Stout

Angel City Rahsaan Rolan Kirk Strich Stout

Augusta Hyde Park Stout

Boundary Bay Dry Irish Stout

Cigar City Marshal Zhukov's Imperial Stout

Deschutes Obsidian Stout

Eel River Organic Raven's Eye Imperial Stout

Elysian Dragonstooth

Founders Kentucky Breakfast Stout

Golden City Lookout Stout

Good People Oatmeal Coffee Stout

Great Divide Yeti Imperial Stout

Guinness Extra Stout

Left Hand Imperial Stout

Lost Coast 8 Ball Stout

New Holland The Poet

Ninkasi Oatis Oatmeal Stout

Oskar Blues Ten Fidy

Rogue Shakespeare Stout

Santa Cruz Dark Night Oatmeal Stout

Santa Cruz Mountain Devout
Stout

Sierra Nevada Stout

Southern Tier Crème Brûlée
Stout

Southern Tier Chokolat Stout

Steamworks Backside Stout

Stone Imperial Russian Stout

Thirsty Dog Siberian Night

Three Floyd's Moloko Milk Stout

Vinos Lazy Boy Stout

Tripel

Allagash Curieux

Biere de Chimay Triple Cinq
Cents

Brouwerij Westmalle Trappist
Tripel

Boulevard Smokestack Series
Long Strange Tripel

Brouerij de Achelse Kluis Achel 8
Blonde

Thirsty Dog Cerberus

Victory Golden Monkey

Winter Warmer

Anchor Christmas Ale

Olde Hickory Christmas Ale

Pyramid Snow Cap

Red Hook Winterhook

Witbier

Alaskan White

Allagash White

Asheville Christmas Jam

Ballast Point Wahoo Wheat

Lost Coast Great White

Marble Wildflower Wheat

Morgan Street Krystal

New Belgium Mothership Wit

Odell Easy Street Wheat

Ommegang White

Upland Wheat

List of Brewers

10 Barrel Brewing Company

Alaskan Brewing Company

Allagash Brewing Company

Alltech's Lexington Brewing Company

Anchor Brewing Company

Angel City Brewing

Asheville Brewing Company

Augusta Brewing Company

Avery Brewing

Ballast Point Brewing Company

Bear Republic

Bells Beer

Bières de Chimay

Big Sky Brewing Company

Boulevard Brewing Company

Boundary Bay Brewing

Brasserie d'Achoufee

Brasserie d'Orval

Brasserie de Rochefort

Brewery Ommegang

Brooklyn Brewery

Brouwerij de Achelse Kluis

Brouwerij Westmalle

Buckbean Brewing Company

Capital Brewery

Captain Lawrence Brewing Company

Carolina Brewing Company

Cigar City Brewing

Clipper City Brewery

Dark Horse Brewery

Deschutes Brewery

Dogfish Head Craft Brewery

DuClaw Brewing Company

Durango Brewing Company

Eel River Brewing Company

Elysian Brewery

Firestone Walker Brewing Company

Flying Dog Brewery

Founders Brewing Company

Four + Brewing

Full Sail

Golden City Brewery

Good People Brewing Company

Gordash Brewing Company

Grand Teton Brewing Company

Great Divide Brewing Company

Great Lakes Brewing Company

Green Flash Brewing Company

Guinness

Hale's Ales

Harpoon Brewery

Hook and Ladder Brewing Company

Independence Brewing Company

Jolly Pumpkin Artisan Ales

Karl Strauss

Kona Brewing Company

Lagunitas Brewing Company

Lakefront Brewery

Left Hand Brewing Company

Live Oak Brewing Company

Long Trail Brewing Company

Lost Coast Brewery

Magic Hat Brewing Company

Marble Brewery

Maui Brewing Company

Mendocino Brewing Company

Metropolitan Brewing

Millstream Brewing Company

Morgan Street Brewery

Moylan's Brewery

New Belgium Brewing Company

New Holland Brewing Company

Ninkasi Brewing Company

NOLA Brewing Company

Northwoods Brewpub

Odell Brewing Company

O'Fallon Brewery

Olde Hickory Brewery

Oskar Blues Brewery

Port Brewing Company

Pyramid Brewing Company

Redhook Ale Brewery

River City Brewing Company

RJ Rockers Brewing Company

Rogue Brewery

Russian River Brewing

Santa Cruz Ale Works

Santa Cruz Mountain Brewing

Shipyard Brewing Company

Sierra Nevada Brewing Company

Ska Brewing Company

Sonoran Brewing Company

Southern Tier Brewing Company

Sprecher Brewing Company

Steamworks Brewing Company

Stone Brewing

Stoudt's Beer

Summit Brewing Company

Terrapin Beer Company

The Bruery

The Lost Abbey

The Pike Brewing Company

Thirsty Dog Brewing Company

Thomas Creek Brewery

Three Floyd's Brewery

Tröegs Brewing Company

Twisted Pine Brewing Company

Two Brothers Brewing Company

Uinta Brewing Company

Uncommon Brewers

Upland Brewing Company

Victory Brewing Company

Vino's Brewpub

Widmer Brothers Brewing Company

Yards Brewing Company

Yazoo Brewing Company